GOD'S
GREAT
SALVATION

GOD'S GREAT SALVATION

by

Wesley L. Duewel

Preliminary Edition

Published by
OMS INTERNATIONAL, INC.
P. O. Box A
Greenwood, IN 46142-6599

GOD'S GREAT SALVATION
Copyright © 1991 by Wesley L. Duewel

Library of Congress Catalog Card Number: 91-90440

Published by
OMS INTERNATIONAL, INC.
P. O. Box A
Greenwood, IN 46142-6599

Printed in the United States of America.

CONTENTS

FOREWORD

In this volume Dr. Wesley Duewel, veteran missionary to India and mission statesman at large, gives us a clear and articulate introduction to the basic elements of Christian theology: God, sin, and salvation. It is an excellent presentation of the basic order of salvation.

It is obvious that the author is treading familiar territory as he leads the reader through these pages. Otherwise, it would be difficult to account for the clarity, the presentation, and the fullness of the references to supporting biblical passages, or the sure yet tender tone as he invites his reader along.

Dr. Duewel knows his subject, his Scriptures, the human heart, and the ways of the Spirit. One can only pray for a wide usage for this basic work.

> Dr. Dennis F. Kinlaw
> Chancellor
> Asbury College
> Wilmore, Kentucky

PREFACE

This book is written with the prayer that God will ground all our holiness people in a biblical understanding of the new birth, entire sanctification, growth in holiness, holy ethics, and holy leadership.

God wants us to have an experience of these mighty works of God's Spirit so definite, clear-cut, and spiritually rewarding that we frequently testify publicly to our own experience of these truths. We must understand the biblical doctrines so completely that we teach and preach them with such clarity that our people understand and experience God's saving and sanctifying grace. Too many sermons are so general that few people are led into the fullness of the Spirit-filled life. Too few of our people can give a clear personal testimony of how and when they received this glorious experience and the difference it made in their life.

These chapters have been written with the conviction that the average pastor seldom refers to his theology books after he graduates from seminary and begins his ministry. I have tried to avoid an emphasis upon theory and have sought to be completely biblical, practical, and understandable by any Bible-studying Christian. While I come from a background of 70 years in the Wesleyan holiness movement, to me the all-important question is always, Is this biblical? I pray that this book may be so readable that it will be referred to again and again.

I have used shorter chapters, shorter paragraphs, and comparatively simple sentences so that it will be more readable, and so that it can be easily translated into the languages of the mission fields. This is a preliminary edition, and I welcome your response as to whether this is helpful or how it might be improved.

It is my prayer that many of our splendid laymen will find this book helpful and instructive. Please join me in getting this volume into wider and wider use.

I am deeply grateful to OMS International for enabling me to have a ministry of writing. The past more than 50 years of OMS ministry as theology teacher, editor, Bible seminary principal, field leader, and headquarters administrator have helped prepare me for this role. I am deeply grateful to Miss Hilda Johnecheck, my fellow missionary and for more than 20 years my secretary, who carries much of the load during writing, publishing, and marketing of my books.

Oh to be used more and more for God's glory!

Prayerfully,

Wesley L. Duewel
P. O. Box A
Greenwood, IN 46142-6599

Dr. Wesley Duewel has been in OMS ministry in India during a span of some 25 years and has since that time served at the OMS headquarters as a vice president and for some 13 years as president. He is now Special Assistant to the President for Evangelism and Intercession. He gives his full time to the ministry of writing and a limited number of speaking engagements.

1

THE IMPORTANCE OF SALVATION FROM SIN

YOU HAVE GOOD NEWS FOR THE WORLD. You have the greatest news ever given to anyone. You have the tremendous responsibility of sharing it and proclaiming it to others so clearly and attractively that they, too, will want to know Jesus and receive His salvation.

This book is written to help you rejoice in the greatness and full blessing of the salvation Jesus died to provide and to supply you with usable material for teaching and explaining it to others. May God help us to lead people into clear, definite, personal experiences of God's saving and cleansing grace. May He help us lead them in constant growth in grace and spiritual maturity. All Christians need to understand and rejoice in the truth of the Gospel and to experience its reality daily in their lives as they walk ever more closely with Jesus.

GOOD NEWS! GREAT NEWS! GLORIOUS NEWS! The wonderful salvation that Jesus provides is all of that and much more. God's plan of salvation through Jesus Christ is good news for every sinner and for every Christian. It is good news for all of life and for eternity.

Every person needs this news. Anyone can be transformed and blessed by it. The more one knows about it, the more wonderful it becomes to him. God's plan for us is complete. It satisfies and thrills. Rightly understood, it never grows old. It changes your life and personality. It is practical and will bless you every day. It is for you.

THIS GOOD NEWS FOR EVERYONE. Jesus' salvation is for everyone. Jesus invites whoever is spiritually thirsty to come and take His free gift of salvation (Rev. 22:17). No one is too sinful, too uneducated, too old, or too bound by sinful habits or by demon powers. No one's life record is too bad. No one has gone so far in sin that he cannot return to God and be forgiven through Jesus.

You can tell anyone you ever meet that God loves him and sent His Son, Jesus Christ, to die for him. Nothing would please God more than for him to come and ask forgiveness and by God's help begin a new life. Jesus said, "Come unto me, all you who are weary and burdened, and I will give you rest" (Matt. 11:28). He was referring to spiritual peace of heart.

People are weary of sin, tired of their moral failures, tired of the life they have been living. New activities, situations, or friends give them joy and hope only for a time, but then often disappoint. Some people become so battered and broken that they begin to despair of life itself. To every weary one Jesus calls with longing love, "Come to Me. Let Me give you peace, rest, and true lasting joy. Let Me forgive you and save you from your sins."

Every Christian has a message of salvation, forgiveness, hope for a new life, and hope for a better world after this life. You as a Christian have this message which the world needs.

THE IMPORTANCE OF THE DOCTRINE OF SIN. A clear understanding of the doctrine of salvation must of necessity include a clear understanding of the doctrine of sin. Christianity is a religion of salvation from sin. People need salvation because they are sinners. The three central themes of the Bible are: God, sin, and salvation.

Satan seeks to rob Christ of His glory, and the sinner of salvation, by giving us a wrong view of sin. He does not want us to know how sinful we are and how deadly sin is. Sin is what God says it is. It made the death of Jesus upon the cross necessary. It is deceiving, destroying, and damning every unsaved person in the world. It is destroying lives, homes, nations, and civilization. We cannot afford to be deceived about sin. It is the greatest danger to every human being. It is the greatest threat to our world.

God is holy. Nothing is more basic to the nature of God than His holiness. God wants us to be holy because He is holy (Lev. 19:2; 1 Peter 1:16). Nothing is more contrary to the nature and will of God than sin. Sin is evil because it is unholy. Sin is anti-God, anti-Christ, and anti-humanity. If sin is to be avoided and conquered, we must recognize sin for what it is. Sin is tragically real. Sin has polluted, deceived, and begun destroying every human being.

The Bible teaches that sin has brought infinite tragedy to heaven in the past and to earth since the creation of man. We need to understand the violence, destructiveness, and sinfulness of sin. We need to understand the helplessness of the sinner and the way sin pervades his personality, blinds his understanding, and enslaves his whole being. The sin problem is the major problem for earth and heaven, humankind, angels, and God.

In order to defeat Satan and deliver human beings from sin, Christ left heaven and became incarnate man. Sin caused Jesus' death upon the cross. Christ has once for all defeated Satan and made it possible for anyone to be saved from sin. The ultimate defeat of Satan, the deliverance for the world from sin, and the eternalness of salvation from sin are guaranteed by Christ's death for us on the cross. The ultimate, final, and eternal defeat of sin is guaranteed by the nature of God's holy being.

God is holy, therefore Jesus Christ His Son provided salvation from sin. God is holy, therefore Satan is doomed and sin will be ultimately destroyed. God is holy, therefore righteousness and holiness will one day reign supreme. God is holy, therefore the long night of sin will end. God is holy, therefore there is deliverance from sin for every child of God, and eventually for God's world.

The glory of eternity, the glory of the new heaven and new earth which God has promised (Isa. 65:17; 2 Peter 3:13; Rev. 21:1) will be the eternal glory of righteousness, holiness, and love. Nothing sinful, impure, or shameful will ever raise its head again (Rev. 21:17).

We now must devote our study to sin and its origin on earth, a brief view of Satan, man's temptation and fall into sin, and the two forms of sin. We will then be ready to study the wonderful salvation from sin which God provided through Jesus Christ our Savior.

2

THE ETERNITY BEFORE SIN
AND EVIL BEGAN

God the Father, God the Son, and God the Holy Spirit have existed without beginning from all eternity in a trinity of holy love. Holy love is the greatest reality of their nature. They can never cease to be God, and they can never cease to be holy love. They are eternally unchangeable in nature.

There came a point in the eternal existence of God that God created angels. God will never create any being contrary to His own nature of holy love. Angels are spirit beings. They were created holy and lived in holy, loving fellowship with God. They serve God in holy love in His holy heaven and fulfill His will throughout the universe.

There came a point when the Triune God decided to create human beings. First, God needed to create a place for humankind to live, because He planned to create them spirit beings with physical bodies and human natures. Once a spirit being (whether angel or human) is created it can never cease to exist. Matter (from which our bodies are made) can be destroyed, but spirit is not material so it can never be divided or destroyed.

The angels and heavenly spirit beings of all kinds already were created when God created earth (Job 38:4-7; Gen. 1:1). Time began with the preparation of the earth for man and the creation of man. Time is like a parenthesis in an eternity which always has been and which never will end. Time, as we know it today, will cease to exist with the destruction of this earth (2 Peter 3:10-13) and the creation of God's new heaven and earth (Rev. 21:1).

God is timeless in the sense of never having had a beginning. He is the beginning of all else (Rev. 21:6; 22:13). In the beginning when God created, through Jesus Christ, also named the Word (Gen. 1:1), Christ was already with the Father and Spirit (John 1:1-3). Only the Triune God never had a beginning.

No sin, evil, or darkness has ever existed in God (1 John 1:5; 3:5). God is infinitely, perfectly, eternally, unchangeably holy, so sin could not have its origin in the nature of God. He never would create a universe or beings sinful or out of harmony with Himself. He who never tempts any being never would create a sinful being (James 1:13). Whatever He would create would be holy, perfect, and good. Sin did not begin as a created state or condition of evil, but by a rebellious misuse of free choice.

God created angels with the power of choice and later created human beings in His own image with the power of free choice. This provided the possibility of the abuse of this freedom by an act of sin. It was so important to God and to the future blessedness of His obedient created beings that they have the power of choice, that God was willing to permit the risk of wrong choice and its evil results.

We cannot perceive today the full reasoning of the infinite and holy mind of God. Until God reveals more to us, we will not be able with our finite minds to understand completely all the glory that our freedom brings to God and all the blessings it will bring to all obedient creatures. While from the perspective of this present time it seems a majority of humankind will be lost, yet this period we call time is but a tiny portion of the unending eternity yet to be. There will continue to be obedient, holy people and nations in the new earth and the New Jerusalem (Rev. 21:24-27).

God's original plan will be fulfilled and the Edenic earth condition which would have existed if Adam and Eve never had sinned will then prevail throughout the new earth. God's original plan will not have been defeated, only delayed by the intrusion of sin. In the new earth there will be no more sin. We have every reason to believe that throughout eternity the new generations of holy people in the new earth fulfilling God's original plan will so outnumber those several billion of lost humanity during the period of earth's sin that the lost will be but a tiny fraction of the blessed beings of the new earth and the new heaven.

God saw all that would follow if He created people with free will and the possibility of sin. But in the light of eternity, He saw that it would be infinitely more glorifying to God and more blessed for all holy beings if they were given free will.

Sin was no surprise to God. Sin was no ultimate defeat to God. Sin was no discouragement to God for His plans. God is eternally opposed to sin. He prepared a plan for redemption from sin for all human beings who will accept His gracious offer and provision. And now He offers this great and wonderful salvation from sin. Let us continue to study it.

3

SATAN'S CREATION AND FALL

In order to understand how sin entered our world, we need to study what the Bible teaches us about sin's beginning.

SATAN'S CHARACTER. Seven books of the Old Testament teach the reality of Satan. In the New Testament every writer teaches his reality and activity. Of the 29 times the Gospels speak of Satan, 25 times Jesus Himself is speaking.

The Hebrew name "Satan" (adversary, one who withstands) is used 34 times in the New Testament. He is called the devil (slanderer or false accuser) 36 times. He slanders God to people (Gen. 3:1-7) and people to God (Job 1:9; 2:4). Other New Testament names include Apollyon (Hebrew: Abaddon)--destroyer (Rev. 9:11); Beelzebub (Matt. 12:24); Belial--worthlessness (2 Cor. 6:15); the god of this age (2 Cor. 4:4); the ruler of this world (John 12:31); the ruler of the kingdom of the air (Eph. 2:2); the ancient serpent (Rev. 20:2); the dragon (Rev. 12:3, 7); the enemy (Matt. 13:39; 1 Peter 5:8; the accuser (Rev. 12:10); the father of lies (John 8:44); murderer (John 8:44); the evil one (1 John 5:19; Eph. 6:16); the morning star, translated Lucifer at times (Isa. 14:12).

Satan has great power and exercises authority over his demons, and to some extent over sinners. He is a finite created being with limited power [only God is almighty] (Luke 22:31; James 4:7; Jude 9), limited knowledge [only God is omniscient], and in only one place at a time [only God is omnipresent]. Therefore, Satan has to work through his demons and depend on them for much of his information and activity. Since he is the father of all lies (John 8:44), he has taught them to lie and deceive, so they no doubt deceive him at times. Satan often makes mistakes. Satan is impure, hateful--the opposite of the holy love of God.

Satan is anti-God, anti-Christ, anti-church, anti-humankind. God valued human beings highly, loved them infinitely and personally, and planned wonderful things for them on earth and in heaven in eternity (Gen. 1:26; Jer. 29:11; Eph. 2:7). Therefore Satan determined to try to ruin God's plan by enticing Adam and Eve to sin.

SATAN'S ORIGIN. But where and when did Satan, the holy angel, become so evil and become the devil? The Bible does not satisfy our curiosity by telling us a lot about angels, cherubim, demons, and Satan. Its primary concern is with us human beings. Some day in heaven God will teach us much more. But for the time being He has given us some hints and sufficient teaching to meet our spiritual needs.

Satan seems to have been originally one of the mighty angels created by God (Job 1:6), probably a cherub (Ezek. 28:14). Remember that Jesus addressed Satan through Peter since Satan had put wrong suggestions in Peter's mind (Matt. 16:23). In the same way, God seems to address Satan through the king of Tyre (Ezek. 28:12-17) and through the king of Babylon (Isa. 14:12-15), because they were being used and manipulated by Satan.

In both of these prophecies originally addressed to the kings mentioned, God helps the prophet discern the hand of Satan behind these kings. Also, the words of Isaiah and Ezekiel go far beyond what could be true of a human king and describe the fall of Satan from his position as a holy angel into a demonic being destined for hell (Rev. 20:10).

Why did Satan fall into such sin when he had been living in the holy presence of God in heaven? Here, too, the Bible gives us answers. (1) He seems to have become proud and conceited over his exalted position (1 Tim. 3:6). (2) He seems to have planned to rival God, be independent of God, and perhaps overthrow God (Isa. 14:13-14). He then tempted Adam and Eve to pride and disobedience (Gen. 3:1-6). He uses the same basic temptations for people today (1 John 2:15-16).

All persons who set up their own self-will against the will of God to some degree reenact Satan's sin. Adam's sin was like Satan's sin. It was planned by Satan, suggested by Satan, and motivated by Satan. Adam thought he was exercising his freedom; in reality he was being deceived by Satan, and by surrendering his obedience to Satan, he was becoming enslaved by Satan.

All sin enslaves us to sin and Satan. All human beings who follow and believe the lies of Satan become Satan's helpers and allies. The father of lies and sins becomes their father in sin (1 John 3:8; John 8:44). Unless those sinners accept God's grace and repent of their sins and turn their allegiance from Satan to God, they will share the same fate as Satan and his fallen angels (Rev. 20:10-15).

When Satan fell into sin and became the archenemy of God, he lost his authority in God's heaven and God's kingdom. He seems to have influenced some of the holy angelic beings to follow him into rebellion and sin. They are the anti-God force in the unseen world today. When God created earth and humanity, Satan plotted to destroy the people God had created. We will study Satan's plot to tempt Adam and Eve and cause them to fall into sin. But first let us look at Satan as he is today--his kingdom and his methods.

4

SATAN'S CHARACTER TODAY

In the mystery of God's wisdom and will He chose not to banish Satan instantly when he sinned. One day He will--temporarily for the one thousand years of the millennium (Rev. 20:1-3) and later, after a brief interval, eternally (v. 10).

God chose to permit Satan to have limited freedom. Even when he led Adam and Eve into sin God did not abandon humankind and wipe them out. The Triune God planned for the second person of the Trinity, God the Son, to redeem humanity by becoming the Son of Man. Having become incarnate, Christ taught us, revealed God the Father to us, and fulfilled all the demands of God's holiness and justice by taking our place and dying on the Roman cross. He defeated death for us by rising from the dead. Then, after confirming the faith of His disciples, He ascended to heaven before their eyes to occupy once more His glorious throne.

At the same time that Christ provided redemption for us on the cross, He defeated Satan. Satan sinned the most heinous sin that any being could ever commit by crucifying the Son of Man. Therefore, Satan will receive God's maximum punishment throughout eternity in the lake of fire (Rev. 20:10).

Satan and his demon followers know the future punishment which will be theirs (Matt. 8:29; 2 Peter 2:4). However, in his malignant hatred to God and humanity he is determined to fight, deceive, and destroy as many others as he can. He desires to cause God and His kingdom as much trouble as possible. He lashes out continually in anger and destruction. His intent, his determination, and his actions are wholly evil. The Bible describes his role today in considerable detail, often using symbolic terms.

1. *Satan is opposed to God the Father, God the Son, and God the Spirit. He promotes the spirit of antichrist.* Thus he denies that Jesus is the Son of God, that He came in the flesh and took our place, and that He defeated Satan at the cross (1 John 4:1-3).

2. *Satan is the "god of this age"* (2 Cor. 4:4). "The whole world is under the control of the evil one" (1 John 5:19). Multitudes in this age are submitting themselves to Satan's will and program. He holds limited control over humankind. That is why he blatantly tempted Christ by offering to turn the homage of the world to Him if Christ would compromise (Matt. 4:8-10).

Satan's authority is usurped, partial, limited, and only temporary. God alone is sovereign. Satan can only work within the limits God sets (Luke 22:31) and the time frame God temporarily tolerates.

The world system of this age is something maneuvered by Satan. He promotes the spirit of this age, the spirit of worldliness, in contrast to the spirit of godliness and eternal reality. Hence, we are warned not to love the world or be influenced by its standards and methods (1 John 2:15-17). The world in this forbidden sense is the world system dominated by Satan.

3. *Satan is the ruler of the kingdom of the air* (Eph. 2:2). Satan is the evil one brooding over our age and world, seeking to bring to birth as much evil as possible. His demon forces cannot arise to heaven. These rulers, authorities, and "powers of this dark world" and "spiritual forces of evil in the heavenly realms" (Eph. 6:12) are described as being an evil atmosphere surrounding humankind and seeking to mislead and pervert our race. They are "the dominion of darkness" (Col. 1:14. Compare Luke 22:53). They are spirit beings who seek to influence and mislead or even dominate human beings.

Some envisage the heavenlies as comprising a succession of levels, with God's throne at the summit, and Satan's spirit forces at the lowest. In between, undoubtedly, are the holy angel beings (Eph. 3:10), and in spiritual reality we are above them, enthroned with Christ (2:6).

4. *Satan is "the spirit who is now at work in those who are disobedient"* (Eph. 2:2). In these human slaves of Satan and rebels

against Christ, Satan is actively and energetically at work (Greek: *energountos*). He seeks to demoniacally counterfeit the Holy Spirit who is at work energizing believers and working actively in them (same Greek verb) to conform them to the likeness of Christ (3:20). The Spirit fills them to "the measure of the fullness of God" (v. 19). As the Holy Spirit helps the believer to grow in grace and Christlikeness, Satan and his demons are actively working to make the sinners more evil and even to inhabit them.

5. *Satan is the believer's "enemy, the devil," prowling around like a roaring lion, looking for someone to devour* (1 Peter 5:8). He seeks to oppose the child of God in every holy desire and endeavor, to frighten and intimidate him by his roaring threats. He watches for any unsuspecting, careless, prayerless Christian.

6. *Satan is the "accuser" of all the Christian brotherhood* (Rev. 12:10), *"who accuses them before our God day and night."* This is illustrated clearly in Job 1:6-12; 2:1-7. He constantly brings accusations against every Christian over every failure or yielding to temptation. Thank God, Jesus Christ is our defense attorney at the right hand of the Father, "who speaks in our defense" (1 John 2:1).

7. *Satan is the monstrous deceiver "who leads the whole world astray"* (Rev. 12:9). Just as he led Adam and Eve into sin, so today he seeks to lead every Christian into sin, and every sinner into ever deeper and ever more enslaving sin (2 Tim. 3:13; 2 Peter 2:19).

8. *Satan is the hater.* His name can be translated "hate" or "oppose." He is the source, motivator, and epitome of all hate. Hatred is essentially incipient murder and has been in the heart of Satan ever since his first sin (John 8:44; 1 John 3:15). He is the demonic source of all hatred, murder, criminal violence, sadism, and cruelty in the world. He seeks to destroy lives, homes, societies, and nations, for he is the arch hater of God and humanity.

9. *Satan is "that ancient serpent"* (Rev. 12:9; 20:2). This undoubtedly refers back to Genesis 3. Did Satan adopt the form of a serpent in Eden in order to deceive Eve? Most commentators believe that he temporarily entered into the serpent and spoke

through the serpent's mouth, even as demons enter, possess, and manipulate some people who surrender to them.

10. *Satan is called Belial in 2 Corinthians 6:15 and in other places in Scripture.* This word is thought to mean worthlessness, but came to mean wickedness. In complete contrast with God and righteousness, he is the ultimate of wickedness.

11. *Satan is Apollyon* (Hebrew: Abaddon)--*destroyer, or the place of destruction.* In Revelation 9:11 he is the ruler of the abyss (Greek for bottomless), the place of evil spirits, where the demons feared to go (Luke 8:31). Satan will be confined there during the millennium (Rev. 20:1, 3). Satan seeks to destroy or pervert all good, truth, beauty, right, and holiness. He is the destroyer of people and civilization.

12. *Satan is the dragon* (Rev. 12:9; 20:2). He is also termed "an enormous red dragon" (12:3), probably symbolizing cruelty and bloodshed.

5

SATAN'S KINGDOM AND METHODS

Satan probably was an angel prince or archangel before his fall into sin. He was not satisfied with his role and authority and lusted for more (Isa. 14:13). Some commentators believe that sometime before his fall into sin and before the creation of man Satan was given authority over the earth since Satan claimed it was delivered over (Greek) to him (Luke 4:6; John 12:31; 1 John 5:19) . Of course, we have to remember that Satan is repeatedly a liar.

Jesus did not dispute Satan's claim, nor did He accept it. He ignored it. Perhaps Satan claimed it was delivered to him by Adam, who had been assigned to rule it under God (Gen. 1:28). Perhaps he meant that when Adam sinned in Eden and accepted Satan's lie and leadership that this transferred earth over to him. Today he only rules over people to the extent that they surrender to him and follow him. God is still sovereign over the universe and can limit Satan whenever He so desires. The earth and everything in it, in reality, are God's (Ps. 24:1).

SATAN'S KINGDOM TODAY. Satan's kingdom today includes fallen angels, demons, and sinners. Revelation 12:4 suggests that about one-third of the angels followed Satan in his original rebellion. These angels today are not free to work according to Satan's will, but are imprisoned in Tartarus (Greek of 2 Peter 2:4) until the judgment day. In Greek thought, Tartarus was the lowest hell, where God gave punishment to the beings there.

There is no provision for forgiveness for the angels who sinned. The reasons suggested are these:

1. They were intellectually superior to human beings and so had less excuse for their sin.

2. They were spirit beings with no material body and, hence, could not be seduced by sensuous allurements in the same way as human beings.

3. They did not sin because they had a sinful nature as human beings have had since the fall.

4. They had greater previous knowledge of God through their access to the heavenlies, hence, their sin was less excusable.

Satan also rules over evil spirit beings called demons. The Greek word for these unclean spirits (Matt. 10:1, Greek) and evil spirits (Luke 7:21) is completely different from the Greek word used for the angels who sinned. Demons are active in the world today and seem to be Satan's chief agents. They seem to prefer to be embodied in people whenever possible (Mark 5:2-16; Luke 8:27-38). Jesus and the apostles, by the authority which Jesus gave, cast them out of people. God still today can deliver from demon indwelling, control, and possession.

God would not have created these beings sinful, so they must have rebelled at some time--perhaps at the time of Satan's fall or perhaps at some other time not mentioned in the Bible. They know what their doom will be (Matt. 8:29). They seem to be related to this earth and to be subject to Satan. Their number must be very great (Mark 5:9). Since Satan can be in only one place at a time and since the fallen angels are imprisoned already, Satan has to depend primarily on the demons and has to work through them. The demons are finite and can be in only one place at a time.

The demons instigate and teach "doctrines of demons"--false doctrines and philosophies (1 Tim. 4:1); attack and afflict people mentally, morally, and physically (Matt. 12:22; Mark 5:1-5; 9:18; Acts 5:16); and deceive people by idolatry and cruel religious zeal and practices (Ps. 106:37-38). Both the Old Testament (Deut. 32:16-17) and the New Testament (1 Cor. 10:20; Rev. 9:20-21) teach that idolatry in all its forms is demon worship. Demons deceive religious teachers and influence them to give false teaching and false prophecy

(1 John 4:1-2). They are the source of all attempts to foretell the future.

Demons of various ranks are organized under Satan to dominate the civilizations and governments of the world as far as they can (Eph. 6:12; Dan. 10:13). Daniel 10:13, 20 suggests that certain demonic beings are assigned to certain groups of people or areas of the earth to fulfill Satan's will there.

There was greater demonic activity concentrated when Christ was on earth, as Satan wanted to defeat Him in every way possible. When the Gospel is preached in new areas where people have long been bound by idolatry, false religion, or the occult, there are many evidences of demon opposition and activity. By the authority of Jesus and His name, Christians can rebuke them and cast them out. Jesus has all authority, and the demons have to obey Him.

Satan also deceives, enlists, and enslaves sinful people. He becomes the father of sinners (John 8:44; 1 John 3:8, 10). He blinds the minds of unbelievers (2 Cor. 4:4), snatches away the gospel seed and truth sown in people's hearts (Matt. 13:19), and traps and makes the sinners his captive slaves (2 Tim. 2:26). If Satan cannot deceive people as an angel of light [as he did with Eve] (2 Cor. 11:14-15), then he will try to intimidate and frighten them (1 Peter 5:8).

SATAN'S GOAL. Satan has not held to the truth. "There is no truth in him" (John 8:44), so he opposes God, God's kingdom, truth, and God's great plan for humanity.

In his self-will Satan chose to oppose God. He failed to exalt himself above God or become equal to God (Isa. 14:13-14). Nevertheless, he determined to establish his own kingdom of sin and evil as a rival of God's kingdom. In the temptation of Christ, he sought to win over Christ to his scheme (Matt. 4:9). He failed completely, and Christ totally defeated him at the cross (Col. 2:15; Heb. 2:14).

Satan's final great attempt will be to become incarnate in Antichrist, the man of lawlessness (2 Thess. 2:3-4; 1 John 2:18; 4:3). The climax of Satan's deception and the climactic attempt of Satan to establish his kingdom will be through the Antichrist. Then Satan's rebellion will be crushed by Christ, and Satan and Antichrist will be cast into the lake of fire, where they will be punished eternally (Rev. 20:10). Sinners who refuse God's plan of salvation will be sentenced to share hell with Satan, where Satan will probably harm them eternally (vv. 10, 13-15).

SATAN'S METHOD. Satan always attempts to hinder God and His plan, to deceive people, and either close their eyes to the Gospel or else he tries to counterfeit the Gospel. He tempts people to sin more and more. He tempts Christians to sin and backslide (1 Thess. 3:5), or to compromise and lose their power and effectiveness. He uses methods to divide families, churches, and Christian organizations, so as to make Christian work and witness less effective. His method is to keep Christians from praying until they prevail (Eph. 6:12, 18), and to be so busy with trivial, less significant activities so that they neglect prayer and God's priorities for them.

As the gospel message reaches more and more of earth's people, Satan adjusts his methods to whatever he hopes will be more successful. Where people are more educated or have been influenced by the Gospel, Satan masquerades as an angel of light (2 Cor. 11:13-15). He will emphasize selected beautiful sayings of a false religion. He will guide false religions to imitate Christian methods that God has blessed--children's meetings, youth meetings, literature, radio, and TV evangelism.

Satan seeks to pervert Christian doctrine through denials of the supernatural elements of Christ's life, ministry, and gospel; through false and heretical teachings, even causing unworthy leaders or teachers of false doctrines to "masquerade as servants of righteousness" (2 Cor. 11:15). He does not hesitate while using the name of Christ to deny the power, inspiration, and inerrancy of the Word; the transforming power of the blood of Christ; the transforming power of Christ's literal resurrection; and the miracle-working power of the Holy Spirit (2 Tim. 3:5; 2 Peter 2:1; Phil. 3:10).

As we near the time of Christ's coming, Satan will deceive through miracles (Matt. 24:24; 2 Thess. 2:9-11; Rev. 13:13-15; 16:14;

19:20). He will even deceive the ones through whom he works miracles (Matt. 7:22-23).

This is one reason it is necessary to test the spirits (1 John 4:1). Anyone whose life shows deceit and sin is not sent by God, no matter what miracles or signs he performs (Matt. 7:23). Such a one will be shut out of heaven (Rev. 21:27).

When Satan fails to defeat by sin, false teaching, compromise, or wrong motives, he will try to hinder in other ways. He uses persecution (John 15:20; 17:15; 2 Tim. 3:12; 1 John 3:13). He tries to hinder by circumstances, accident, or illness (Job 1:8-12; 2:3-6; 2 Cor. 12:7; 1 Thess. 2:18). He even tries to accuse Christians before God to stop God's blessing and power from resting on them (Rev. 12:10).

6

HUMAN CREATION AND THE FALL

THE CREATION AND HOLY STATE OF ADAM AND EVE.
The Bible gives a simple, clear, but highly significant account of the
creation of human beings.

1. The creation of the first human beings required the attention
and personal involvement of each member of the Trinity. "Then God
said, 'Let us make man in our image, in our likeness'" (Gen. 1:26).
The plural "us" was not used in any other aspect of creation.

2. The creation of the first human beings is the only place
where thoughtful deliberation announces the first step before taking
it. In all the other acts of creation it simply states, "God said."

3. No other creation is said to be in the image and likeness of
God. This point is so important that it is repeated twice in verse 27.

This means having some similarity to God but lacking the
fullness. Perhaps never until we meet Jesus in heaven will we fully
comprehend all included in being in the image of God. The full
meaning of this involves two aspects--natural and moral. The natural
or essential image of God, though later crippled by Adam's fall into
sin, was not lost. To lose this would be to cease to be human. The
natural image is the basis of the moral image. Surely it includes our
being created with full personality--with the power to choose, to
comprehend intellectually, to respond emotionally, to communicate
with others--even with God, and to share all the holy desires and
emotions of God. We are more than body; we are spirit.

But the image is much more than that. It includes sharing in a
finite and limited sense in the moral attributes of God (sometimes
called the communicable attributes). These include wisdom, justice,
holiness, righteousness, love, goodness, grace, truth, and faithfulness.

This moral image of God involved character and the indwelling of the Holy Spirit. Our spirit was created to be indwelt by the Holy Spirit who imparts holiness of character. Adam's sin forfeited the indwelling presence of God, and thus the moral attributes were seriously impaired and Adam was no longer holy and fit to commune deeply with God.

Human beings were created for God--for communion and fellowship with God. This was only possible because they were created holy and innocent. They were also created to serve God, to do His will and work. The moral image which was lost through the sin of Adam and Eve is restorable through salvation. Redeemed humankind in heaven will enjoy communion with God and service of God forever and ever.

4. This creation was a twofold act (Gen. 2:7). This is said of no other created being and is true of no other creation. (1) "God formed the man from the dust of the ground and (2) breathed into his nostrils the breath of life, and the man became a living being" (Gen. 2:7). Here alone God's specific breathing is mentioned. Physical life was given to animal creation.

A human being is thus constituted a creature of two worlds--the material world and the spirit world, earth and heaven. We are related to space and time, yet also to eternity. We are created from the dust of the earth (and science proves that all the elements in our body are found in the top portion of the earth) and the breath of God--showing our special relation to God's love and plan.

5. Only human beings are created immortal--spirit as well as body. Spirit is immaterial. Once created, spirit can never die. Our first parents were created immortal in spirit--created in the image of God's eternity. Our spirit lives eternally somewhere, and God has provided for each human being who will accept His redemption to spend eternity with Him in the joy, fellowship, beauty, music, glory, and fulfillment of His heaven. Only sin prevents that future, so God has made provision for each person to be saved from sin if he will accept God's provision.

6. God provided Adam and Eve with holy spiritual life. God does not create sinful beings. He breathed into Adam the breath of lives (plural in Hebrew). He became alive with human life--a gift of God, and spiritual life--a created holiness imparted by the indwelling Holy Spirit qualifying him for fellowship with God, also God's gracious gift. Adam and Eve were alive to God spiritually until they sinned. Sin brings spiritual death.

7. God gave Adam and Eve rulership and dominion (Gen. 1:28). They were to rule earth and all created life upon it on God's behalf as His vice-regents. They were responsible to be stewards of earth, its environment, and its animal creation. The New Testament reveals that the salvation of God provided by Jesus includes our sharing with Christ His future reign as His royal fellow-rulers under His sovereign jurisdiction (2 Tim. 2:12; 1 Pet. 2:9; Rev. 2:26; 3:21; 5:10; 20:4; 22:5).

THE ACCOUNT OF THE FALL. Satan's temptation of Adam and Eve in Eden and their yielding to temptation and sinning against God is called "the Fall." This account is recorded in Genesis 3.

Jesus, in John 8:44, teaches that Satan lied, that he is father of sin and lying, and that sin brought death. Paul affirms that the serpent deceived Eve (2 Cor. 11:3; 1 Tim. 2:14), that sin entered the world through Adam and death through sin, and thus sin and death pervaded the whole human race (Rom. 5:12). Paul builds a strong theological message on sin and salvation on this truth (Rom. 5:12-21). The historicity and truth of the Fall are basic to the whole doctrine and experience of salvation.

THE ACCOUNT OF THE FALL IS HISTORICAL. Although there is deep symbolical truth in the account of the Fall, it is fully historical fact.

1. *Genesis 3 is part of a historical book.* This account is an integral part of a continuous historical record. Genesis is an inspired historical book accepted by Christ and the believing church.

2. *It is written in a factual way.* The Bible record is simple, clear, and factual. It is not written in the form of parable, allegory,

or myth. When compared with the early accounts of humanity in nonbiblical writings, the strong contrast and evidence of the truthfulness of the Bible account is obvious.

3. *It is an essential and integral part of Bible history.* No account of God, humanity, and salvation could be complete without an explanation of how human beings became sinners. No account of redemption and salvation through Christ could be complete without showing how salvation became necessary.

4. *The Bible facts of the Fall are appropriate to the first condition of humanity.* All the specific elements are appropriately adapted to newly created humanity:

    a. God placed them in a garden where all their needs were easily supplied.

    b. God established a simple probationary law to establish their loyalty and obedience. This was symbolized in a clear, visual way.

    c. Satan used a living animal familiar to them and present in their environment through which to speak to them, without startling them and making them more cautious.

    d. Satan used psychological steps to tempt Eve and approached her rather than Adam.

    e. The account of Adam and excuse-making as Adam and Eve sought to shift responsibility are straightforward.

    f. The punishment in exclusion from the garden is logical.

5. *Both Old and New Testament writers build upon its historicity.* The truthfulness and historicity of the details of this account are assumed or referred to in both Testaments. Note:

    a. Satan's use of the serpent (Matt. 10:16; 2 Cor. 11:3; Rev. 12:9; 20:2).

    b. The fact that Eve, rather than Adam, was deceived (2 Cor. 11:3; 1 Tim. 2:14).

    c. The fact that sin came into the world through disobedience (Rom. 5:12-19).

    d. The fact that Adam tried to conceal his sin from God (Job 31:33).

    e. The curse on the serpent (Isa. 65:25).

    f. The crushing of the serpent's head (Rom. 16:20).

    g. The pain of childbirth (Gen. 3:16; John 16:21).

    h. The punishment of death passing to all humankind through Adam (1 Cor. 15:21-22).

    i. The human body's return to dust after death (Gen. 3:19; Eccl. 12:7).

    6. *This historical truth is basic to New Testament doctrine.* Essential doctrines are based on this account:

    a. Satan is the tempter (Matt. 4:3; 1 Thess. 3:5).

    b. Man fell into sin through deception (2 Cor. 11:3; 1 Tim. 2:14; Rev. 12:9; 13:14).

    c. The wages of sin is death (Rom. 6:16, 21, 23).

    d. The world is under the control of Satan today (John 12:31; 14:30; 17:15; 1 John 5:19).

    e. The second Adam was victorious where the first Adam failed (Matt. 4:1-11).

    f. The curse brought on the world by the first Adam is destroyed by Christ, the second Adam (Rom. 5:15-21; Rev. 22:3).

NOTE THE CONTRAST BETWEEN GENESIS AND REVELATION. In Genesis Satan enters the world through the serpent; in Revelation as the dragon-serpent he is removed (20:3). In Genesis death enters the world because of sin; in Revelation sin and death are removed from the world (20:13-14; 21:4). In Genesis the curse is pronounced on the earthly Eden; in Revelation the curse is removed and a new edenic paradise is unveiled (2:7; 22:1-3). In Genesis sorrow and laborious toil are part of the curse brought by sin (3:16-19); in Revelation rest from labor is bestowed (14:13) and sorrow is no more (21:4). In Genesis humanity is banished from God's presence (3:23-24); in Revelation redeemed humanity is welcomed to God's presence and immediate fellowship (21:3; 22:4). In Genesis humanity is driven from the tree of life (3:24); in Revelation the tree of life and full right of access is reinstated (22:2, 14).

7

THE PROBATION IN THE GARDEN

A probation is a period of testing to ascertain fitness, loyalty, and character. It can involve not only testing but also preparation and training. Scripture teaches that all of life is a probation. Human probation begins with the testing of Adam and Eve in Eden. It continues throughout the life of all human beings as they build character and qualify for rewards in heaven or for varying degrees of punishment in hell.

We are morally responsible to use our opportunities for God, right, and His kingdom. As free agents we have responsibility for our choices. Duty involves moral accountability. This life is a probation filled with duty and responsibility for moral choice, and for all moral choice we will be accountable to God (Exod. 12:13-14; Rom. 2:16; 14:12; 2 Cor. 5:10; Rev. 20:11-13).

THE NECESSITY OF PROBATION. God created Adam and Eve without sin. They were innocent and holy. God requires us to be holy because He is holy (Lev. 19:2; 1 Peter 1:16). Moral holiness requires moral freedom, freedom of choice. We must choose to love, fellowship, and obey God. The highest blessing God can give any human being is His fellowship and love. But only freely accepted love, love fully responded to, is moral love.

Quality love requires full personality--intellect, sensibility, and will. Sensibility is the capacity for sensation, feeling, emotion. The higher the degree of intellect, sensibility, and will, the greater the degree of fellowship and love that is possible. It is beyond our finite comprehension why God loved humankind enough to create us with the freedom, greatness, and God-likeness of personality which makes holy fellowship with God possible. What condescension for Him to create us in His own image! Yet having done so, there is no logical way God could avoid giving us choice, choice which would be tested.

If a person is free to choose fellowship and obedience to God, he must also be free to reject and choose self rather than God. If he is created dependent on its Creator, he must be subject to his Creator. Fellowship requires harmony of interest, nature, and will. When God gives a human being free will, the power to choose, then the person must prove his love and choice of fellowship by placing his will in harmony with God. A human being has no greater obligation than this. It is his most simple and most moral law of duty.

Duty is only duty when choice is possible. A robot or machine has no duty. Only people capable of moral choice can have duty. But duty involves probation. Where there is probation there is the possibility of disobedience and sin. Before there can be permanent fellowship on the highest level there must be at least a temporary period of probation, with the power to accept or reject the conditions of fellowship.

THE PROBATIONARY LAW. God as the creator of free moral beings, with the purpose of fellowship and cooperation, had the right and necessity of testing those beings. As Creator and Sovereign, He had the responsibility to choose the form of testing or probation. The probationary law had to be such that it tested the human being's personality (including intellect, sensibility, and will). The test, temptation, or choice had to come through his personality.

But since the human being was innocent and holy, that temptation had to originate outside his being. Furthermore, to be a fair test the appeal to his personality had to be regarding something innocent in itself and only wrong because God had forbidden it. Anything unattractive or inherently wrong or evil would have no appeal and would not be a fair test of loyal obedience.

There are only two kinds of laws or commands--moral and positive. A moral command is one with a reason you innately feel to be right since you have a moral nature. It has within it inherent rightness or goodness. A positive command, in contrast, is one you are not able to reason out. Its moral basis is not evident to you. It is only wrong because it is forbidden.

Adam and Eve as innocent, pure beings, having no sinful nature, could be truly tested only by a command they had ability to obey but which was positive rather than moral. Obedience to a positive command proves respect, loyalty, faith, and love.

THE FAIRNESS OF EDEN'S PROBATIONARY LAW. God in His holy wisdom and love made the probationary law for testing Adam and Eve completely fair. His infinite justice could not do otherwise.

a. His command was plain and clearly understood. It tested their loyalty to God their Creator and Lord. They had only one prohibition. They were clearly warned of the serious consequences of disobedience. Nothing could be more reasonable, simple, and right.

b. Adam and Eve were innocent and pure. They were undoubtedly indwelt by the Holy Spirit, for the only holiness we have is that communicated to us by the Holy Spirit.

c. The environment was adequate and satisfying. Not only was every need supplied, but there was an abundance of what delights the senses.

d. They had access to God. Not only were they indwelt by the Holy Spirit, but God seems to have been in daily communion with them in the evening. They could ask for explanation or clarification of His will. They could have inquired of God concerning the tempter and his statements. We do not know how long after their creation they fell into sin, but obviously they had continued fellowship with God for some time, for Adam had time to get acquainted with all of creation and give appropriate names to all of the animals. They had been taught their responsibilities, and they recognized the voice of God.

e. They had strong reasons for trust and obedience to God. They knew God was their Creator. They knew and had already experienced in some variety (Gen. 2:19-20) His power, wisdom, and love as manifested in His creation. They knew they owed their existence to God and that they owed Him obedience. He had proved His trustworthiness and love already in providing Eve for Adam and probably in many other ways. They knew God had given them only one simple law or command to obey.

THE PROBATION WAS BOTH FACTUAL AND SYMBOLIC. God conducted the probation through command and through symbol. The probation and fall into sin are a moral lesson for the universe. For Adam and Eve and for the universe each symbol, whether an object, person, or act, had tremendous significance. Note the following:

The enclosed garden--there is safety in the will of God.

The tree of life--symbolizing communion with God. Continuous life depends on continuous obedient partaking. God provides eternal life of fellowship with God.

The tree of knowledge--knowledge is experiential in nature. We learn by obedience and by doing.

The command of God--God is the source of moral law. "Man does not live on bread alone, but on every word that comes from the mouth of God" (Matt. 4:4).

The only command--the unitary nature of God's law. You become a lawbreaker by breaking one law (James 2:10).

The serpent--the subtlety, external attractiveness, deceitfulness, swiftness, and fatal nature of temptation to sin, and of Satan, the tempter.

The death penalty (Gen. 2:17)--the fatal nature of sin.

The lie of Satan--Satan, the father of lies (John 8:44).

Eve yielding while alone--sin is an individual act.

Eve giving to Adam--the social influence of sin.

Fig leaves--the inadequacy of human efforts to cover and hide sin.

Hiding from God--guilt brings shame and fear.

The voice of God--God lovingly searches for lost ones.

Questions of God--confession of sin to God cannot be escaped. Either we confess to God now or we will to God before the whole universe at the Judgment (Dan. 7:9-10; Rom. 14:12).

The curse--the punishment of sin is inevitable.

Snake in the dust--the humiliating effects of sin.

Curse on earth, animals, and man--the totality of sin's effect.

Banishment from Eden--sin separates from God and good.

Garments of skin--the only covering for sin acceptable to God is that which required sacrifice in atonement for sin.

Flaming sword at gate of Eden--without holiness no one will have access to God (Ps. 24:3-4; Rev. 21:27) or see the Lord (Matt. 5:8; Heb. 12:14).

Thus the account of the Fall is totally historical but at the same time deeply symbolical. The spiritual interpretation of the historical account must be understood in order to comprehend the full significance of Adam and Eve's act of rebellion against God.

Many believe that prior to God's curse upon it the serpent was one of the higher animals, perhaps the highest, and was therefore desired by Satan as his instrument. Satan to this day makes frequent use of others as his instruments to voice or do what he wants done (Matt. 16:23; Luke 22:3).

8

THE STEPS IN THE
TEMPTATION AND FALL

SATAN'S METHOD IN TEMPTING. Satan uses every method, every law of psychology, every deceitful appeal which he believes will help in accomplishing his goals. God wants us to be aware of Satan's schemes (2 Cor. 2:11). It is instructive to note the methods he used with Eve.

1. *Satan appeals to innocent appetites.* He takes advantage of any weakness and tries to pervert legitimate human appetites, drives, and needs to his purpose. He used Eve's desire and enjoyment of fruit (perfectly legitimate in itself) as part of his temptation.

2. *Satan injects doubts about God.* He begins by exaggerating what God said. "Surely God did not say that! Did He really say you must not eat from any tree in the garden? Is God really keeping you from all these beautiful trees and their delicious fruit? How could God have said that? Is He that kind of God?"

Satan begins by slandering the character of God. He casts doubt on God by implying that He is treating Adam and Eve in some kind of an unjust way. He is distracting Eve's attention from the abundant provision God has made and focusing on one seemingly small, trivial restriction.

3. *Satan tries to create desire for what God has forbidden.* He motivates them to disagree with God. He focuses attention on the forbidden. The more a person focuses attention on something forbidden, the stronger the desire can become. Satan is seeking to motivate self-will to be expressed in independence from God.

4. *Satan injects doubt about the truthfulness of God.* "God surely did not really mean what He said. He must have just been

threatening you." He cast doubt on the seriousness of sin. He motivated them to presume on the mercy of God.

5. *Satan attributes false motives to God.* He continues his slander of God's character and integrity. This is his strategic warfare against God. The longer Eve talks with him, the bolder Satan becomes in his anti-God statements. He implies that God is deliberately depriving Adam and Eve of their rights. God is actually trying to keep them ignorant!

Satan always appeals to one's self-benefit and emphasizes right rather than duties. All social relationships depend on the law that right depends on the fulfillment of duty. All efforts of Satan and sin seek to cause neglect and failure to fulfill duty and to give improper insistence upon rights.

Satan's basic appeal is to pride, sinful ambition, and carnal self-will. The essence of all sin is the self-seeking spirit which was evident in Satan's first sin and the first sin of Adam and Eve. The essence of victory over sin is the forgiveness of sin and the crucifixion of self by the Spirit's sanctifying, cleansing work.

6. *Satan appeals to exert independence from God.* He promises Eve she will become like God in knowledge if she insists on her own rights and does what God has forbidden. Satan camouflages his full purpose. If he had said, "Renounce your relationship with God, deny His sovereignty over you, and in place of God accept me as your Lord," she would not have yielded to his temptation. Satan suggests what seems to be a simple action, but it is contrary to God's command. The doing of it, in effect, renounces God's sovereign authority. Satan makes a person think it is important to maintain some independence. Actually, such an act makes one the slave of Satan and sin. To exert independence of the will of God and act contrary to it is to reject God.

To this day Satan makes the same deceitful appeal: "Do what you think is best for yourself." Actually, it is the worst possible act for the person to take, but what is best for Satan. The best action for anyone at any time is that which is the will of God, for God is all-wise, unselfish love.

THE STEPS IN YIELDING TO TEMPTATION. These are the steps which Eve took in yielding to temptation. The same basic steps are taken again and again when people yield to Satan's temptation to sin. Every yielding to temptation is a sin against God and a victory for Satan.

1. *Mental consideration.* Eve should have instantly cast aside Satan's suggestion since it was contrary to God's expressed will. She should have remembered who God is and His goodness to her. Instead, she paused to consider it. She accepted the possibility that her reason might be more helpful than God's will. She began to weigh in her mind and think over what Satan had said.

We can never avoid thoughts of evil coming to our mind, but we do not need to entertain and consider them. By God's help we can instantly reject any thought of evil as soon as it comes. If we do that, we will never be overcome by temptation and will never fall into Satan's suggested sin and thus become guilty. It is never safe to converse with the devil.

2. *Doubt.* A wholesome question is not sinful in itself. God is willing to answer sincere questions when our faith needs evidence. He gave miracle credentials to Moses, the prophets, Christ, and the leaders of His church.

The doubt that leads to sin is the doubt that questions the validity or truth of what God has commanded. It is the first logical step after listening to Satan that can lead to the act of sin. It is questioning the wisdom, justice, love, faithfulness, or power of God. This is the kind of doubt that Eve yielded to. It is the kind of doubt which leads to sin today. It is a form of unbelief that is the great sin of which the Holy Spirit convicts the world (John 16:9). All forms of unbelief are a dishonor to God and are a step to disobedience.

The shield of faith is available to the Christian to extinguish all the flaming arrows of Satan (Eph. 6:16).

3. *Desire.* Satan leads from doubt to desire. He tries to make the sinful object or action seem attractive, rewarding, and desirable. Every sin is the result of yielding to some kind of wrong desire.

James 1:14-15--"Each one is tempted when, by his own evil desire, he is dragged away and enticed. Then, after desire has conceived, it gives birth to sin; and sin, when it is full-grown, gives birth to death."

Often innocent desire is changed into evil desire through a wrong motive. The desire for good, beautiful fruit was not wrong in itself, but when desire became the hope that it would make them "like God," it became evil. Even the desire for spiritual power can become a deadly sin when it springs from carnal ambition, pride, or some other sinful motive (Acts 8:18-23).

4. *Consent.* Sin only becomes sin through the consent of the will. The first step to consent is doubt. The second is desire. But the crucial, decisive step is the consent of the will. That is what brings guilt, even if the circumstances do not permit the actual act. Once the will consents, the person is already guilty in God's sight (Matt. 5:28). The social consequences of sin are not as great if the act is not committed, but the person is already guilty in heaven's records--guilty of a sin of the heart.

THE THREE AVENUES OF TEMPTATION. All temptations come to human beings through one of three ways: the cravings of the sinful person, the lust of the eyes, or the boasting of what he has and does (1 John 2:16). These three together constitute "the world" (v. 15). This term "the world" is a summary term for all that is contrary to the will of God. We are forbidden to love the world or anything of the character of the world [i.e., worldliness] (1 John 2:15). We are not to conform to the pattern of the world (Rom. 12:2) or live by the standards of this world (2 Cor. 10:2).

The cravings of the sinful person refer to the cravings of the carnal ego, the self-first mentality, the self-sufficient independence from God, and the lust of the flesh--including sinful physical and sexual desire. The lust of the eyes refers to the desire for visible splendor and show, the desire to accumulate material things, coveting, and greed in all its forms. The boasting of what one has and does refers to the pride of life, self-display in an ostentatious way of life, empty bragging, and all proud boasting.

The temptation of Adam and Eve was along these three lines. Eve saw that the fruit of the tree was "good for food," "pleasing to the eye," and "desirable for gaining wisdom" (Gen. 3:6). The temptation of Christ was also related to these three: "Tell these stones to become bread," "Throw yourself down" from the highest part of the temple in view of all the worshipers, and "All the kingdoms of the world and their splendor . . . I will give to you if . . . " (Matt. 4:1-11). Christ, the second Adam, was victorious at each point where the first Adam fell. Through Christ we also can be victorious over all temptation (1 Cor. 10:12-13).

QUESTIONS REGARDING THE FALL AND TEMPTATION

1. *How could a holy being fall?* Sin is always something of a mystery. It is so irrational and immoral, why would anyone sin? Even God does not explain this in detail to us, but God conquers it in Christ, wipes it out (Acts 3:19), and destroys it along with the other works of the devil (1 John 3:8).

Since God does not explain sin as an entity, He does not detail an explanation for the sin of Satan or Adam. In both it was a grasping for spiritual and moral autonomy. Thereby it manifested unbelief and the spirit of rebellion. It was a transgression of the law of God's holy nature, the law written in conscience and memory, and the law as spoken or written by God (1 John 3:4).

The Bible account of Adam and Eve's fall into sin is the only rational explanation of how sin came into the world. Sin is here. It has to be accounted for in some way. The Bible account is simple, clear, rational, and trustworthy.

There is only one explanation of how a holy being can sin-- through the wrong exercise of free will, wrong choice. This was the only way Satan could become a sinner, and it is the only way Adam and Eve could become sinners.

God is not the author of sin, neither is sin its own author. Sin results from the wrong use of free will. That is the cause of sin today. A holy being has a will inclined to obedience toward God. But he is free to choose disobedience. There is no such thing as temptation unless there is power of contrary choice. Such power of choice may exist in a holy or in a sinful being. Christ was holy, yet He was tempted in every way just as we are (Heb. 4:15).

2. *Why did God permit the temptation?* To say that God permits temptation is not to state that God ordained, decreed, or compelled yielding to temptation. No temptation is irresistible (1 Cor. 10:13). God did not compel, encourage, or desire the fall into sin. Neither did God consent to Adam and Eve's yielding to temptation. God had created them with power of choice and did not forcibly prevent Satan from tempting them or their using their power of choice.

God permitted the temptation because He permitted human beings to be free. Freedom of will is the most Godlike aspect of human personality, of the natural image of God in human beings. God did not choose even a neutral setting for the temptation where it would be as easy to sin as to obey. He put Adam and Eve in an ideal environment, was daily present with them for fellowship, and preserved an environment of peace and plenty. They had many forms of satisfaction--beauty, variety, enjoyable activities (ruling the animals). There were no external pressures or strains.

God gave them only one simple test of loyal obedience. He gave them clear, easily understood instructions. He created them with original innocence and holiness of nature. That holiness resulted from the presence of the Holy Spirit indwelling them--all holiness is personal and is imparted by God's presence. When in spite of all this they abused their freedom, withdrew their trust, and deliberately violated God's command, the seriousness of their sin and rebellion is apparent.

Temptation, when resisted, yields moral character. If Adam and Eve had been continuously obedient to God, continuously fellowshiping with God, then their positive created holiness would have merged into ethical holiness. By loyal love and faithful obedience to God they would have been united in ever-closer and blessed fellowship with God.

Perhaps after a period of such steadfastness in the midst of temptation individuals would have been translated to heaven without passing through death. Temptation, when resisted and overcome, becomes a means of strengthening and growth of character and ethical holiness, of spiritual growth and blessing, of ever-deepening communion with God, and makes possible God's bestowal of reward.

Also remember that God did not permit the Fall without a provisional "back-up" economy of redemption. God is love, so He chose human persons for glorious fellowship and a blessed eternal role (since spirit once created can never cease to exist). Having created persons with the gracious privilege but awesome responsibility of free will, God in love provided the possibility of redemption which would be available for them if they did disobey and fall into sin.

Therefore Christ is the Lamb of God that is "slain from the creation of the world" (Rev. 13:8), that is, God's redemptive plan was complete with Christ already willingly accepting His atoning role from the time the world was prepared for Adam and Eve.

Through Christ's redemption provided for fallen humanity, which God provided at such infinite cost, the infinite grace and love of God is demonstrated and proved to the whole universe. God did not wish human beings to fall, but God made full provision to reclaim from the Fall all who accept His gracious provision. His is a redemption of grace and glory.

God thus demonstrates what is clearly stated in Romans 8:28, that God is able to work for the good of those who love Him, in spite of any and every circumstance. In His infinite wisdom, love, and power God can cause even the wrath of people to praise Him (possible translation of the Hebrew in Ps. 76:10). While permitting human beings to remain free, He achieves His ultimate purposes and brings infinite good and blessing to all who accept His loving provision and obey Him.

God always more than overcomes any evil done by Satan. There is no way Satan can ultimately benefit or succeed. God permits each person to exercise his free will, and the person can destroy his character, forfeit every opportunity to repent, and refuse God's will. But God will carry out His eternal plan and purpose in spite of this.

God is never surprised, never discouraged, and will never be ultimately defeated.

9

THE DEFINITION AND
NATURE OF SIN

DEFINITIONS AND DESCRIPTION OF SIN. Sin is an act or state of our being that separates us from our holy God. The ultimate sinfulness of sin is that it is against God. It is an act against the law and will of God and, hence, against God Himself. It is an attitude against God, which comes from a nature that is not only unlike God but is hostile to God. So sin has to be defined in relation to God, our holy Sovereign. For a discussion of Hebrew and Greek terms for sin, see Appendix A.

Sin severs our relationship and fellowship with God. This distorts and depraves our personality, which was created to be related to God, and enfeebles, pollutes and disintegrates our own self. It also corrupts, interrupts, and estranges our fellowship with others.

The root of sin is fourfold: unbelief (self-confidence, distrust in God), pride (self-idolatry), disobedience (self-will, inner rebellion), and sensuality (self-gratification). These interrelate in the inner nature of the person. At times one of these may seem to dominate or be more basic, and at times another. Their inner expression is in attitude, and their outer expression is in willful transgression. All sin is the expression of self against God, His holiness or His law, which is based on His holy nature.

In the Old Testament sin is breach of covenant relation with God, which the prophets saw as outright wicked rebellion against God. In the New Testament there are at least 28 synonyms or terms for sin, of which five are discussed in Appendix A.

Sin is both pollution and guilt, state and act, motivation and expression. It can be deceptively lurking in the inner nature, yet audacious and strident in deed. It is darkness in soul and dark deeds.

Note these definitions:

Wm. B. Pope: "Sin is the voluntary separation of the soul from God."

J. Wesley: "Sin is the voluntary transgression of a known law."

A. H. Strong: "Sin is lack of conformity to the moral law of God, either in act, disposition, or state. . . ."

Westminster Catechism: "Sin is any want of conformity to, or transgression, of the law of God."

In summary, we may define sin as twofold in nature. Sin as an act is a willful transgression of God's law. Sin as a state is unholiness of nature motivating sinful acts. Since sin is twofold in nature, God has made a twofold provision of salvation.

1. *Sin as an act.* A willful transgression of a known law of God is always sin. It may be a willful commission or a willful omission. It may be expressed by thought, word, or deed.

The law of God is written in the Bible and, to some extent, on a person's conscience. An act becomes sin to man and brings guilt on him when he knowingly sins against God's holy nature or His revealed will.

The Bible recognizes what is called "unintentional sin" (Lev. 4). This is a sin of ignorance. It is sin from the standpoint of God's perfect holiness, but the person becomes responsible to confess and ask forgiveness when he becomes aware of the sin committed (Lev. 4:28). From God's perspective the person has unknown guilt. From the person's standpoint, he senses no guilt and is not responsible to confess the guilt until he is convicted by new light and the ministry of the Spirit.

Romans 4:15--"Where there is no law there is no transgression."

Romans 5:13--"Before the law was given, sin was in the world. But sin is not taken into account when there is no law."

We are responsible for the light we receive. The familiar saying is, "The measure of light is the measure of responsibility." If we walk in the light the Spirit gives us, our fellowship with God remains unbroken and the blood of Christ cleanses us and covers us (1 John 1:7). We will not be condemned by God's judgment for these forgiven, cleansed, and covered sins.

The condemnation of God, the primary experience of conviction of guilt by the Holy Spirit, is for the known sin willfully committed in spite of light from conscience and from God. This is the sin that separates from God.

The light of God is progressive. As the person walks in the light given by the Holy Spirit, through God's Word, conscience, memory, or the guidance or restraint of the Spirit, he understands ever more clearly the nature of God and what is contrary to that nature. The person begins to recognize some things as sin which up to that time had not been perceived to be sin. From then on the person is responsible to walk in that new light. This is fully scriptural (Acts 14:16; 17:30).

Things God at one time permitted humankind to do are now clearly covered by God's light as over the centuries God revealed Scripture and enlightened Christian conscience. Examples are polygamy, marriage within near kinship, and divorce. Similarly, the church has recognized light progressively and has developed Christian standards on things like slavery, use of intoxicants, and responsibility to one's local church.

2. *Sin as a state.* Sin also exists as a state or condition of our nature. This will be studied more thoroughly under the topic of "The Sin Nature." The Bible teaches that Adam's sinful choice brought a defiling change to his spiritual nature. All of Adam's descendants-- our entire human race--are born with a sinful inherited nature. Today all sinful acts or manifestations are expressions of the sinful nature of the person.

a. The Greek terms in the New Testament are used for both the act and the state of sin:

Hamartia--an act of falling away or missing the mark (1 John 3:4) or a state of having fallen away or missed the mark (Rom. 6:12).

Parabasis--an act of transgression (Matt. 15:3) or a state of transgression (1 Tim. 2:14). Note: *paraptoma* is used only for the act of transgression.

Adikia--an act of unrighteousness (1 John 5:17) or a state of unrighteousness (Rom. 3:5).

Anomia--In 1 John 3:4 *anomia* is used twice, both for the lawless deed and for the state of lawlessness.

Asebia--In Jude 15 *asebia* is used twice, both for the ungodly nature and the ungodly deeds.

b. Both thoughts (acts) can be evil (Matt. 15:19) and heart (nature) can be evil (Heb. 3:12).

c. It is sin as a state or nature which motivates persons to acts of sin (Rom. 7:8).

d. Sin reigns in people (Rom. 5:21; 6:12).

e. Human language proves that humanity believes in the fact of a sinful nature. People speak of bad character, a vile nature, and a cruel heart.

f. This sinful nature is manifested even in innocent children.

g. Many Christians who know their sins are forgiven still find a sinful nature within them.

God's condition to receive forgiveness for our sinful acts is confession of these acts (1 John 1:9). God's condition for cleansing of this hostile inner nature is total surrender of our selfhood (Rom. 12:1). Consecration is not only giving one's self to God as a gift; it is the total surrender of the inner self to God. Heart purity can only be received from God after total surrender, full consecration. That is why eternal fellowship with God is conditioned upon heart purity (Matt. 5:8). Without that it will be impossible to see the Lord (Heb. 12:14).

10

THE CONSEQUENCES OF SIN
(PART 1)

The results or consequences of sin were serious, far-reaching, and devastating in their effect upon human beings personally, upon human beings socially, and thus on human society in general, and even upon earth and nature.

Adam and Eve not only lost the indwelling presence of the Holy Spirit and their innocence and purity, but there came an instant alienation from God. They became sin conscious and convicted by the Holy Spirit. They felt shame before God and before each other. They immediately wanted to hide from God. Their trust in God, love for God, and the freedom of sonship with God suffered tragic loss.

Created to be indwelt by the Holy Spirit, they were now empty with a void that none but God could fill. Created to fellowship and commune with God, they now dreaded His presence. Liberty, joy, and trust were replaced by shame and fear. For the first time they experienced reproof, condemnation, curse, and expulsion from the Sovereign God. God still loved them but justly could not have the same relation to them. God cannot be neutral or fail to react against sin. He cannot contradict His holy nature (2 Tim. 2:13).

There were far-reaching social consequences and racial consequences. When their blessed relationship with God was disturbed, God's elevating and holy presence was lost and their personalities defiled. When depravity began, Adam's relation with Eve and with his descendants could not but be disturbed. Murder began in their immediate family. Soon there was polygamy, more murder, vengeance, and sexual perversion. The human race rapidly became so sinful that God wiped out all but eight people by judgment in the form of the Flood. In a sense God gave humanity a new start (Gen. 6-9), but almost immediately drunkenness and sexual sin are recorded. God's description of human beings was, "Every inclination of the thought of his heart was only evil all the time" (Gen. 6:5). And we further read, "The earth was corrupt in God's sight and was full of violence" (v. 11).

All the problems of contemporary civilization trace back to the corrupting and destructive influence of sin and the long, tragic history of the havoc of sin. Hatred, crime, breakup of the home, cruelty, abuse, pornography--all forms of corruption, immorality, violence, and war witness that sin destroys.

And what shall we say of the destruction of our globe turning countryside into desert, polluting the water of rivers and ocean, contaminating the air we breathe, wiping out many species of animals and fish life, and endangering even the atmosphere that surrounds our earth. The beautiful cosmos that God created so congenial to human beings has become a place of pain and conflict. "The whole creation has been groaning as in the pains of childbirth right up to the present time" (Rom. 8:22). It awaits God's day of redemption to be applied to all life (Isa. 11:6-9). Then there will be no more curse (Rev. 22:3). The law of the jungle will no longer prevail. Might will not determine right, and all will be harmony and peace under God's eternal reign.

Let us now note the three tragic results of sin for human beings:

1. GUILT. Guilt is personal blameworthiness because of an act of sin. The guilty one deserves punishment because he has broken God's law. It is the legal and moral condition resulting from the wrong act. Guilt always involves a) responsibility for an act of sin; b) the condemnation of God and hence the sinner's condition of guilt; and c) accountability and liability to punishment because of the sin.

The basic Hebrew word for "to be guilty" is *asham*. It includes all these three aspects of guilt. *Hypodikos* in the New Testament means to be guilty (Rom. 3:19).

Guilt is strictly personal. It is not transferable to others. The sin of a father may bring evil consequences for the whole family, but only the father is guilty (Ezek. 18:20; 32:33).

The sin of a ruler may bring evil consequences on the whole nation, as we see frequently in the Old Testament, but no other one in the nation is guilty for that sin unless he associates himself with the ruler in it. There is such a thing as national or group sin and corporate guilt which brings corporate consequences (Lev. 4:13; Num. 32:23; Deut. 9:16; 1 Kings 8:33, 50; 2 Kings 17:7; Jer. 50:4). This then calls for group or national repentance (2 Chron. 7:14). A righteous person can identify himself with the sin of his people and repent and pray vicariously for the nation (Dan. 9:4-11). This is one aspect of the way Jesus identified with humanity and interceded for us all (Isa. 53:12).

Guilt brings a sense of personal condemnation, a sense of personal shame and remorse for the sin committed, an awareness of alienation from God because of the sin. The Bible gives examples of people sensing, confessing, and bearing remorse over their guilt (Adam and Eve--Gen. 3:7-8; Cain--Gen. 4:8-9; Saul--1 Sam. 15:30; 28:15; David--2 Sam. 12:13; Ps. 51).

But guilt is not just feeling. It is a biblical reality because sin is against God. Scripture emphasizes that each person is accountable to God for his acts. Each person must bear the moral and often other consequences of his wrong choice and act. He reaps what he sows, and there is no way to escape the moral reaping except by forgiveness. Even then, he may reap other consequences of his sin (Gal. 6:7).

God longs to forgive the sin that makes us guilty. This is why He provided for atoning sacrifice in the Old Testament. Sacrifice pointed to Christ's true and final sacrifice which provided the basis for our forgiveness and acquittal and which enables God to justify us by His grace. We are no longer guilty and no longer under God's condemnation, nor do we feel that sense of condemnation after we are forgiven (Rom. 5:1; 8:1).

Jesus took upon Himself the punishment for our sin which was rightly ours, but that did not make Him guilty. He was still the sinless one. Guilt is always personal. If Jesus, by taking upon Himself the punishment for our sin, had thus become guilty, His death could not be substitutionary. Only one who is himself not guilty can voluntarily take the punishment for someone else.

The Christian forgiven of his sins is a sinner saved by grace, but he can never be restored to innocence. He will always be a forgiven sinner. A person can be forgiven and cleansed of his sin, but innocence and spiritual virginity, once lost, never can be restored. Each infant is born innocent but impure. He is not guilty of committed sins, but he has a sinful nature. Only Adam and Eve came into the world both innocent and pure.

There is a difference between guilt and the consciousness of that guilt (Lev. 4:27-28). Various circumstances may increase or diminish the person's feeling of guiltiness. Sin deceives the person, blinds him to the seriousness of his sin, and hardens his conscience (Eph. 4:18). Often the more a sinner repeats a sin the less compunction he feels as he sins again. But his guilt is increased every time he sins, whether his conscience bothers him or not.

No sinner recognizes his full guilt before God nor the seriousness of that guilt. It is the work of the Holy Spirit to convict of sin, and He may do that any moment. Only the Holy Spirit can help us realize our guiltiness before God.

Since there are degrees of guilt which God will recognize at the Judgment, there will be degrees of punishment in eternity (Matt. 10:15; 12:31; Luke 11:29-32; 12:47-48; John 19:11; Rom. 2:12; Heb. 2:2-3; 10:29).

2. DEPRAVITY. Depravity is the moral state of Adam and Eve after their sin. Their act of sin not only made them guilty, it had a profound effect upon their inner nature. The moment they sinned the Holy Spirit withdrew from their hearts. They had been created innocent and holy. But holiness, like depravity and sin, does not have real existence of its own. It is not a physical thing or spiritual entity.

Holiness is a characteristic of a being, the quality of the nature of the being. There is only one innately holy being--God. All holiness in man is derived from God's indwelling us by His Holy Spirit. So Adam's created holiness was the residence of the Holy Spirit in him--for he was created to be indwelt by the Holy Spirit. Without the indwelling Spirit a person's inner nature is empty and restless and never can be fully satisfied.

When the Holy Spirit was withdrawn from Adam, his inner nature was without the lordship of the Spirit, without any holiness imparted to him. Separation from God is spiritual death. So spiritual death began to work within his nature. He had no strength of character developed. He succumbed to the thoughts and temptations with which Satan bombarded him. His own firstborn son became a murderer. It does not take depravity long to spread and pervert a person.

We may not know fully how to explain the nature of sin, but we all know its reality. A sin affects the whole of our being. The conscience is wounded and hardened. The understanding and intellect are blinded, darkened, and deceived. The ability to reason is enfeebled and disabled. The sensibilities are diverted from God's intended role and become deranged, depraved, and enslaved. The will is enfeebled, to some extent bound and constrained to serve sin and Satan. Our whole spiritual being is profaned, debased, disorganized, and in many ways perverted.

Since this is the subject of the next major topic in chapter 12, further discussion is deferred to that section.

11

THE CONSEQUENCES OF SIN
(PART 2)

3. DEATH. The penalty of sin is death (Gen. 2:17). Penalty is the punishment that follows sin. Depravity is not a punishment; it is the result of sin. Sin deprives and depraves. The penalty, however, is inflicted by the Moral Ruler of the universe. A penalty is a suffering of pain, or loss of rights or property directly inflicted by a lawgiver in vindication of his justice which has been outraged by the violation of his law. God may inflict punishment through natural, moral, or spiritual laws, or through direct decree.

God is not only immanent in the universe, He is transcendent and personal. To fall into the hands of the living God (Heb. 10:31) is not merely to fall into the hands of the law but also of the Law-giver. Penalty has a personal element--the holy wrath of the Author of the law, the Moral Ruler, the Judge. God's attitude toward sin is shown in Christ's cleansing of the temple with a whip in His hand (John 2:15), in His denouncing the hypocrisy of the Pharisees (Matt. 23:13-33), in His weeping over Jerusalem (Luke 13:34-35; 19:41), and in His agony in Gethsemane (Luke 22:39-44).

There is no alternative--God's holiness must react against sin with full penalty. Sin deserves God's judgment. Sin and defilement must be banished from God and those who love and serve Him. God must be just or cease to be holy. God's imposing the penalty for sin is the necessary expression and vindication of His holy character as Sovereign and Lawgiver.

The primary purpose of penalty is not to reform but to enforce justice. God must be just even though He is holy love. The reforming influences which God gives are His grace accompanying His justice. Punishment, in the Bible, is not attributed to God's love but to His justice (Ezek. 28:22; 36:22-23; Heb. 12:29; Rev. 15:1, 3-4).

> **Revelation 16:5**--"You are just in these judgments, you who are and who were, the Holy One, because you have so judged."
>
> **Revelation 19:2**--"True and just are his judgments."

If the primary purpose of penalty was to reform the sinner, then punishment would not be just if the sinner (for example, Satan) could not be reformed. Chastisement and correction (God's discipline for Christians) is reformatory. Punishment is not primarily so. Chastisement proceeds from love, punishment from justice. God may first act in a form of disciplinary chastisement. But if the person refuses to heed, God will eventually punish.

Punishment can serve three purposes: 1) prevention, 2) reformation, or 3) retribution. God's penalty on sin is mainly just retribution. His penalty is not primarily to prevent or deter. God in His goodness often secures more than one result, but He never punishes a person merely for the good of society. No punishment ultimately benefits society unless it is just in itself.

The only reason God punishes is because punishment is deserved, but while thus giving deserved punishment God often graciously uses it to prevent or deter others from sinning. Sin merits punishment and God is just, so He is compelled to punish sin whether good results from it or not. God must be just or He ceases to be holy.

God's justice has no passion or unpredictable quality. It is calm and judicial, the expression of His infinite, unchangeable eternal holiness and righteousness. God must and does vindicate His justice, but He is not a revenging Being just waiting to show His wrath. Without holy vindication of His justice and righteous law, there could be no righteous government and God would not be God.

The penalty of death, according to Scripture, is threefold: physical death, spiritual death, and eternal death. All death involves separation. "Sin when it is full grown, gives birth to death" (James 1:15). Death in its totality is the punishment for sin.

A. PHYSICAL DEATH. Physical death is the separation of the spirit from the body. Death is not annihilation. The body disintegrates, but the spirit lives on forever. Physical death is part of the penalty for sin, but not the primary part. The moment Adam sinned, the grace and mercy of God prevented his instant physical death, but he began that moment to die physically.

Since Christ is "the Lamb that was slain from the creation of the world" (Rev. 13:8; 1 Peter 1:19-20), the merits of His blood became immediately effective when Adam and Eve sinned. The gift of God's grace (Rom. 5:15-17) was ready and available even before they sinned. Thus God could be at the same time the God of justice and the God of grace. So the full strength of God's condemnation of sin was met by the full strength of redemptive grace. God could begin the first sacrifice (the garment of skins--Gen. 3:21) as soon as He had Adam and Eve's confession.

The penal nature of physical death and the shadow it casts on humankind is clearly recognized in the prayer of Moses (Ps. 90:7-12), and in Paul's statements (Rom. 5:12, 14-17; 6:23). Probably if neither Adam nor any of his descendants had sinned, all human beings would have been translated like Enoch and Elijah. Sin turned what could have been normal into a very rare exception.

The fear of death and what may follow it is a slavery for humankind (Heb. 2:15). We are now destined to die (9:27). The Christian is now delivered from that fear (Rom. 8:15-16). Death is still something of a mystery. The uncertainty of when and how it will occur may intimidate even a Christian, but for him death has been changed by the New Testament teaching and the death and resurrection of Christ (1 Thess. 4:13-14).

B. SPIRITUAL DEATH. The second part of the penalty of sin is spiritual death. This occurred instantly when Adam and Eve sinned and still takes place instantly when a person sins willfully. Spiritual death is the separation of one's spirit from God. The primary penalty of sin in Eden was spiritual death. Sin not only deprives of the presence of God, the favor of God, the knowledge of God, and the desire for God, but also blinds and enslaves the spirit.

What fellowship can light have with darkness, God with sin (1 John 1:5-6)? The term "death" is often used in the Bible in this spiritual sense. The withdrawal of the Holy Spirit from the soul results in spiritual death. Without God's presence, life, and power, the spirit of man is spiritually dead and needs to be made spiritually alive from the dead (Luke 15:32; John 5:24; 8:51). The sinner is dead in trespasses and sins (Eph. 2:1-2; Jude 12), darkened by sin (Eph. 4:7-18), but God can make any sinner alive (Col. 2:13). When the Holy Spirit withdraws from a person these results are instantly present:

1) *Spiritual death.* The Holy Spirit is the only source of spiritual life. "The Spirit gives life" (John 6:63; 2 Cor. 3:6). It is the law of spiritual existence that sin brings death. The law of the spirit of life sets free from the law of sin and death (Rom. 8:2).

2) *Powerlessness.* When the Holy Spirit withdraws His presence He withdraws His power. The person must depend on his own strength to resist temptation and do good. Even the Bible loses much of its power and effect in the life, because the Bible is the sword of the Spirit (Eph. 6:17). Jesus' promise to His disciples was, "You will receive power when the Holy Spirit comes on you" (Acts 1:8). Paul emphasizes that the power which works in the Christian is the power of the Spirit (Rom. 15:13-19; Eph. 3:16, 20).

3) *Emptiness.* God created human beings to be indwelt by the Holy Spirit (our only source of holiness). When the Holy Spirit leaves one, his heart's temple is empty. It is empty of the presence of God, fellowship with God, and the fruit of the Spirit (Gal. 5:22-23). The person is not the full spiritual being God created him to be, so the person's spirit is restless, hungry for what only God can supply. He is not the full being God intended him to be. He is spiritually deprived.

Thus man's whole inner being becomes lonely. Life has lost a major part of its reason for existence, so the person gropes for the meaning of life. The person was intended to be guided by the Spirit in developing habits of life and in developing beautiful personality characteristics which can become the fruit of the Spirit. Under stress and strain the person lacks the Holy Spirit's strengthening of the will and assistance in self-discipline, lacks the guidance of the Spirit, and becomes much more susceptible to Satan's suggestions and hindering activity.

God's mercy does not entirely leave the person. God's grace still, to some extent, blesses the person, and conscience, though dulled or hardened, is still somewhat active. So-called "natural virtues" are evident to some degree, but they lack the beauty, strength, purity, and perseverance which only the Holy Spirit can give. So they are not the fruit of the Spirit in any full sense.

4) *Idolatry.* When the Holy Spirit is displaced from the throne of the soul, self immediately assumes the throne. Self which could be the home of the Spirit becomes the residence of sin and Satan. Self becomes the sinful, carnal self and usurps the place that rightfully belongs to God alone. This carnal ruling principle or law is described in Romans 7:14-23. This is the carnal self that needs to be crucified by the power of the Spirit (Gal. 2:20).

5) *Lust.* When the Holy Spirit leaves, self becomes misled, depraved, and dominated by sin. Evil desires develop. The self-will always remains active, but its activity, instead of being Spirit-guided, Spirit-motivated, and Spirit-dominated, becomes self-centered, self-dominated, and selfish. This results in evil desire and lust in the general sense of the term.

The sensual nature tends to dominate over the rational and spiritual in the sinner. We speak of such a person being carnal, with a sinful mind-set. Paul makes it clear that we either live according to the Spirit or according to the sinful nature (Rom. 8:4, 9).

Galatians 5:16-17--"Live by the Spirit, and you will not gratify the desires of the sinful nature. For the sinful nature desires what is contrary to the Spirit, and the Spirit what is contrary to the sinful nature."

C. ETERNAL DEATH. Eternal death, also called the second death (Rev. 2:11; 20:14; 21:8), is the third and final part of the penalty of sin. Those who remain in spiritual death during their lives and who do not receive Christ's salvation from sin die in their sin (John 8:21, 24). The wrath of God which is upon sin remains upon them (John 3:36).

Eternal death is the final judgment of God upon sin. It is the separation of the soul from God made permanent and more total because all influences of God's grace and mercy cease at physical death. It is a death for which the human spirit requires a special resurrection to provide a form of spirit-body adequate for eternal existence in the lake of fire. Jesus calls this to "rise to be condemned" (John 5:29). The sinner will stand before Christ's judgment throne and be sent to eternal punishment (Matt. 25:46).

Into the lake of fire all the wicked dead (those who died in their sins) will be cast since their name is not in Christ's register in the book of life (Rev. 3:5; 20:12-15). This book is also called "the Lamb's book of life"--that is, the book of those redeemed by Christ's blood shed at Calvary (Rev. 21:27). It is referred to by God when He spoke to Moses (Exod. 32:32) and to Daniel (Dan. 12:1).

The lake of fire is what Jesus repeatedly termed "eternal fire" (Matt. 18:8; 25:41, 46), the "fire of hell" (Matt. 5:22), hell, "where the fire never goes out" (Mark 9:43), where "the fire is not quenched" (Mark 9:48). Isaiah prophesied about it as the place where those who rebel against God are and where their conscience "will not die nor their fire be quenched" (Isa. 66:24). Jude refers to it as the punishment of eternal fire (Jude 7).

Jesus used the same word "everlasting" to speak of eternal life for the saved and eternal punishment and eternal fire for the unsaved. Paul used the same word to speak of the eternal encouragement for Christ's own (2 Thess. 2:16) and eternal destruction for the unsaved. "They will be punished with everlasting destruction and shut out from the presence of the Lord and from the majesty of his power" (2 Thess. 1:9). Hell will be just as everlasting as heaven.

Eternal death includes future eternal banishment and eternal separation from God and all which God can bestow, all that is good, holy, and rewarding, and from all fellowship with righteous beings. It includes also eternal punitive infliction of divine wrath according to the requirements of the infinite justice.

The Bible describes it with such figurative terms as destruction of soul and body [i.e., the resurrected body of the sinner specially prepared for enduring hell fire] (Matt. 10:28). Isaiah calls it "consuming fire" and "everlasting burning" (Isa. 33:14). John explains, "The smoke of their torment rises for ever and ever. There is no rest day or night" (Rev. 14:11). Hebrews explains, "It is a dreadful thing to fall into the hands of the living God" (Heb. 10:31).

12

THE SIN NATURE

THE DEFINITION OF DEPRAVITY. Various terms have been used to describe the sinful nature which a child inherits from Adam through his parents. It has been called original sin, depravity, the Adamic nature, and the sin nature. In practical life, it is often called carnality, the old self, or the old man (Rom. 6:6; Eph. 4:22; Col. 3:9).

Depravity is that pollution and corruption of the selfhood and inner nature of all Adam's descendants by which the self is impure and inclined to evil. It is not an essential aspect of human nature or selfhood as created by God. That which is abnormal to human beings as created by God has now become normal in human experience. Though the original image of God is not destroyed, it is defaced and marred. The human nature can be either holy through the indwelling Holy Spirit, as Adam and Eve were created, or depraved, as sin in the absence of the Holy Spirit perverts the human nature.

Jesus, speaking to His disciples, said: "Though you are evil" (Matt. 7:11). Thus this depraved selfhood remains in the heart of a true believer until cleansed by the Spirit. Our whole human race is fallen and inclined to sin. The new birth brings the forgiveness of our committed sins and the cleansing from their defilement. But until the Holy Spirit cleanses the believer by the blood of Christ in response to total self-surrender and faith, the believer continues to be sinful in nature. Thank God, there is a deeper, fuller cleansing portrayed in the Bible for believers (Acts 15:9; 2 Thess. 5:23; 1 Peter 1:2; 1 John 1:7).

Depravity is not an aggregate of separate sins associated together in various chance combinations--such as anger, jealousy, deceit, lust, and hatred. It is a unitary principle of sinful reality. It is a moral condition of the soul. The moral image of God (holiness) is absent or is only partial because the Holy Spirit does not indwell in His fullness or not at all.

The Holy Spirit's absence, coupled with the personal and inherited effects of sin, have disrupted the inner harmony with which human personality was created by God. The person's faculties are abnormally weakened, perverted, and comparatively uncontrolled. Now he is perverted by a radical tendency to evil which may try to express itself at any time. It is perversion, not the expression of the person's true nature. Sin has infected every part of the being. Fallenness is interpenetrating the personhood even when it is not realized.

Since the Holy Spirit is not present and the personality is disordered, the sensuous may be undisciplined and dominate the rational. The will may be disproportionately independent and self-assertive. Sin becomes easy. The most obvious--the material, the allurements of "the world" (1 John 2:15-16)--can easily entice the personality and usurp dominance.

The soul was not created to be empty but to be indwelt by the Holy Spirit. When the Spirit is absent, the person is left with nothing but self to rule him, except as he surrenders his self to Satan. Since the Spirit does not rule, the predisposition of the soul is not toward God but toward its own faculties. Reason, sensibilities, or will--any one of these or any combination of these--may dominate the soul. Since they are each somewhat perverted by the Fall, they are an even more dangerous guide or master. The personhood of the person is now subject to the ungoverned, unharmonized, perverted, and somewhat anarchic rule of self-will, appetite, passion, and unsupervised and unenlightened reason.

THE MEANING OF TOTAL DEPRAVITY. The term "total depravity" is frequently used to describe our fallen condition. This is not a Bible term but is used by evangelical theologians. We need to understand clearly what the Bible teaches about our total depravity and also what we do not imply by this term.

1. *The whole soul is affected.* The entire personality, the selfhood, is influenced by sin. Every ability, power, and faculty of the human spirit, soul, or body are impaired and debased to some extent. The whole person is affected. The feelings and emotions are alienated and deranged. The mind is darkened (Eph. 4:18). The will is enfeebled and perverted (Jer. 3:21) and even enslaved (Titus 3:3). All the mental powers--imagination (Gen. 6:5; Isa. 65:2; 66:18), memory and reason (Matt. 16:8; Mark 2:8)--are affected. The conscience is weakened (1 Cor. 8:7), wounded (1 Cor. 10:12), defiled (1 Cor. 8:7), corrupted (Titus 1:15), or even seared (1 Tim. 4:2).

2. *The soul lacks all positive good.* "I know that nothing good lives in me, that is, in my sinful nature" (Rom. 7:18). In spiritual things, apart from the grace of God, a person is helpless. "By the grace of God I am what I am" (1 Cor. 15:10). To do good work for God the person must be aided and equipped by God (2 Tim. 3:17). In himself no one can do the good works God desires (Titus 2:14; Heb. 10:24). All our righteous acts, apart from God's grace, are like filthy rags in God's sight (Isa. 64:6). Even in seeking to serve God we often have a mixture of desire for self-glory and for the glory of God. No human deed can be perfectly done with the purest, most worthy motive apart from the aid of the Holy Spirit.

3. *The soul is continuously depraved.* The influence of the depraving, enfeebling, darkening power of the sin nature continually affects the being and power of each person. He is continually inclined to choose his own will and way, to depend on his own resources and strength, and to be open to consider tempting suggestions at least momentarily. His nature is in a continuous state of potential or latent aversion to God or even hostility to God (Rom. 8:7). From Eden on, there is a latent aversion in sinners to God's will and even to God's presence (Gen. 3:8). It may become active and visible at any time. The sinner tends to make no room in his thinking for God (Ps. 10:4). Paul stated it, "I find this law at work: when I want to do good, evil is right there with me" (Rom. 7:21).

4. *The soul is subject to a law of progressive evil.* Evil people go from bad to worse (2 Tim. 3:13). Unless checked by grace, sin becomes more natural, more habitual, more bold, and more vile. Sin continuously depraves, so the drag on the soul is constantly away from God and deeper into spiritual neglect, disobedience, and evil in any form.

Sin reproduces itself. One form of sin in the nature opens the door for other forms of sin. The nature of sin's infection is to keep spreading. Sin hardens and so the same sin can be repeated with less and less compunction of conscience.

Not all forms of sin are equally tempting to any one person. Sin is always personal, and the sin nature has its manifestations in very personal ways. One person may be able to discipline himself or even reform himself in some sins. But always the sin nature is there and everyone has his own weakest areas. In some, it may be sins of the flesh--gluttony, sexual temptation, and sloth. In others, it may be sins of the spirit--pride, self-will, and resentment.

God's prevenient grace mobilizing conscience, God's providence, and the Spirit's restraint may help in the suppression of some of the aspects of the sin nature. Thank God for this restraining work of the Spirit. Thank God even more for the deliverance which we will describe later (Rom. 7:25).

5. *The soul's depravity is incurable apart from God's grace.* Some self-discipline, reformation, and development of true character are possible. A person may control many of the outward acts, but he cannot cleanse his own heart. Unless God saves, he will die unsaved. Unless Christ delivers, he will die a slave of sin and Satan. Unless the blood of Christ cleanses, he will die impure. No one can transform his own inner nature. No one can be his own savior.

THINGS NOT IMPLIED BY TOTAL DEPRAVITY. It is as important to understand what total depravity does not mean as to understand what it does mean. We will see later that it is as important to know what Christ does not cleanse as what He cleanses.

That is why our definition of sin was also very important. Remember, total depravity does not mean the following five things:

1. *Total depravity does not mean that the person cannot become more evil.* The term "total" is used extensively, rather than intensively. Depravity is progressive. The sinner can always become more and more sinful (Gen. 15:16; 2 Tim. 3:13). Sin can become ever more complex, more enslaving, and more debasing. There can be almost endless progression in depravity.

2. *Total depravity does not mean that every person is prone to every form of sin.* Some people have a commendable form of morality which keeps them from some of the coarser, more blatant forms of sin. This may be due in part to home training, self-discipline, the influence of godly people, and the influence of so-called Christian civilization (more accurately the diffusion of Christian light). Some sins tend to exclude other sins--the sin of greed may restrain the sin of luxury. The sin of carnal ambition may restrain the sin of indolence. The sin of pride may restrain some sins of lust.

3. *Total depravity does not mean that the person is without a conscience.* Conscience in every person remains the voice of God within the soul. Even in uncivilized pagans, conscience demonstrates that at least some sins are repugnant. God's moral law is, to some extent, written in every person (Rom. 2:14-15). Many unsaved people have a strong sense of right and wrong, of justice and injustice. Sinners often show some sorrow for sins they have committed. Conscience combines with compassion to motivate some good acts. Consciousness of sin and a sense of guilt demonstrate that the person can still repent and be saved, but these are not proof that the person will do so.

4. *Total depravity does not mean that the sinner is without pleasing qualities.* Jesus Himself recognized good qualities in sinners (Mark 10:21). The morality of some people is commendable as far as it goes. However, when such morality is compared to God's holiness in the light which the Holy Spirit sheds upon the heart, each person realizes how sinful he is and how much he needs Christ the Savior (Isa. 6:5).

5. *Total depravity does not mean that the person is untouched by God's grace.* God's prevenient grace, combining with God's love and mercy, continues to seek the attention of every person and incline them to do right and respond to God's inner call. God seeks to warn the person of the consequences of sin. He seeks to remind the person of His goodness and providence, and thus draws the person to respond to His loving voice. God seeks to bring the person to repentance and obedience (Rom. 2:4).

To a certain extent Christ, the Light of the world, lights every person in the universe (John 1:9), and the Holy Spirit continually seeks to speak to every sinner's conscience. Though He does not indwell the sinner, He does strive or contend with the sinner through his conscience (Gen. 6:3). He convicts him of sin (John 16:8-9), rebukes (Job 13:10; Jer. 2:19), and calls him to come to God (Rev. 22:17).

13

THE PROOFS OF DEPRAVITY

If anyone doubts the reality of depravity in the human race, he needs but to read Scripture or look at the history of humankind.

1. *The Universality of Sin.* The Bible teaches clearly that all persons are sinners and that all have a sinful nature. Many references state this fact, and throughout the Bible this fact is assumed. The Bible warnings are to all people as sinners, and the promises of salvation are to all people as sinners.

In this regard, the Bible distinguishes between just two classes of people--those who have been saved from their sins by Christ and those who have not been saved from their sins. These latter are lost in sin (Matt. 18:11; Luke 15:1-7), are of the world (John 17:9, 16, 18), in darkness (John 1:5; Acts 26:18; Rom. 13:12; 1 Peter 2:9), and controlled and enslaved by Satan's power (John 8:34-36; Acts 26:15). In the first two chapters of Romans, Paul proves that the whole world is in a sinful state and goes on to prove that no one is saved from sin apart from Christ.

Not only does the Bible assert the universality of sin, but human history illustrates and proves the prevalence of sin, wrong, and injustice in every race, nation, and tribe of people. History knows no sinless person except Christ. Muslims agree that Christ was the only sinless prophet.

The scientific method develops generalizations from uniformly observed results. No scientist, therefore, could rightly oppose the statement that human beings are universally sinful. If all people are sinning, there must be a universal cause. Environment, circumstances, and history change. The cause cannot be outside people. It must be located within people, within human personality. This the

Bible clearly states: Ps. 130:3; 143:2, Isa. 53:6; 64:6; Rom. 3:10; 3:23; Gal. 3:22; 1 John 5:19.

2. *The Persistence of Human Beings in Sin.* Sin is not only universally prevalent, it is continuously prevailing in people and in society. People not only sin in times of great stress and turmoil, they sin in the most ordinary of times. They sin when they observe the evil example of others, and they sin in the presence of the good example of others. People sin in private and in public, in thoughts, attitudes, words, and acts.

People sin when warned not to sin and when promised reward if they abstain from sin. People promise not to sin, determine not to sin, yet succumb to temptation or habit and sin anyway (Rom. 7:15-24). People sin in their childhood--even showing the beginnings of sinful tendencies before they can explain sin. They sin in their youth before habits are firmly established. They sin in maturity when they already recognize the consequences of sin.

People sin in spite of education, wealth, prestige, or position. They sin regardless of occupation or of need. They sin regardless of environment. Such persistent sinning on the part of all people everywhere can only be explained by a deep and permanent depravity of soul.

3. *The Rejection of Christ and God.* The consciences of all people remind them that there is a Supreme Being to whom they are responsible. Their consciences continually remind them and rebuke them for sin which they commit. This often is proved by their attempt to hide their sins. Nevertheless, they continue to do things their conscience tells them are wrong. They continue to disregard the Supreme One to whom they know they are responsible. On the whole, people live without God and in disregard of God. "In all his thoughts there is no room for God" (Ps. 10:4).

People try to convince themselves that if there is a God He will not see, reprove, or punish them. There is a state of irritation against God, at the thought that He is observing them, or might hold them accountable (Rom. 8:7). This hostility to God is proved continually by puny man's neglect of God, disobedience to God, and rebellion against God.

Even more amazing is the rejection of Christ. "He came to that which was his own, but his own did not receive him" (John 1:11). The beautiful, good, holy, loving life of Jesus Christ is accepted and acknowledged by almost all sinful people who have heard of Him. Jesus was altogether merciful, loving, and kind. He went everywhere doing good, healing the sick, and sharing blessings and truthful teaching to people of all levels of society (Acts 10:38).

Sinful people, noted scholars, and perceptive people, regardless of religion, agree on the nobility of Christ's character, the goodness of His life, and the purity of His teachings. They admire Him but usually refuse to accept Him or obey Him. Christ is praised, but His claims about Himself are rejected. His love is clearly recognized, but is continuously spurned. Despite His spotless life, His constant, impartial love, His miraculous power, His holy teachings, and His dying love, humanity as a whole ignores Him, profane and despise His name, and hate both Him and His followers.

The attitude and conduct toward, and the ignoring and rejection of Christ are an incontrovertible proof of the depravity of the human race. What more could He have done to bless humankind? The truth of Scripture is obvious: "Whoever does not believe stands condemned already because he has not believed in the name of God's one and only Son. This is the verdict: Light has come into the world, but men loved darkness instead of light because their deeds were evil" (John 3:18-19). What greater sin could there be than the willful rejection of the pure love, holy life, and undeniable truth taught by the Son of God.

4. *The Unreformability of Human Nature.* The sinful nature of human beings is utterly incorrigible. No one is able to cure himself of his sin. Repeatedly persons recognize their wrongdoing and determine to quit one or many of their sins. But in spite of good resolves, the person succumbs to temptation again and again. He, at times, detests some or all of his sins, becomes disgusted with his own sinfulness, indeed, becomes sick of his own sinful self. Yet he knows

in personal experience the description Paul gives of the sinful nature in Romans 7:15-23.

People have tried to cure themselves of sin or to control themselves so that they do not sin. They have used many forms of self-denial, penance, and at times even torture of their own bodies. They have tried to follow the teachings and forms of worship of their own religion--even the Christian religion. They have tried to escape their past by fleeing to distant places where they are not known and beginning life all over again.

Some people have tried to conquer sin by withdrawing from normal social relations, abstaining from marriage, and maintaining an ascetic life. But no one can escape from his sin except by way of the cross. Some have pled guilty and gladly accepted punishment for their sin, hoping this would give deliverance from defeat by their sin. But Scripture still stands confirmed again and again: "The evil man brings evil things out of the evil stored up in his heart" (Luke 6:45). "Can the Ethiopian change his skin or the leopard its spots? Neither can you do good who are accustomed to doing evil" (Jer. 13:23). If a tree is known by its fruit, then the human being, apart from God, is evil of soul.

5. *The Manifestation of Sin in Infants.* Infants so young that they have learned nothing by example from others, so young that they are not yet able to speak clearly, or so mentally immature that they do not yet know right from wrong or do any careful reasoning, show manifestations of anger when frustrated. As soon as an infant is old enough to recognize itself as a self distinct from others, selfishness is evident. Stubbornness of will can be clearly demonstrated before the little child can speak.

Even before the child is capable of moral action it gives evidence of a sinful inner disposition. There is no possible explanation of these innate tendencies apart from a sinful nature. Deceit seems to be learned almost automatically at a very early age. Disobedience often seems more natural than obedience. Note: Gen. 8:21; Ps. 51:5; 58:3.

THE HEART AS THE SOURCE OF EVIL. Scripture clearly teaches that the source of a person's sinful acts is within himself. Environment, the people about the person, can help provoke the expression of sin, but the person himself is responsible. His own will makes the choice of resisting or yielding to temptation. The person's sinful nature reproduces itself in sinful thoughts, attitudes, words, and deeds.

It is because our nature is sinful that God insists on a new spiritual birth, a regeneration, a transformation of nature, a complete change of the personhood of each individual. Salvation does not result from external rituals (such as baptism or the Lord's Supper). It is not obtained by joining a Bible-teaching church. It is not a matter of faithful attendance of worship services, financial support of the church, or any other external act--no matter how good. A hypocrite can do all of these and still be untransformed.

Salvation is a spiritual transformation, a change within the inner nature of a person which is produced by God's supernatural grace. Since sin is located in the nature of the person, salvation must change that nature. Note: Jer. 17:9-10; Matt. 12:34; 15:18-20; John 3:6; Gal. 5:17, 19-21; James 1:14.

THE INNER NATURE OF SALVATION. From the time when Adam and Eve sinned, each human being has been spiritually dead until made alive by the power of God. Spiritual death means separation from God and a state of spiritual sinfulness and absence of all spiritual life. Salvation means a spiritual resurrection from spiritual death to spiritual life (John 5:24; Rom. 6:4; 1 John 3:14). Salvation consists of becoming a new creation (2 Cor. 3:17).

The fruit of the Spirit will come from within, just as the acts of the sinful nature come from within (Gal. 5:19-23). The result of salvation will be streams of living water from within the person, provided by the Holy Spirit (John 7:38-39).

The work of salvation which transforms the inner sinful nature into a holy nature is a work of washing (Titus 3:5), purifying (Matt. 3:11-12; Acts 15:8-9; 1 John 1:7), and cleansing (Ps. 51:7; Heb. 10:22).

This is strong Bible proof that our nature is sinful until God cleanses us through the work of the Holy Spirit, applying the cleansing of Christ's blood. Christ's work is an inner baptism of fire that burns up the chaff and impurity of our inner nature. Note: Matt. 3:11-12; Rom. 12:2; 2 Cor. 5:17; 7:1; Eph. 4:22-23; 5:25-26; 1 Thess. 5:23; Heb. 12:14; 13:12; 1 John 1:7; 1:9.

14

THE TRANSMISSION OF DEPRAVITY

How is depravity passed through the human race from Adam to us today? Depravity is inherited as a part of our fallen humanity. Certain effects of the Fall automatically become ours because we are part of the fallen human race. Flesh gives birth to flesh (John 3:6).

1. *We are a member of the guilty race.* Whose sins crucified our Savior? The sins of our race. Our personal sin was included, but also the sin of all other human beings. As a part of our solidarity with all of humanity, we share the corporate guilt of our race. We may rejoice personally in the forgiveness of our own committed sins, yet, identifying ourselves with our race, we must pray, "Forgive us our sins" (Luke 11:4).

Each of us as a member of our nation shares a corporate unity with our whole nation. Regardless of our personal disagreement with a particular act of our nation, we share in the consequences of that act. In the same way, we as a part of humanity inherit an earth cursed because of the sin of Adam and Eve, the ancestors of humanity. We enter life as human beings, minus the indwelling Holy Spirit, with a personality deprived, depraved, and pervasively influenced by the Fall and humanity's depravity.

Note the clear scriptural teaching: Adam was the natural head of our race. He was also in some sense the representative head of our race. "Sin entered the world through one man, and death through sin, and in this way death came to all men, because all sinned" (Rom. 5:12).

2. *We are members of a race for which Christ died.* Counterbalancing what is lost in Adam is the grace we receive through Christ.

Not only do we lose through the sin of Adam but we gain through the grace and mercy that flow from Christ's redemptive death.

Christ is the Lamb of God available and already committed from before the universe was created (Rev. 13:8) to die in our place should humanity sin. Because God's plan of the role of Christ was conditionally prepared and accepted by Christ, God's eternal mercy was able to express itself the moment of the first sin. God's overarching prevenient grace began to operate instantly. Thus the benefits of God's grace were immediately available to our race.

3. *Humanity was not instantly wiped out.* The wages of sin is death (Rom. 6:23). God had said, "When you eat of it (the forbidden tree of the knowledge of good and evil) you will surely die" (Gen. 2:17). Adam and Eve both died instantly spiritually. Physically, death began to work in their bodies from that instant, although they survived many years before actual physical death. To this day, death begins to work in the human body from the time of birth. But we are given varying amounts of time to repent and make our personal peace with God. If we fail to do so, eternal death will surely come to every sinner (Rev. 20:14; 21:8).

4. *Humanity retained God's natural image.* There was instant loss of the moral image and likeness of God (from holiness to sin), but God's natural image (our personality, with our mental, emotional, and volitional powers) was preserved even though affected by the Fall. Thus humanity is redeemable even though sinful. We can still be saved and restored to fellowship with God. We can still be prepared and welcomed to an eternal role and home in heaven.

5. *God's prevenient grace began to operate for humanity.* God's covenant of grace was announced to Adam and Eve in Eden in the first promise of the Messiah (Gen. 3:15). Woman's offspring (Note: Messiah would come specially through woman--a veiled hint of the Virgin conception and birth) would crush the serpent (symbolizing Satan who had plotted the Fall).

The more humanity has sinned the more God's superabundant grace has abounded. "Where sin increased, grace increased all the more" (Rom. 5:20). This was only possible because Christ was

already the available Lamb of God waiting for God's perfect time to
die in our place.

6. *Christ is God's provision available as extensively as Adam's sin
had its cursing influence.* Not all humankind will accept God's
provision, but it is God's great gift to more than counterbalance
Adam's sin.

> **Romans 5:18**--"Just as the result of one trespass was condemnation for
> all men, so also the result of one act of righteousness was justification
> that brings life for all men." Note also: Rom. 5:15; 5:16; 5:21.

7. *While the sin nature is transmitted genetically, salvation is
provided graciously but must be appropriated personally.* The
transmission of sin is not a judgment or penalty from God. It is the
outworking of the law of heredity. It is more important to know
God's answer to the sin nature than to be able to explain fully how
we receive that nature. As far as we know, if Adam and Eve had
continued in obedience to God and had not sinned, the Holy Spirit
would have been able to indwell their children from birth. They
would have transmitted to their children an undepraved nature and
the Spirit would have given them primitive created holiness. Now the
sin nature is transmitted to all of the race, whether they are born of
pagan sinful parents or to godly Christians.

All salvation through the atonement of Christ is by the grace of
God. But we cannot transmit grace to our children. Grace must be
individually appropriated. Children of godly parents are born with a
sin nature, for we cannot transmit or control the Holy Spirit. Neither
can we transmit character. Heredity cannot transmit acquired
characteristics or character. Each person develops character as he
responds to the grace of God.

Sinners do not transmit their sins or the responsibility for their
sins to their children (Ezek. 18:20). Neither do Christian parents
transmit their righteousness and virtues. They probably do transmit
some dispositional characteristics as are manifest in personality. The
environment of the home and their personal example can be a great
blessing to their children.

15

ATONEMENT THROUGH CHRIST

God's great salvation is based on the atonement provided by the death of Jesus Christ upon the cross. His atonement provides the sinner a way back to God. Other religions are based on a creed, an ethical code, or religious or ceremonial requirements. Our salvation is centered in our Savior. No other religion provides a Savior from sin. All other religions emphasize salvation through works. Bible salvation emphasizes the grace of our Lord Jesus Christ.

The simple yet profound truth of the Atonement is stated in two verses: "While we were still sinners, Christ died for us" (Rom. 6:8). "Christ died for our sins" (1 Cor. 15:3). Our sins had separated us from God, and our guilt made us under God's wrath and the sentence of death. "The wages of sin is death" (Rom. 6:23). This is what God told Adam when He created him (Gen. 2:17).

Christ, the sinless Son of God, became human in the incarnation that He might take our punishment and die in our place.

John 3:16--"God so loved the world that he gave his one and only Son, that whoever believes in him shall not perish but have eternal life."

Christ's death in our stead enabled God to be holy and just in giving the full punishment for our sins to our Substitute, yet loving and merciful to us if we meet His conditions for forgiveness. Those conditions are fair, logical, and gracious. We must repent of our sins and accept Christ as our Substitute and our Savior.

Ephesians 2:8--"It is by grace that you have been saved through faith--and this not from yourselves, it is the gift of God."

The Atonement reconciles the sinner to God. He who had been God's enemy by his sins is now forgiven and transformed into a child of God and received into God's family as His child.

Colossians 1:21-22--"Once you were alienated from God and were enemies in your minds because of your evil behavior. But now he has reconciled you by Christ's physical body through death to present you holy in his sight, without blemish, and free from accusation."

The word "atonement" literally means AT + ONE + MENT. We have become one with God again. The first word God used in the Hebrew Old Testament for atonement gave the thought of ransom money, or a ransom substitute. From this came the understanding of atoning by offering a substitute. The sinner was reconciled and accepted by God through providing the death of an animal substitute.

In the Old Testament, atoning sacrifice symbolized a substitutionary exchange of the life of a sacrificed animal for the life of the worshiper, innocent life taking the place of the guilty. It was only effective as the sinner placed his hand on the head of the sacrifice, confessing his sins which had separated him from God and for which the sacrifice was given as a means to reconciliation and atonement. This enabled forgiveness and acceptance.

The idea of atonement was much emphasized in the Old Testament. The sinner was repeatedly sinning and deserving God's just wrath. He needed repeated atonement to reconcile him to God and free him from his sin. Therefore, God provided an elaborate system of sacrifices and ceremonies.

We do not have space for a detailed discussion, but all of these symbolically taught important truths:

The nature of God--holy, just, sovereign, merciful.

The responsibility to God the Holy Sovereign--responsible obedience, indebtedness to God for all.

The seriousness of sin--all sin ultimately against God the Sovereign and deserving the death of the sinner.

The need of the sinner to be reconciled, forgiven, cleansed.

The costliness of atonement and reconciliation, requiring the death of a substitute.

The need of the sacrificed animal to be without blemish, perfect.

God's plan of salvation based on atonement was completed even before creation (1 Peter 1:18-20; Rev. 13:8). The disclosure of this plan of atonement to humankind was gradual and progressive. This was done during Old Testament times through the symbolism of Old Testament sacrificial ritual and ceremonies, and by the prophetic teaching of the prophets. All symbolism pointed to the great and final atoning sacrifice of Christ in His death on the cross.

Non-Christian sacrifice illustrated the universal human recognition of the need of atonement. Only the cross of Christ provides an adequate basis by which God can be perfectly holy, perfectly just, yet perfectly loving and provide a perfect forgiveness. Because the death of Christ upon the cross was planned before Adam was created, all the sacrifices in Old Testament times were provisionally accepted by God until the time when Christ would actually die for our sins. The first sacrifice occurred in Eden itself when God provided garments of skin for Adam and Eve (Gen. 3:21).

It was impossible for these sacrifices and ceremonies in themselves to take away sins (Heb. 9:9-10; 10:4). It was only because they were offered in obedience to God's carefully detailed plan and in confession of their sin, bringing a substitute sacrifice that God for the time being accepted them as a basis for forgiveness.

The sinner in Old Testament days repented and offered a sacrifice which looked forward to the Cross. God accepted it on that basis, though the sinner did not understand Christ's coming incarnation and death on the cross. The repentant sinner today confesses his sins and looks back to the Cross and accepts Christ's atoning sacrifice by faith. Christ's death upon the cross is the one and only sacrifice that ever atoned for sin.

God's holiness necessitated either His judgment upon sin or an atonement for sin. God in His grace provided the atonement through His own Son. In His infinite and all-wise love He provided a sacrifice of infinite value, though it was at infinite cost. Because of Christ's sacrifice of Himself on the cross in our stead, God can now remain perfectly just and yet be merciful to whoever accepts Christ's atoning sacrifice.

The atonement which Christ provided in His death on the cross is profoundly wise, amazingly complex, and yet beautifully simple for us to receive by God's grace through faith. The Bible gives many terms and metaphors in explaining this to us. All of these help us understand the wonderful Atonement. They portray Christ as our Sacrifice, our Substitute, our Ransom or Redemption, our Deliverer, our Reconciliation or Atonement, and the Propitiation for our sins.

A. TERMS AND METAPHORS POINTING TO CHRIST'S SACRIFICE

1. Christ as a Lamb. Isa. 53:7; John 1:29, 36; 1 Peter 1:19; Rev. 5:6, 12, 13; 7:14; 12:11.

2. The Blood of Christ. Heb. 10:29; 13:20; 1 Peter 1:19; 1 John 1:7; Rev. 1:5; 7:14.

3. Christ as an Offering. Heb. 9:14, 28; 10:10, 14.

4. Christ as a Sacrifice. Eph. 5:2; Heb. 9:26.

5. Christ our Passover. 1 Cor. 5:7.

6. Christ our Altar. Heb. 13:10.

7. Christ our Scapegoat. 1 John 3:5 (Lev. 16:8, 10, 26).

8. Christ our Sin Offering. 2 Cor. 5:21 (Exod. 30:10); Heb. 13:12.

B. TERMS AND METAPHORS POINTING TO CHRIST OUR SUBSTITUTE

1. Although the actual word Substitute is not used, the meaning is clearly there. Isa. 53:5; Heb. 2:9; 13:12; 1 Peter 4:1.

2. Christ bore our sins. Isa. 53:11; 54:12; 1 Peter 2:24; Heb. 9:28.

3. Christ gave Himself for us. John 10:11; Gal. 1:4; 2:20; Eph. 5:25; Titus 2:14.

4. Christ laid down His life for us. John 10:15; 15:13-14; 1 John 3:16.

5. He was delivered to death for us. Rom. 4:25; 8:32.

6. He died for us. Rom. 5:8; 14:15; 1 Cor. 15:3; 2 Cor. 5:15; Heb. 2:9.

7. He became a curse for us. Gal. 3:13.

C. TERMS AND METAPHORS POINTING TO CHRIST OUR RANSOM OR REDEMPTION

1. Christ is our Ransom. Matt. 20:28; Mark 10:45; 1 Tim. 2:5-6.

2. Christ purchased us. Matt. 13:44-46; Acts 20:28; 1 Cor. 6:20; 7:23.

3. Christ is our Redemption. Rom. 3:24; 1 Cor. 1:30; Gal. 4:4-5; Eph. 1:7; Col. 1:14, Titus 2:14; Heb. 9:12; 1 Peter 1:18-19; Rev. 5:9.

To redeem is to buy back, to ransom, to liberate from slavery, to deliver from captivity or death by payment of a price. It is a ransom paid in order to deliver. It is not a price from which God receives personal advantage. It satisfies public law and justice and makes the remittance of the sentence possible. Christ redeems us not by commercial equivalent but by a rectorial equivalent of penalty. The motivating cause of redemption is the love of God. The procuring cause is the substitutional death of Christ.

D. TERMS AND METAPHORS POINTING TO CHRIST OUR DELIVERER, VICTORIOUS FOR US

1. Christ is our Deliverer. Luke 4:18; Rom. 7:6; 11:26; Gal. 1:4; Col. 1:13; 1 Thess. 1:10; Heb. 2:14-15.

2. Christ sets us free. John 8:36; Gal. 5:1.

3. Christ defeated Satan. John 12:31 (Luke 11:21-22); Heb. 2:14; 1 John 3:8.

4. Christ was Victor for us. 1 Cor. 15:57; Eph. 5:23; Col. 2:15; 2 Tim. 1:10; Rev. 5:5.

E. TERMS AND METAPHORS POINTING TO CHRIST OUR RECONCILIATION OR ATONEMENT

1. Christ brings us near to God. Eph. 2:13, 18; Heb. 10:19; 1 Peter 3:18.

2. Christ reconciles us. Rom. 5:11; 2 Cor. 5:18-19; Eph 2:16; Col. 1:20-22; Heb. 2:17.

3. Christ is our Mediator. 1 Tim. 2:5; Heb. 8:6; 9:15; 12:24.

4. Christ is our Peace. Rom. 5:1; Eph. 2:14-15; Col. 1:20.

Sin had made us God's enemies. The Atonement makes possible our being reconciled to God (2 Cor. 5:19-21).

F. TERMS AND METAPHORS REFERRING TO CHRIST AS PROPITIATION

The Greek word *hilasterion* means to appease and render favorable. It is the turning away of wrath by an offering. The Old Testament emphasizes the wrath of God 585 times. The sinner has incurred the wrath of God for his sin. Sin's punishment is not an impersonal law of sowing and reaping. All people are under the condemnation of God and the sentence of death because of their sins (Rom. 1:18, 24, 26, 28). Christ's death removes God's wrath. God sent His Son to remove that wrath (1 John 4:10). Christ became our High Priest to remove that wrath (Heb. 2:17). Not all translations use the word "propitiation," but the Greek clearly used the word in the following references:

1. Christ is the propitiation for our sins. Rom. 3:24-26; Heb. 2:17; 1 John 2:2; 4:10.

2. God is merciful (the Greek: *propitious*) to sinners. Luke 18:13; Heb. 8:12. Propitiation is God's gift to us. Because He longs to be propitious, He sent Christ to be the propitiation for our sins.

CHRIST IS OUR ATONING SAVIOR. Christ's central role to us is that of a Savior. He fulfills many roles. He is Prophet, Priest, King, Teacher, Elder Brother, Friend. But all of this is possible because Jesus is a Savior. The most important message of the Bible is "Jesus saves." He saves not by His omnipotence, not by His sovereignty. He saves us by His atoning death. As the atoning Savior, He fulfills all the Old Testament prophecy of a suffering

Messiah, and all the Old Testament symbolism. He makes possible our great salvation. It is a salvation for the whole world.

ATONEMENT FOR THE WHOLE WORLD. God created the whole world. He loves the whole world, provides atonement adequate for the whole world, and freely and fully offers salvation to the whole world upon the basis of the atonement provided in Christ. God is the Creator-Father of all men. But in the spiritual sense, He is the Father only of the saved. If He did not provide salvation for the whole world, He could not be the universal God. Because He provided salvation available for all, He commissions us to go to every nation with this great salvation.

1. *God the Father desires the salvation of all.* He loved the world enough to provide atonement for all (John 3:16), for His Son to be the Savior of the world (John 3:17). God desires all to be saved (1 Tim. 2:4), desires to have mercy on all (Rom. 11:32), and reconciles the whole world to Himself through the atonement in Christ (2 Cor. 5:19).

2. *Christ made atonement for the whole world.* He is the atoning sacrifice for the sins of the whole world (1 John 2:2), does not want any to perish, but all to come to repentance (2 Peter 3:9), and is the Lamb of God who takes away the sin of the world (John 1:29). He tasted death for everyone (Heb. 2:9), gave His body for the life of the world (John 6:51), and gave Himself a ransom for all (1 Tim. 2:5-6). He wants all to come to the knowledge of the truth (1 Tim. 2:4), and has provided justification which can provide life for all (Rom. 5:18).

Whereas Adam's sin brought death to all, Christ's death on the cross brought the gift of grace available for all (v. 15). Romans 5:15-21 makes this abundantly clear.

3. *Christ's atonement is sufficient and available for all.* Christ's provision is sufficient for all but is effective only for those who accept it on God's conditions. It is effective for all men potentially, for no man unconditionally, but is personally effective for whoever freely wills.

Whereas Adam's sin brought potential judgment for all, Christ's atonement at the cross brought provisional life for all. Infants are saved without their consent, just as they inherited the results of Adam's sin without their consent. Children are born not only under sin, but also under the Atonement. They remain under it until they become old enough to repudiate it by their personal choices and acts of sin. Children are thus in a state of gracious security. When a person reaches the age where he is mentally fully competent to understand and accept the benefits of the Atonement, he becomes responsible to exercise saving faith in Jesus Christ.

16

THE GRACIOUS CALL OF GOD

The atonement of Jesus Christ becomes effective in the salvation of people through the ministry of the Holy Spirit. He has been called the executive of the Trinity in the administering of salvation. The atonement of Jesus Christ provided salvation and made it available. The Holy Spirit applies it to people and makes salvation real in their lives. It is as necessary for the Holy Spirit to work in us as it was for Christ to die for us. The preliminary aspects of God's grace in which the Holy Spirit leads us to and prepares us to receive the new birth are:

1. God's gracious call
2. God's prevenient grace
3. Conversion
4. Repentance
5. Saving faith

These ministries of the Holy Spirit are sometimes termed preliminary workings of God's grace.

THE GOSPEL CALL. The Greek verb *kaleo* means, first of all, to call, invite, summon. It is specially used of God's call to receive the blessings of redemption. The noun *klesis*, calling, is always used in the New Testament of that calling which is heavenly in origin, nature, and destiny. It is specially used for God's invitation to people to accept the benefits of salvation.

Those who respond are "the called." We are "those whom God has called" (1 Cor. 1:24), "those who are called" (Heb. 9:15). All who have responded to God's call are called according to God's purpose (Rom. 8:28), a purpose that includes all of God's gracious work of the Spirit to conform us to the likeness of God's Son (v. 29). Thus the moral image and likeness lost in Eden is to be restored to us by God's grace.

The inclusiveness of God's call is indicated by the many ways Scripture uses it. God's salvation call is to repentance (Luke 5:32), out of darkness into God's wonderful light (1 Peter 2:9), by the grace of Christ (Gal. 1:6), to peace (Col. 3:15), to freedom (Gal. 5:13), to fellowship with Christ (1 Cor. 1:9), and to eternal life (1 Tim. 6:12).

Having been called to belong to Jesus Christ (Rom. 1:6), we are then called to holy living (1 Thess. 4:7; 2 Tim. 1:9), called saints (Rom. 1:7, Greek), called to godliness (2 Peter 1:3), and to inherit blessing (1 Peter 3:9). God calls us to one great hope (Eph. 4:4), which includes all God's plans for our future. We are called to Christ's eternal kingdom and glory (1 Thess. 2:12; 1 Peter 5:10) to share in the glory of our Lord Jesus Christ (2 Thess. 2:14), and to share God's heavenly rewards (Phil. 3:14).

Thus God's whole scheme of grace is described as our heavenly calling (Heb. 3:1), although we by obedience must eagerly make our calling sure (2 Peter 1:10). We should therefore live worthy of God's calling (2 Thess. 1:11; Eph. 4:1). Every Christian is also called to serve God in ways which the Holy Spirit will guide (John 16:13).

The church is termed the *ekklesia*; that is, "the called out ones" (*ek*--out and *kaleo*--call). By accepting and obeying God's call, we have been called out of the generality of people to belong to Christ.

There are two aspects to God's call:

a. The universal or indirect call is the influence of the Holy Spirit on the conscience of all people apart from His ministry through Scripture.

b. The direct or immediate call is the ministry of the Holy Spirit calling people to salvation through Scripture or Christian ministry.

In the Old Testament the direct call was primarily to Israel, the race chosen (elected) from among the peoples of the world for God's special role of preparing for Christ's coming. In the New Testament the call is universal and is to all. Those who respond with repentance and saving faith, the believers, are God's elect.

THE ELECT. *Eklektos* (from *ek*--from and *lego*--to pick out, select) is the Greek word for chosen. The Bible emphasizes God's sovereign choice. It speaks both of God's choice and our choice. Christ is the elect of God for our salvation (Luke 23:35; 1 Peter 2:4). The Cross is God's chosen or elected means of atonement. Repentance and faith are God's chosen means of obtaining salvation through the Atonement.

Whoever will may come (Rev. 22:17) and receive salvation through God's elected or chosen means. They then become the elect of God. God chose for us to choose and believe and for the Spirit to apply the Atonement to us. So now we have been baptized by the Spirit into the Church, the body of Christ (1 Cor. 12:13), and the Church is now the chosen people of God (1 Peter 2:9), even as Israel was in the Old Testament.

There are three aspects of God's election found in God's Word:

1. *Individuals are elected (chosen) to perform a particular service or to fill a particular office.* For example: Aaron--as high priest; Saul--as king; Peter, James, and John--as apostles; Paul--as an apostle; even Judas--as an apostle. People are not saved by election for an office (Note: Saul, Judas).

2. *Groups or nations are elected to special religious privileges* (Israel; the Church). In Israel's case, those privileges (ceremonies, Scriptures, laws) were granted to all Israel without regard to prior righteousness. The purpose of this choice was blessing and ultimate good to all nations (Gen. 12:3), but membership in Israel, the chosen nation, did not guarantee salvation for anyone. They had to personally commit themselves to God and fulfill His will.

3. *In the New Testament sense there is election of specific individuals to become children of God on the basis of God's condition:* receiving Christ by faith. "To all who received him, to those who believed in his name, he gave the right to become children of God--children . . . born of God" (John 1:12-13). God chose the means of

their salvation--atonement through Christ, the conditions of receiving Christ--faith, and the person chooses to obey, come to Christ, and believe.

> **2 Thessalonians 2:13-14**--"From the beginning God chose you to be saved through the sanctifying work of the Spirit and through belief in the truth. He called you to this through our gospel, that you might share in the glory of our Lord Jesus Christ."

Note how clearly Paul expresses this truth. God called them to salvation through the Gospel preached by Paul (v. 14) so that they might share in Christ's glory. He chose from the beginning, that is, from creation, from the time when Christ accepted God's plan to be the Lamb of God slain to provide atonement (Rev. 13:8). He chose that this be available through the provision of the sanctifying work of the Holy Spirit, on the condition of the person believing in the truth. God chose, Christ chose, the person chose, and the Spirit chose.

Sanctification is by faith (Acts 26:18), thus making election dependent upon our faith. "If you do not believe I am the one I claim to be, you will indeed die in your sins" (John 8:24). Remember also John 3:16 and verse 36: "Whoever believes in the Son has eternal life, but whoever rejects the Son will not see life, for God's wrath remains on him" [i.e., because of his sin which only Christ can take away] John 1:29).

God does not choose to irresistibly save some in spite of their sin and choose to leave the rest to be condemned and subject to the wrath of God. He provides His perfect plan of salvation but conditions it on the person's free choice to accept God's gracious provision. He chose (elected) this plan for salvation even before the world and human beings were created. Old Testament people could be saved by repentance and bringing the sacrifice which God prescribed to point to God's plan of salvation through Christ, the perfect sacrifice. Today we can be saved by looking back to Christ and His cross and repenting and believing in the finished work of Christ our redeeming Savior.

17

GOD'S PREVENIENT GRACE

Grace is an essential and permanent attribute of God. God revealed Himself to Moses as "the Lord, the Lord, the compassionate and gracious God" (Exod. 34:6). Peter calls Him, "the God of all grace" (1 Peter 5:10). One of the most frequent salutations in Paul's letters is found in almost identical words ten times: "Grace and peace to you from God our Father and the Lord Jesus Christ" (1 Cor. 1:3). The grace of Christ is mentioned many times, and the Holy Spirit is called the Spirit of grace (Heb. 10:29). God's throne is called the throne of grace (Heb. 4:16).

While grace and truth came through Jesus Christ (John 1:17), God has eternally been the God and source of all grace. God's grace is infinite and eternal.

1. The interrelations of the members of the Trinity were ever relations of grace.

2. Grace provided the plan of incarnation of Christ and atonement through Christ from before the creation of the world (Rev. 3:18; Eph. 1:4; 1 Peter 1:20).

3. Grace provided the order, beauty, variety, and perfection of the world at the time of creation.

4. Grace provided all revelation of God prior to the birth of Christ, including the entire Old Testament.

5. Grace called and prepared Israel to be the chosen people through whom Christ would come.

6. Grace provided the Incarnation in the fullness of God's time (Gal. 4:4) and the atoning death of Jesus Christ as the fulfillment of God's plan.

7. Grace provided all the gracious outworking of God's comprehensive plan, including such aspects as salvation from the penalty and power of sin, growth in grace, prayer, New Testament revelation, and the Church.

8. Grace provides God's future plan of Christ's return, glorification for the body, the lifting of the curse, a new heaven and a new earth, and God's eternal fellowship with redeemed humanity. God's holy being is the basis of all God's grace.

COMMON GRACE. The general grace of God unconditionally manifested and given to benefit all humankind and to some extent to all creation is often termed the "common grace" of God. The common grace of God benefits all human beings universally whether righteous or unrighteous, regardless of their response to God's gracious provisions. These unconditional benefits are based on the nature of God's being and on the atonement provided by Christ. They are related to God's goodness, love, and mercy. They include:

1. *Man's preservation after the sin of Adam and Eve.* While spiritual death was instant, God delayed physical death and began a process of death in the human body. While the moral image and likeness of God was instantly lost, what has been called the "natural image" was retained, though it too was detrimentally affected by sin. Human personality retained its mental, emotional and volitional capacity, conscience, and capacity to be saved and again be indwelt by the Spirit of God. It is by grace that humankind continues to have the free will given to him in creation. All is due to the grace of God.

2. *The scheme of providence.* God's providence is His gracious activity by which He cares for all creation. It includes three aspects:

a. Conservation is God's maintaining in existence the physical universe and all inanimate things (Col. 1:17; Heb. 1:3). The whole plan evident in the mathematical basis of the cosmos, the manifold "laws of nature," the cycle of seedtime and harvest, the orderly seasons, the amazing construction of the human body, and many other things that we take for granted are due to God's common grace.

b. Preservation is God's provision for and sustaining care of all living things up to and including human beings (Ps. 145:15-16; Matt. 5:45; Acts 17:28).

c. Government is God's direction and control of humanity according to His plan and moral purpose. It includes His permission, His restraint, and His overruling of human beings and all His sovereign, loving rule.

3. *The common influences of the Holy Spirit.* Human government, the moral codes of the great civilizations, the fragments of wisdom and truth found in non-Christian religions and great philosophers, the discoveries of science--all to varying degrees are due to the mercy, common grace, and goodness of God. "Every good and perfect gift is from above" (James 1:17).

All that is good in people and society can be to a large extent attributed to the workings of God's grace. Many unsaved people's answers to prayer in times of need, sickness, or danger are due to the goodness, grace, and mercy of God.

God's common grace administered by the Holy Spirit preserves humanity from far greater manifestations of depravity, cruelty, inhumanity, war, and chaos. The Holy Spirit through conscience restrains people from many more terrible expressions of sin that are conceived in the heart but not fully enacted.

The desire to achieve, the desire for freedom, the desire for peace in human relations, the concepts of honor, dignity, justice, respect for goodness and integrity, right and wrong, the sense of some form of a God or higher being, the sense of human dependence and responsibility, friendship, family awareness, human love, parental love, desire for human society and fellowship, humor, artistic and music ability--these and other similar concepts and attitudes are all due to the common grace of God mediated by the Holy Spirit. They may be more evident or more limited in one individual than in another, but they are a common heritage of our humanness that we owe to the grace of God.

Innumerable daily blessings benefit all people, even though many do not recognize that God's grace is their source. The amazing provisions of the human body which enable it to be renewed after sickness, to rest, sleep, and enjoy variety in taste in food are due to grace. Grace has provided for human creative ability, memory, and human inventiveness. Grace provides color, sound, and ten thousand delights that improve the quality of life. God's grace permits, assists, and guides in innumerable social, educational, psychological developments. All of the world is dependent upon God, indebted to God, and constantly blessed by God.

PREVENIENT GRACE. Common grace at times has been termed prevenient grace (grace coming before). We probably more accurately should restrict the term prevenient grace to those aspects of God's infinite grace which come before salvation and prepare the soul for receiving God's saving grace.

Prevenient or preliminary grace is that grace of God which the Holy Spirit supplies as He seeks to prepare a person to experience spiritual birth. His preparation of persons to come to repentance by God's mercy, goodness, discipline, providence, and restraint combine to help the person understand, recognize, and respond to God's grace and be saved. Perhaps some are granted more prevenient grace than others. This may be related to such factors as the prayers of God's children and the responsiveness of the person to God's grace. Note such Scriptures as Matthew 13:12-15; Romans 2:4. God's grace as given in salvation thus begins long before the regenerating and sanctifying power of God transforms the person "from darkness to light and from the power of Satan to God" (Acts 26:18).

All grace is the one grace of God. But for purpose of more fully understanding its holy working, we may speak of common grace, prevenient grace, saving grace, sanctifying grace, keeping grace, and glorifying grace. The Holy Spirit ministers to us God's grace in all its manifestations and forms (1 Peter 4:10).

Every person in himself is spiritually helpless and hopeless apart from the ministry of the Holy Spirit and the grace of God. When our foreparents sinned, they lost the indwelling Holy Spirit, the source of their created holiness. The depraved nature they passed on to their descendants cannot in itself please God (Rom. 8:8).

Whatever of light and moral principle is found in a person's conscience, whatever desire for God and righteousness is experienced by the person, whatever strength of will to desire the right and a restored relationship with God are the result of the faithful Holy Spirit expressing God's prevenient grace.

For the person's spiritual darkness the Spirit of grace provides light in illuminating God's mercy, God's goodness (Rom. 2:4), God's Word (Ps. 119:105, 130), and the person's spiritual duty and responsibility (Ps. 51:1-4). For the person's carelessness and sinfulness, the Spirit provides awakening (1 Cor. 15:34; Eph. 5:14) and conviction of guilt before God (John 16:8-11). For the person's hopelessness, the Spirit calls (Rev. 22:17), illuminates God's promises (2 Cor. 1:20), and encourages with new hope (Rom. 15:13; Heb. 6:18-19). For the person conscious of his powerlessness (Rom. 5:6), He provides enabling power (Isa. 40:29).

But God's grace through the Holy Spirit does not work irresistibly as He seeks to lead the person to repentance. The person can show contempt for the Spirit's gracious working (Rom. 2:4-5) and remain stubborn. God draws by His Spirit (John 6:44), but the person can grieve the Spirit and rebelliously refuse to respond (Isa. 63:10; Eph. 4:30). The Spirit contends with the sinner (Gal. 6:3), but the sinner can resist Him (Acts 7:51) and test Him (Acts 5:9). The gracious Holy Spirit can convict of sin, righteousness, and judgment (John 16:8-11) and seek to guide into truth (John 16:13), but the person can insult the Spirit (Heb. 10:29).

The Bible clearly teaches that our human will must cooperate with God's grace. This is called synergism. However, the Bible clearly gives preeminence to God's grace which takes the initiative in our salvation. "This is love: not that we loved God, but that he loved us and sent his Son as an atoning sacrifice for our sins. . . . We love because he first loved us" (1 John 4:10, 19).

God's grace has provided us the capacity for God. God draws and convicts. We must use the God-given capacity, yield to the Spirit's drawing, and submit to His conviction. Although we may refuse to respond or submit to the Spirit's activity, we cannot entirely avoid or escape that activity. Every human being to some extent and at some time feels the Spirit's conviction of sin and a restlessness or guilty conscience until he comes to Christ, the only Savior.

Prevenient grace touches the total personality of the unsaved person. It gives light to the intellect, conviction to the conscience and feelings, and strength to the will. However, God respects our personality and our freedom to choose, for that is how He created us. Therefore, the Holy Spirit influences, speaks to our heart, strives with our conscience and will, and convicts without compelling.

Apart from God's prevenient grace, our blind eyes would not see and recognize our spiritual need. Our deaf spiritual ears would not hear God's call and voice, nor would our dead conscience feel the drawing and striving of the Spirit. But apart from the cooperation of our free will, our soul will remain in sin and without Christ's salvation in spite of seeing, hearing, and feeling the Spirit's ministry through God's prevenient grace. "For it is by grace that you have been saved, through faith" (Eph. 2:8). "As God's fellow workers we urge you not to receive God's grace in vain" (2 Cor. 6:1).

> **John 1:9, 11**--"The true light which gives light to every man was coming into the world . . . He came to that which was His own, but His own did not receive him."

> **Matthew 13:15**--"This people's heart has become calloused; they hardly hear with their ears and they have closed their eyes. Otherwise they might see with their eyes, hear with their ears, understand with their hearts and turn, and I would heal them."

18

CONVERSION AND REPENTANCE

CONVERSION. The word conversion is used in various ways by evangelical speakers and writers. It is often used in a comprehensive and general way to include all involved in the initial work of saving grace in the soul--justification, regeneration, adoption, initial sanctification, and receiving the witness of the Spirit to the new life in Christ. Sometimes it is used only to include primarily the turning to God in repentance and faith.

The concept of conversion is based on the Hebrew word *shub* (to return, to turn), implying motion towards, and the New Testament Greek words *strepho* (to turn) and *epistrepho* (to turn about, to turn towards). It implies a turning from and a turning to. Conversion is the turning of the soul from sin to God.

From the age of accountability on, the sinner lives with his back toward God and is following Satan. Upon conversion the person turns from sin and turns to God to repent, believe, and be born of God. In turning away from sin, conversion is related closely to repentance. In turning toward God it is related closely to saving faith. Conversion is thus the turning point in the spiritual life. It is the soul's decision to forsake sin and Satan and to come to Christ. In this sense, conversion may be a tentative turning or a decisive turning. More than turning is required to be born of God. However, turning is very essential.

Conversion is a work of God's grace in which God's initiative and the person's response combine. The Holy Spirit through prevenient grace applies His holy influence on the heart, enlightening it, convicting it of its sin, and drawing it toward God and God's will. The Spirit strengthens the will in its resolve to turn to God, but the actual decision is personal choice. It is the result of divine initiative, divine enabling, but not divine compulsion. The person's free will must determine by God's help to place itself in submission to God and in harmony with His will.

Turning, or conversion, is occasionally referred to in Scripture as the work of God (Jer. 31:18; Lam. 5:21). God's part in turning is mentioned 15 times in the Old Testament but not directly in the New Testament. However, when the returning refers to a definite spiritual change, it almost always is shown as an act of the person (Isa. 55:7; Ezek. 33:11; Matt. 18:3). God appeals to us to turn, to come to God, to listen to God, to seek God.

Conversion has its double meaning. Negatively, it is turning away from sin. Positively, it is turning to God. Increasingly in the Old Testament, and predominately in the New Testament, it is the positive aspect of turning to God that is emphasized. It is thus the first step in beginning the Christian life or in the restoration of backsliders. Conversion is more than a change of beliefs. It is a turning to God. It is not merely an experience which one feels, but an act, something which one does. It is a change in commitment, a new commitment to Jesus. From the time of conversion, the person is a convert.

> **Isaiah 55:7**--"Let the wicked forsake his way and the evil man his thoughts. Let him turn to the Lord, and he will have mercy on him, and to our God, for he will abundantly pardon."
>
> **Ezekiel 33:11**--"Turn, turn from your evil ways! Why will you die?"
> Note also: 1 Chron. 28:9; Isa. 55:2-3; 55:6; Amos 5:4; Matt. 11:28; John 5:40; Rev. 22:17.

REPENTANCE. Bible repentance is one of the fundamental doctrines of both the Old and the New Testaments. It is an absolutely essential step to the new birth. It is closely interrelated with conversion, for turning from sin to God is a part of repentance.

Two Hebrew words are used in the Old Testament for a person's repentance. *Naham*, meaning "to pant, sigh, or groan," came in time to mean "to lament, grieve, regret bitterly, repent" (Job 42:6; Jer. 8:6).

The type of repentance which God desires from the sinner is more commonly expressed by *shub*, meaning to turn or return. So it is used for conversion and for repentance. In the New Testament the Greek words *metanoia* (change of mind, repentance) is used 23 times and *metanoeo* (to change one's mind or purpose) is used 34 times. So the Old Testament concept of repentance was to lament, grieve, regret bitterly one's sinful actions, to turn away from them, and return to God and doing God's will. The New Testament concept emphasized turning from sin, along with a deep sorrow for sin.

Repentance is that inner change of one's whole selfhood--mind, affections, convictions, and commitment--as a result of true regret and sorrow for sin against God. It is a change of one's whole being from following sin to following God.

Repentance is an essential part of the evangelical gospel. It was almost the entire content of John the Baptist's message (Matt. 3:2). It was the beginning message of Jesus (Matt. 4:17). It was the initial message of the early church and resulted in the salvation of 3,000 at Pentecost (Acts 2:38-41). This is the message Christ commanded to be preached as a primary part of the Gospel to all the world (Luke 24:46-48). This was the message of Paul (Acts 17:30).

Repentance is godly sorrow for sin (2 Cor. 7:10) that leads to forsaking and renouncing sin and turning to Christ for forgiveness of sin and salvation from sin. In real repentance the sinner's heart is broken because of his sin and that leads to separation from the sin. Repentance involves the whole personality.

1. *The sinner's mind is involved.* The intellect is illumined by the Holy Spirit to begin to comprehend the holiness of God (Isa. 6:1-5), the rebellion involved in his sin (Ps. 5:3-4; Rom. 1:32), the personal guilt for his sin (Luke 15:18), and the defilement of his sin in all its heinousness to God (Job 42:6). The sinner senses how helpless and hopeless he is apart from God's mercy and grace.

2. *The sinner's emotions are involved.* It is possible to have knowledge of sin without abhorring it. A changed emotional attitude toward sin is essential in true repentance. The sinner must realize how harmful his sin is to others, to humanity in general, and how

offensive and obnoxious it is to God. Sorrow for sin is not the whole of repentance, but there is no genuine repentance without it (2 Cor. 7:9-10). A sinner's emotions can move him powerfully to seek deliverance from sin (Ps. 32:3-5).

3. *The sinner's will is involved.* The most important aspect of repentance is the volitional element. The other elements of repentance are incomplete without it. The change of mind, of purpose, of attitude, and the godly sorrow for sin must lead to an actual turning from sin to God for salvation from sin. Loud and repeated lamenting of sin and tears over sin are no substitute for abandoning sin, returning to God, and casting one's self totally upon God's mercy and help.

Repentance does not cause us to merit salvation. It is the necessary condition for God to bestow saving grace. It is God's prevenient grace which enables the sinner to know his sin, sorrow for it, and turn from it to God.

THE NECESSITY OF REPENTANCE. "God . . . commands all people everywhere to repent" (Acts 17:30). Many verses of Scripture teach repentance; it is not optional to anyone (Luke 13:3, 5). Repentance and saving faith are both so essential to salvation that often the Gospel almost can be condensed into these two concepts-- repent and believe (Matt. 21:32; Mark 1:15). They are so interrelated that sometimes the Gospel is condensed even more and one or the other stands for both. Believing can be a synonym for salvation (Luke 8:13; John 1:7, 12; 7:39; 12:36). So can repentance (Luke 15:7, Acts 11:18; 20:11).

Repentance is not efficacious without saving faith and implies faith as the next step. We turn from sin (repentance) to God (faith). But faith in itself is not efficacious without repentance as its basis. To urge people to believe in Christ without repenting from their sin is to build upon sand (Matt. 7:26-27). However, in leading people from other religions to salvation, the acceptance of Christ as God and Savior, saving faith is often the crucial issue. In such a case the full understanding of sin may not come until after their commitment to

Christ. Once they have committed themselves to Jesus they may find obedience to the new light comparatively easy. For people with some Christian background, surrender and obedience may be the crucial issues.

The necessity of repentance is based upon these facts:

1. *God's Word commands it.* "God . . . commands all people everywhere to repent" (Acts 17:30). Note also: Ezek. 18:30-31; Matt. 4:17; Mark 1:15; Luke 13:3; Acts 3:19.

2. *Unrepented and unforsaken sins separate from God and all holy beings.* God is holy love. Only the pure in heart see God now or eternally (Matt. 5:8). "Without holiness no one will see the Lord" (Heb. 12:14). Holiness and sin are opposites. Nothing is more abominable to God than sin. Note: Deut. 18:12; 25:16; Prov. 12:22; 15:9.

Unrepented sin is an active force in a person and constantly seeks to express itself. Sin seeks to enslave and exercise dominion over the sinner. God's justice, holiness, and wrath cannot tolerate a rebel, rival, and enemy. The least possible requirement of God is that every sin be repented of. Apart from God there is no future peace or safety for any being. Until a person repents, he is opposed to God and a rebel against God. Unrepented sin will separate from God forever.

3. *Repentance is essential to enter heaven.* All sin defiles and is an abomination to God.

Titus 1:15--"To those who are corrupted and do not believe, nothing is pure. In fact, both their minds and consciences are corrupted." Note also: James 3:6.

No defiled or impure person will enter heaven. It was sin that changed the harmony and perfection of Eden into the suffering, injustice, conflict, and chaos of our world today. Unrepented sin means unconfessed and unforgiven sin, and totally bars from heaven and God's mercy.

Revelation 22:15--"Outside are the dogs (the unclean), those who practice magic arts, the sexually immoral, the murderers, the idolaters, and everyone who loves and practices falsehood." Note also: Rev. 21:8, 27.

4. *Repentance is necessary to receive mercy at the judgment throne of God.* Every unconfessed sin must be accounted for there. God "has set a day when he will judge the world with justice" (Acts 17:31). Everyone is destined to face judgment after death (Heb. 9:27). "We must all appear before the judgment seat of Christ, that each one may receive what is due him for the things done while in the body, whether good or bad" (2 Cor. 5:10). Every sin will be faced, either at the Cross or at the Judgment Day.

We are now ready to discuss the five phases or steps in repentance: Holy Spirit conviction, sorrow for sin, confession of sin, restitution, and forsaking of sin.

19

HOLY SPIRIT CONVICTION

Conviction is a work of the Holy Spirit revealing to the sinner his sins, his sinful nature, his guilt before God, the righteous standard of God's holiness and truth, and the certainty of God's future judgment of his sins on the basis of the record of his sins. The Holy Spirit works through the mind, conscience, and emotions of the sinner. The Spirit brings a recognition of sin as being unrighteous and wrong, of its defiling, enslaving, deceptive effect, and the resulting guilt and need of God's mercy and forgiveness.

Apart from the Holy Spirit, no one realizes the enormity of his sin or what an abomination it is in the sight of God. The experience of sin does not make us more sensitive and alert to sin; rather, it is like a narcotic, deadening and hardening our conscience (Ps. 95:8; Mark 10:5; 1 Tim. 4:2). Only the Spirit can show us the seriousness of sin.

The Spirit helps the sinner realize how his sin appears in the light of God's holiness and righteousness. Up to the moment of the Spirit's convicting work the sinner may have been so blinded by his sins and so morally and spiritually deadened or unawakened that he considered himself relatively a "good" person. Only by the illumination of the Holy Spirit as He sheds God's light on the heart can the sinner realize his full spiritual need (Ps. 90:7-8; Heb. 4:13). Isaiah's experience is an example of the convicting work of the Spirit in the life of one who is already a believer committed to God (Isa. 6:1-5).

The idea of the Spirit's conviction is a major theme of Scripture, even though the word is not often used. Pharaoh was repeatedly convicted of his sinful treatment of Israel but continued to harden his heart (Exod. 9:27, 34). Aaron and Miriam were convicted of their sin by God's judgment on Miriam (Num. 12:11). Balaam was convicted (Num. 22:34). King Saul confessed conviction (1 Sam. 26:21; 28:15). David showed deep conviction (2 Sam. 12:13; 24:10, 17; Ps. 51:4). Judas showed conviction, but he did not repent (Matt. 27:4). On the Day of Pentecost the Holy Spirit convicted the people (Acts 2:37). See also Gen. 6:3; Ps. 32:3-5; 51:1-17; John 8:9; Rom. 7:7-25.

The Holy Spirit has various methods of awakening, illumining, and convicting the soul:

1. *The Holy Spirit convicts by pointing out the goodness of God* (Rom. 2:4). When the person is helped to realize the kindness, long suffering, patient goodness, and love of God, his heart may become more tender. When the Spirit can reveal the sufferings of Christ on the cross, whether by word, picture, or film, the Spirit can often melt and convict and lead to the sinner's turning to Christ for salvation. Suddenly he realizes that Jesus took his place, suffered in his stead, and died for him. The Spirit can reveal how absolutely personal Christ's love for him is.

2. *The Holy Spirit convicts by showing how sinful sin is* (Rom. 7:13). When the Holy Spirit convicts the sinner, suddenly he realizes how utterly sinful his actions have been. Not only so, but the Spirit shows how loathsome and abhorrent sin is in its absolute vileness and evilness. He shows how hateful and despicable sin is. He can make the sinner so despise his sin that he is sick of it and loathes it.

The Spirit can show how sin is destructive of love, peace, and all good, how it destroys his own welfare and that of his friends and loved ones. He can show how opposed it is to the moral nature and law of God and to all of God's holiness. The Spirit can show how sinful sin is to crucify Jesus and then can convict the person with the awesome revelation that it was his own sin which nailed Jesus to the cross.

The Spirit can convict the person of the vast accumulation of his sins over the years--sins of thought, word, and deed. Often He brings to memory sins long forgotten and can cause them to stand out vividly in all their hatefulness, vileness, and abomination. The sinner begins to realize how right and just it is for God to judge his sins. He sees his personal guilt in all its alarming dimension (John 16:8-9).

3. *The Holy Spirit convicts of righteousness* (John 16:8, 10). He shows the sinner the holiness, righteousness, and truth of God, especially as revealed in Christ who is known by demons (Mark 1:24) and men (Acts 3:14) as "the Holy One of God." He is "the Righteous One" (1 John 2:1). He is "the Truth" (John 14:6). All sin is judged from the standpoint of His righteousness.

The Holy Spirit convicts the sinner of the infinite gap between the righteousness of God and Christ and his own sinful acts and nature. This revelation is necessary to show sinners the absolute need of a Mediator-Savior.

In the Old Testament, righteousness was defined by God's law. Now it is defined in God's Son. The sinner recognizes that all his own claimed goodness and righteous acts are as "filthy rags" in the light of Christ's righteousness (Isa. 64:6). Thus the Spirit brings the sinner to the point of abhorring his own sinfulness as seen in God's holy light (Job 42:5-6; Isa. 6:1-5).

4. *The Holy Spirit convicts of judgment* (John 16:8, 11). As the Spirit reveals the sinfulness of sin and the righteousness and holiness of God and of Jesus Christ, the sinner cannot but recognize the justice of God's judgment on sin and Satan. He realizes that he himself deserves nothing but the just judgment of the Holy God.

The Spirit impresses that Satan is already judged in principle and that he will one day be ejected from the universe and confined to the fire of hell (Rev. 20:10). The Spirit convicts that the unforgiven sins of the sinner will banish him eternally with Satan in hell after he faces God's judgment day (Rev. 20:11-15; 21:8, 27).

The Spirit shows that the Christ who died to be his Savior, if he rejects His offer of forgiveness and Christ's role as Savior, will then be his Judge (John 5:22, 27; Acts 10:42; 2 Cor. 5:10; 2 Tim. 4:1; 1 Peter 4:5; Rev. 6:15-17; 20:11-15).

The Spirit convicts the sinner that the judgment will include his thoughts (Ps. 19:14; 94:11; 139:23-24; Prov. 15:26), attitudes (Heb. 4:12), motives (1 Cor. 4:5), secrets (Rom. 2:16; Heb. 4:12), words

(Matt. 12:36-37; Jude 15), and actions (Prov. 24:12; Matt. 16:27). There will be no excuse because the complete record of every person is recorded in the books of heaven (Rev. 20:12). Thank God, through Christ sin can be forgiven and the record of sin blotted out (Ps. 51:1; Isa. 43:25; Acts 3:19).

The Holy Spirit may use many means to bring conviction of sin and of the need of salvation. Among the means used are:

Providence, chastisement	Job 33:14, 29-30
Dreams and visions	Job 33:15-18
Sickness and pain	Job 33:19-27; Ps. 119:67
Holy lives	Phil. 2:15; Titus 2:8; 1 Peter 2:12; 3:16
Christian songs	
Testimony	
Christian literature	
The Word of God	Eph. 6:17

Scripture is the great sword of the Spirit (Eph. 6:17) which He uses whenever people have access to the Word or read the Word. The Holy Spirit may combine conviction through the Word with any of the others listed above. If the sinner has read or heard God's Word, the Spirit can bring this to his memory through dreams, visions, sickness, providence. In Christian testimony, literature, songs and preaching, the Word quoted, explained, or its general truth incorporated in what is said gives special convicting power. It is important to sow God's Word, because at any time of crisis the Spirit may bring it to memory and use it as His sword (Heb. 4:12-13).

Holy Spirit conviction can cut to the heart (Acts 2:37), arrest people in their sinful ways (Acts 9:4-5), pierce and penetrate through all the mental defenses (Heb. 4:12), and uncover all the personality and past of the person under God's gaze (Heb. 4:13). But the convicted person still has to yield and accept or else he will resist and reject.

People can refuse the Spirit's convicting efforts and the persons the Spirit uses (Acts 7:54). Pharaoh confessed his sin but hardened his heart (Exod. 9:27, 34). Balaam confessed his sin (Num. 22:34), but went on in his stubborn way. Instead of dying the death of the righteous, as he desired (Num. 23:10), he died the death of the wicked (Num. 31:8). Achan (Josh. 7:20), Saul (1 Sam. 15:24), and Judas (Matt. 27:4)--each confessed to having sinned, but none of them fully repented and received forgiveness.

One of the great spiritual needs of our time is true and strong Holy Spirit conviction for sin. Without conviction the sinner and society become increasingly corrupt. Conviction is necessary in any true spiritual awakening and revival (Neh. 9:1-3; 2 Chron. 7:14). A major reason we have so little conviction for sin is that there is so little anointed preaching on sin, righteousness, and judgment. No minister can be truly faithful to his calling and be truly prophetic and scriptural without preaching at times on sin, righteousness, and judgment.

Holy Spirit conviction always includes an element of hope. Uncompromising condemnation for sin is accompanied by reminder of God's gracious provision and promise in Scripture. The Spirit does not convict to make people burdened with guilt and then abandon them. His purpose is to lead to repentance (Rom. 2:4). This is why the great prophets not only gave strong condemnation of sin, but also great invitations to return to God, accompanied by great promises if the people would only repent.

Conviction, when accepted humbly and yielded to, produces "repentance that leads to salvation" (Rom. 7:10). Conviction resisted adds to the guilt, and the unrepentant one is really "storing up wrath" (Rom. 2:5) and God's judgment against himself, for the greater the light, the greater the responsibility (Luke 12:48). Rejected light hardens and leads to God's judgment (Prov. 29:1; Jer. 19:15; Zech. 7:11-12; Heb. 3:13, 15).

20

SORROW FOR SIN, CONFESSION, RESTITUTION, AND FORSAKING

SORROW FOR SIN. Holy Spirit conviction of sin if not resisted always will lead to a godly sorrow for sin (2 Cor. 7:10). Conviction does not stay in the realm of the purely intellectual. It can have a profoundly emotional element. It is sometimes accompanied by physical manifestations, like sleeplessness, because of a troubled conscience or because God keeps the person awake and quiet so He can speak more personally and directly (Esther 6:1; Ps. 32:4; Dan. 2:1; 6:18). Sometimes the convicted person loses appetite for food (Job 33:20, 23-30; Ps. 102:4-7; 107:17-19). He may lose interest in normal activities and pleasures.

Often the person becomes restless, more easily irritated and frustrated as he tries to "kick against the goads" of God's dealing with him (Acts 26:14). The person may become more stubborn (Ps. 81:11-12; Jer. 7:24; Rom. 2:5), more hateful and sinful for the time being. Apparently Saul of Tarsus, trying to disregard the dying testimony of Stephen, became even more violently anti-Christian just before God stopped him on the road to Damascus.

Sorrow for sin is more than fear of the consequences of sin, sorrow for being caught in sin, shame over the guilt of sin, or sin's aftermath. A person may have all of these and still stubbornly cling to sin. Such sorrow may be only a self-pity and a selfish sorrow. A person may be disgusted with himself and may despise himself without humbling himself before God and being truly repentant.

Selfish sorrow over sin and self-pity may lead to remorse and despair. Paul calls that the worldly sorrow that brings death (2 Cor.

7:10). Judas was driven by such worldly sorrow to commit suicide. So did King Saul (1 Sam. 31:4). The Holy Spirit never includes despair when He convicts of sin. All such despair and hopelessness is from Satan, who desires to drive us to death and hell.

Godly sorrow leads to the humbling of one's self before God and genuine fruit of repentance, what John the Baptist called "fruit in keeping with repentance" (Matt. 3:8). Paul called it proving repentance by deeds (Acts 26:20).

David terms the repentant heart a broken and contrite heart (Ps. 51:17). He assures us that God will not reject such a repentant one. Such brokenhearted ones Christ binds up (Isa. 61:1), heals (Ps. 147:3), saves (Ps. 34:18), revives (Isa. 57:15), and esteems (Isa. 66:2).

CONFESSION OF SIN. A person who is convicted of his sin, who truly sorrows for his sins, will want to take the next step of repentance by confessing his sins to God and asking God's forgiveness. Confession is the acknowledging of personal guilt. One cannot turn to the God he has sinned against without turning from sin. David testified, "I acknowledged my sin to you and did not cover up my iniquity. I said, 'I will confess my transgressions to the Lord'-- and you forgave the guilt of my sin" (Ps. 32:5).

The new moral consciousness of sin which results from conviction and sorrow for sin leads the sinner to accept God's attitude toward sin. He begins to hate sin and submit himself to God and His will. He naturally expresses this in a twofold confession: (a) his personal guilt and defilement, and (b) his utter helplessness and impotence to save himself from sin.

1. *Confession to God.* Since God is the Sovereign of the universe and since all sins are against God's nature and God's law, our primary confession of sin must be to God, the One we have sinned against most seriously. Although David had grievously sinned against others, the overwhelming awareness that it was God who was Sovereign and it was God who he had most dishonored caused David to pray, "Against you, you only, have I sinned and done what is evil in your sight" (Ps. 51:4).

Since all salvation is through Christ and since Christ is our only Savior, the confession of sin is closely related to the receiving of Christ as Savior. To confess Christ is to confess that Christ died for our sins (1 Cor. 15:3) and that He died for my sins personally. To confess my sin in humble repentance is to look to Christ for forgiveness (1 John 1:9). John the Baptist was sent to prepare people to receive Christ by leading them to repentance for their sins. The Holy Spirit leads us to the confession of our sins to Christ and to the confession of Christ as our Savior (1 Cor. 12:3).

2. *Confession to people.* Confession of sin is a moral obligation to God and also often to people. If we have sinned against others, it is often essential to ask their forgiveness (Matt. 25:23-24) and perhaps to make restitution where that is possible.

In the Old Testament confession of sin was often a public act. The public could see the sinner going to the temple with his sin-offering. The sinner was required to confess and make restitution to the one wronged or to any relatives who were harmed by the sin (Num. 5:6-8).

The general rule would seem to be that all sins which are brought to our memory by the Holy Spirit should be confessed to God, and all sins against an individual or group should be confessed to them as far as possible, unless God gives special guidance otherwise. We are not asked to confess the sins of others. Confession is a personal act. Therefore, if by the confession of our own sin we involve others it is probably not wise to make a confession in such a way that the other person can be identified.

Confession of sin was a national as well as a personal obligation (Lev. 26:40-42). Forgiveness of the nation (2 Chron. 7:14) or the individual is conditioned upon confession (1 John 1:9).

God providentially controlled circumstances so that Joseph's brothers were compelled to confess before their father Jacob. Pharaoh had to confess before Moses, and no doubt his officials all heard the confession. Achan was required to confess before all Israel.

Confession to God and generally to other people should be detailed and specific (Lev. 5:5). The person who does not open his heart fully to God or to others in confession is neither fully convicted nor fully sorry for his sins. His repentance is incomplete. As a sinner comes to Christ for salvation, the Holy Spirit often brings sins to mind which were long forgotten, and as long as He reminds us of more sins we should be obedient in continuing to confess them.

A mere general confession that "Yes, I am a great sinner" is usually very superficial. The fuller the confession, if given discreetly, the fuller the sense of forgiveness and release will be. It may not be wise to give sordid public details of past sins which would be offensive or polluting to listen to. But when it is possible to make a direct confession to the person, it should be full enough and deep enough to re-win the confidence of the person sinned against.

When sin is faced and not confessed, the person becomes all the more accountable to God and more guilty in God's sight. Cain refused to confess, and God cursed him (Gen. 4:11). Ananias and Sapphira refused to confess when opportunity was given them, and they were struck dead (Acts 5:1-11). God clearly states that mercy is not available until sin is confessed (Prov. 28:13; Hosea 5:15).

RESTITUTION. Restitution is a phase of repentance which is closely related to confession of sin. A truly repentant person is willing to make restitution wherever it is possible. To make restitution is to restore to its rightful owner anything we have stolen or to make amends by giving some equivalent or compensation for loss, damage, or injury.

The Old Testament basis for restitution is given in Exodus 22:1-6; Leviticus 6:2-5; Numbers 5:6-8. This command is recognized by Samuel (1 Sam. 12:3) and David (2 Sam. 12:6). It is commanded by God again in Ezekiel 33:15. In the New Testament it is undoubtedly included in the "fruit in keeping with repentance" in Matthew 3:8 and Luke 3:8. Christ accepts and thus endorses the principle in Luke 19:8.

For property stolen or money taken falsely there had to be full compensation, with a specified additional amount added (Exod. 22:7; Lev. 6:5). Perhaps there is no stronger testimony to the genuineness of repentance than asking forgiveness and making restitution. Every honest person recognizes the moral correctness of such actions. The lack of these casts serious doubt on the repentance being genuine.

It is not possible to make restitution for certain types of sins. Purity cannot be restored. Life destroyed cannot be restored. It is very difficult to restore a good name ruined by slander. When full monetary restitution is not immediately possible, the genuineness of the repentance can be shown by partial regular payments from time to time until the whole is repaid--as long as the repentant one fully pays according to his ability.

FORSAKING OF SIN. Sorrow for sin and repentance is incomplete unless it leads to the forsaking of sin. Repentance is proved negatively by a separation from sin and positively by an attitude and life of obedience. This forsaking of sin and life of obedience is only possible because of the grace of God provided as the gift of Christ (Rom. 5:15-17) and the help of the Holy Spirit sent by Christ to accomplish Christ's redemption in us. As in all other aspects of repentance and salvation, there must be human cooperation with God's gracious initiative.

In conviction of sin and sorrow for sin there is emphasis upon the feeling. In confession of sin, restitution, and the forsaking of sin there is emphasis upon the will. The sinner must act. Without both the mental recognition of sin and the will to turn from sin to obedience, repentance is not genuine. A child has defined repentance as "being sorry enough to quit."

> **Isaiah 55:7**--"Let the wicked forsake his way and the evil man his thoughts. Let him return to the Lord, and he will have mercy on him. . . . he will freely pardon." Note also: Prov. 28:13; Ezek. 14:6; 18:21; 19:27; 18:30-31; 33:11.

Genuine repentance is comprehensive. It covers all sins committed. It may begin because of conviction for one particular sin, but it must lead to the total forsaking and renouncing of all sin. Sin is a unity and the change of attitude and the will essential to true repentance means that all sin is repudiated without exception--sinful thoughts and attitudes, sinful words, and sinful actions. If even one sin is cherished and retained, repentance does not result in forgiveness and the new birth (Luke 14:33; 16:10; James 2:10).

Repentance as an act leads to penitence as a state--a permanent attitude of forsaking sin and turning to God. None of these phases or steps in repentance result in spiritual merit before God. In no sense do they earn salvation. They are God's conditions and requirements for the soul who desires salvation.

21

SAVING FAITH

What is faith? The Hebrew word for faith gives the idea of firmness, certainty, or assurance. To believe is to be sure about, to be assured. The Greek word *pistis* (faith) means firm persuasion, a firm conviction, trust based on hearing.

Faith is a firm persuasion, a confiding, trusting belief in the truth, veracity, or reality of a person or thing. Hebrews 11:1 gives this definition: "Faith is being sure of what we hope for and certain of what we do not see." The Old Testament and New Testament give primary emphasis upon faith as trust in God, and almost always include the thought of reliance on God.

Saving faith is the act of the whole person. Psychologically we can analyze this into separate aspects of our being. We can say we understand and assent with our mind. We respond with our emotions. We respond with gratitude for God's provision, begin to recognize hope for our salvation, which kindles the joy of anticipation. We sense an inner conviction of God's truth, become favorable to that truth and willing to accept it, and begin to sense a foretaste of peace. We believe with our "heart." That refers to us as a whole person, with our natural emotional response included.

We also respond with a clear decision to accept and claim God's promise and enter into God's provision. When we will to obey, we have responded in the natural entirety of our personhood. Saving faith is reasonable, emotionally satisfying, and personally, decisively exercised.

THE NATURE OF FAITH. Faith has both divine and human aspects. Both of these must be recognized.

Faith is God's ordained condition of salvation. God chose to save us on the condition of faith. It is not faith in faith. It is faith in Christ as Savior. By faith we become part of God's elect. Faith has no merit in itself. God in grace credits (imputes) our faith as righteousness. "Abraham's faith was credited to him as righteousness" (Rom. 4:9). To credit or impute does not mean to substitute, but that faith is accepted as the condition for righteousness.

We were not righteous. Our best motives in seeking salvation are tainted by our carnal self. All our self-produced righteous acts are imperfect and "like filthy rags" in the sight of God (Isa. 64:6). But God graciously and mercifully accepts our faith as meeting His condition for imparting righteousness to us. We do not have a works righteousness. Faith is not a work producing salvation. We have a faith righteousness entirely by God's grace.

We do not deserve salvation. We could never earn it. Faith in itself could not make us righteous if God had not ordained that faith in Christ for salvation would be accepted by Him as meeting His conditions. By grace God has chosen to justify and regenerate those who believe.

The Holy Spirit makes faith possible. God the Holy Spirit leads a person to the point where faith becomes possible. He prepares the heart to recognize its sin and need, to understand God's gracious provision, and assist the heart to repent. He assists the person to take the three steps involved in true faith--assent, consent, and appropriation. God's grace provided Christ's atonement for our sin and the Spirit's aid in our repentance.

The Holy Spirit provides the revealed truth to which we must assent. He strengthens our will to consent and act upon it. The Spirit aids our faith throughout. Then He assures us that we have taken these steps and witnesses to our salvation. This witness is the inner assurance that God in faithfulness to His Word has accepted us on the basis of our faith. So we are saved by grace through faith (Rom. 3:24-25; 4:16; Eph. 2:8).

Faith is the personal act of the believer. The provision of grace and the Spirit's aid in believing and the actual act of believing are separate things. The Holy Spirit does not repent for us or believe for us. He is ready to help us, but we must act personally. Even though the Spirit is available, we may reject accepting His aid.

That is why the Bible repeatedly commands us to come, to repent, to believe. The Bible also warns us against failure to repent and to believe, and gives examples of God's judgment upon those who did not believe.

God gives, by grace, the ability or power to believe, but we must use that power. If we did not have the power to believe and it was all the work of the Holy Spirit apart from our cooperation, it would be the Spirit's faith, not ours. If we did not have the power to believe, we would not be a responsible moral being. We have the power to listen to God's Word or read God's Word, the power to see God at work, and the power to believe. But God exercises none of these powers for us. We can refuse to read, listen, see, or believe.

FAITH IS BASED ON CHRIST AS SAVIOR

Faith is based upon an object. Faith needs light. Faith implies previous knowledge of that which we believe. Faith is really a form of knowledge. The basic principles and laws of science are statements of faith. Faith is not opposed to reason but is based on reasonable evidence. To believe something apart from reasonable evidence is not faith, it is presumption. The impossible and irrational cannot be believed.

Spiritual faith is based on evidence of God's existence and God's revelation which we have accepted. It is reasonable for a child to accept the wisdom of a father and for a creature to accept the evidence of its Creator.

Saving faith is based upon Christ as Savior. Saving faith involves a general acceptance of God's truth, but it is specially focused on Christ as Savior. Saving faith is not mere faith in a record or a doctrine. It is personal trust in a personal Christ. It is the act of a person (the repentant sinner) who commits himself to and trusts another Person (Jesus Christ the Savior). All Bible truth is important, for it reveals that Person and is a revelation from and of that Person.

Justification is by faith, but it is a special kind of saving faith in Jesus Christ as Savior (Rom. 3:22). Salvation is not by faith in Christ as Creator or as our Example or Teacher, but in Christ as Savior. Christ is Savior only through His atoning death; that is, through His blood (Rom. 3:24-26).

Saving faith upon Christ as Savior is based on the Word of God. The Gospel, as contained in the Bible, is to be believed. The Gospel is the power of God for the salvation of everyone who believes it (Rom. 1:16). Belief is through the Word (John 17:20). Faith comes from hearing the Word (Rom. 10:17). The Word is written so we may believe and have spiritual life by believing it (John 20:31). God chose for us to be saved through belief in the truth (2 Thess. 2:13).

Saving faith in the Savior is the result of faith in the Bible as the revealed Word of God. Faith in the revealed Word is strengthened and confirmed by saving faith.

Faith is both receptive and active. Faith receives the Bible as the Word of God. Faith receives the revelation of the Word concerning sin and self. The conviction of the Holy Spirit strengthens this. Faith accepts the promise of salvation through Christ the Savior. But this faith must become active and act upon the light received as well as the conviction of sin felt, and then trust Christ as personal Savior.

22

THE STEPS OF FAITH

There are three steps in saving faith. Many people only take the first or the first and second steps, and thus claim salvation without experiencing true saving faith which brings salvation from sin. However, many persons who reach through to God are unaware that there were actually three aspects or steps in their faith. Logically, the three steps are separate. Chronologically, the person may take all three steps in rapid succession almost in the same moment.

STEP ONE: BELIEF OR INTELLECTUAL ASSENT. The mind must receive and assent to the truth. Faith has an intellectual content. The person must believe that God exists, that Christ is the Savior. "Anyone who comes to him must believe that he exists and that he rewards those who earnestly seek him" (Heb. 11:6). All faith has to start at this level. But the level of belief alone will not save. "You believe that there is one God. Good! Even the demons believe that--and shudder" (James 2:19). To only go this far in faith is to remain unsaved.

There must be an intellectual perception of and assent to what is revealed in God's Word. The Bible clearly teaches (a) human sinfulness, (b) Christ our atoning Savior, and (c) salvation from sin.

To believe in Christ as a person is to believe what the Bible teaches about Him, that He is truly God yet truly man, that He provided salvation by His atoning death, and that He invites the sinner to repent and believe and receive forgiveness of sins. The Bible provides truth for us to believe; God provides us a mind and expects us to use it in believing.

There must be a historical faith in these facts of Scripture. The understanding must assent to this Bible truth. Such historical faith is similar to the faith in other facts of history or life. It is merely an acceptance of fact. Demons cannot avoid such belief in God (James 2:19), but it does not save them.

Mental acceptance does not save us, but it is the first and necessary step in saving faith. It requires more than that to be justified by faith and to become a transformed child of God.

STEP TWO: CONSENT, OR SURRENDER OF THE WILL AND BEING. The person by his will must fully and completely consent to God's plan of salvation. He must accept the truth that he is a sinner and that there is no way he can save himself. He must surrender his whole selfhood to God's terms of salvation, renouncing all other hope and effort.

This voluntary act of the will guarantees that salvation is a moral transaction. It does not permit continuing in the practice of known sin. Saving faith is closely related to repentance and can only be exercised on the basis of repentance.

This second step in full faith is self-surrender to God and to God's will. It is submission to God's standards and God's way. This surrender involves the person's whole being. It is an act of his whole soul, so it has a deep emotional element. Love for sin must become hatred for sin. Now there is love for holiness. This deep surrender means a fundamental, clear-cut decision by the person's will. It may well involve an emotional struggle. It always brings emotional release.

STEP THREE: APPROPRIATION, OR SPIRITUAL TRUST AND PERSONAL RECEPTION. There must be an active, personal appropriation of pardoning grace. The person must lay hold of God's promise. The final logical step in full saving faith is exercising one's will to take salvation and forgiveness from Christ by faith just now. In one sense this volitional element of saving faith is so comprehensive and so dependent on the first two aspects that it includes all of saving faith.

Yet a person can take the first two steps and not really believe savingly. He may fail to reach out and appropriate for himself. Many people intellectually accept the truth, emotionally welcome and approve it, but do not volitionally appropriate it. Their faith is incomplete and leaves God's saving grace unapplied to their heart. God will not accept incomplete faith. We were created as full persons with power to appropriate or reject by our own choice, and unless we take this final step of response in cooperation with God's grace we remain untransformed.

The will must do two things which God will not and cannot do for us--surrender and personally appropriate Christ as Savior. Until we surrender in true commitment to Christ we cannot appropriate by faith. Forsaking all false hopes of salvation, or all false gods, all religiosity, all efforts to save ourselves, we must turn totally and eternally to Christ.

Then as a whole being--our mind, our emotions, our will--we must reach out our hand of faith and take the salvation which Jesus has provided and offers by His free grace. The Holy Spirit has convicted us, illumined us, drawn us, and brought us to the brink of salvation. But we must accept and use His help to reach out our own hand of faith and take it personally.

When Israel came to the Jordan and the feet of the priests carrying the Ark, in obedience to God's command, touched the water, the way through was cleared by God's miracle power (Josh. 3:15). Reaching the brink of Jordan did not open the river. The moment the feet in faith touched the water, God acted. When they acted in faith, God acted in miracle. In the same way, until the will takes the step of appropriating faith, all the previous steps are only preliminary and do not bring the miracle of salvation. But the moment the sinner stretches out his spiritual hand in appropriating faith, he is saved that instant.

There is always a danger that some people go through a kind of formula for salvation, or take the steps to salvation but do it all intellectually and emotionally without the full surrender of their will and the personal appropriating choice. They take the steps superficially, but not from the depths of their whole being. They make an intellectual commitment but not a full, whole-souled commitment.

David, expressing his whole-souled worship of God, said, "Praise the Lord, O my soul; all my inmost being praise His holy name" (Ps. 103:1). Even so, faith is still formal and only nominal until the person can say with all the innermost being--mind, affections, and will--"Jesus, I receive You now. I take Your forgiveness and saving grace now." This full-souled faith of commitment and appropriation can also be called trust. Trust is that final stage of saving faith where the soul rests in total confidence in Christ as Savior.

Assent and consent may be primarily related to the truth and God's requirements, but trust relates us to God as a person. Saving faith necessarily includes both. In salvation we as a person receive Christ as a Person. We establish a personal relationship of trust. We not only become a believer in truth, we become a member of God's family.

Saving trust involves the whole personality. Its commitment is far deeper than feelings, but naturally results in the deepest and profound emotions of the soul. It always expresses itself by love (Gal. 5:6).

The exercise of saving faith is so definite and complete and brings such spiritual transformation of personality and character that everyone can know that he has thus believed unto salvation. If he is not certain that he has taken this step, it is normally certain that he has not.

Saving faith leads to the witness of the Spirit within the soul. God's Spirit witnesses with our spirit to our salvation and sonship (Rom. 8:16). Until the level of personal trust has been reached, the person may have taken only the first step--intellectual assent and agreement. Saving faith includes all three steps.

SAVING FAITH AND GOOD WORKS. Salvation is always a gift of God's grace. Nothing we could ever do could merit or earn salvation. Salvation does not come through our righteous actions. Repentance and saving faith are not works which cause us to merit salvation. But both are necessary conditions of salvation. No one ever has been saved because he deserved God's saving grace, but no one ever has been saved until he met God's conditions of salvation. Saving faith is the final condition God requires in order to receive salvation.

Saving faith necessarily leads us to good works. The surrender to God's will which prepares the heart to believe unto salvation makes us available to do God's will. Saving faith is proved by a saved life. Good works in loving obedience to God and in joyous service of God are the natural outflow and fruit of saving faith.

Any claimed faith which does not result in a transformed life of obedience to Christ is a superficial or incomplete faith. The Bible uses the term "dead faith" for any faith which does not lead to obedience. Such faith does not save (James 2:14-26).

The good works, which are the fruit of saving faith, please God because:

a. They are performed in obedience to His will.

b. They are done through the enabling power and grace of God as the Holy Spirit works through us.

c. They witness to His saving power and thus glorify Him.

Saving faith is inconsistent with continued practice of willful sin. Jesus came not merely to forgive us but to save us from our sins (Matt. 1:21), not in our sins. The Son of God appeared to destroy the devil's work in the lives of people (1 John 3:8). That is why "No one who is born of God will continue to sin" (v. 9). That is how we know those who have exercised saving faith and become children of God (v. 10).

Faith implies obedience because of surrender to Christ and the enabling power of the Holy Spirit. It implies the acceptance and practice of all known truth. It implies walking in the light God gives us (1 John 1:7). If anyone falls into sin, he must immediately flee to

Jesus and confess that sin. Then Jesus Christ will speak in his defense to the Father (1 John 2:1). But he dare not continue the practice of sin, or he ceases to walk in the light and is once more in the darkness of sin. He needs saving grace to establish him in the light, for if we walk in darkness and claim to be in fellowship with God we lie (1 John 1:5-6).

SAVING FAITH AND THE LIFE OF FAITH. Saving faith is the final step in receiving God's wonderful transforming grace. Prevenient grace at that point becomes saving grace. The faith which saves becomes the law of our spiritual life and we now live by faith. Note: Rom. 1:17; 11:20; 2 Cor. 5:7; Gal. 2:20; Eph. 3:17; Col. 2:7.

The initial act of saving faith becomes the permanent attitude of the regenerated person. He is now in "the obedience that comes from faith" (Rom. 1:5). It is "a righteousness that is by faith from first to last" (v. 17). As believers we are now "in the faith." "Examine yourselves to see whether you are in the faith" (2 Cor. 13:5). Also Philippians 1:25. This faith can be increased; it is the fruit of the Spirit. Note: Luke 17:5; 2 Thess. 1:3; 1 Tim. 6:11; James 2:18.

23

THE NEW BIRTH AND JUSTIFICATION

The first transforming work of God's grace in a person's soul, i.e., the new birth, is called by many names in the Bible. But perhaps one of the most common and most general names is the new birth. Saving faith in Christ brings new spiritual life to a soul that was dead in sin.

The doctrine of a new spiritual life from God is one of the most basic doctrines of the New Testament. It is referred to as a new creation of life (2 Cor. 5:17), a spiritual resurrection from spiritual death (Eph. 2:6; Col. 2:12), a being made alive with Christ (Eph. 2:5), and a spiritual birth into spiritual life (John 3:3, 7).

Sin is deadly. The wages of sin is death (Rom. 6:23). Sin puts the sinner to death spiritually (Rom. 7:11, 13). Sinful acts lead to spiritual death (Rom. 6:16, 21; 7:5; Heb. 6:1; 9:14). Sin when it is full grown results in death (James 1:15). The sinner is dead in trespasses and sins (Eph. 2:1, 5; Col. 2:13). Sin and spiritual death become almost synonymous (Rom. 8:2). Even the mind of sinful people is death (v. 6).

Jesus referred to this when He said, "Let the dead bury their own dead" (Matt. 8:22). In His parable He taught that when the prodigal son returned, he who had been dead was now alive again (Luke 15:24, 32). It is possible to claim to be a Christian but to be still spiritually dead (Rev. 3:1).

The Bible teaches that a person's salvation is dependent upon the Holy Spirit giving life to the soul that is spiritually dead. Thus, to be saved is to pass from death to life (John 5:24; 1 John 3:14). When the sinner turns to God he is saved from spiritual death

(James 5:20). He has been brought from death to life (Rom. 5:13), and is now alive from the dead (Rom. 6:13).

Human language is inadequate to describe God or to describe the work of God in a person's soul. Therefore, the Bible uses many terms in order to picture in various understandable ways the wonderful spiritual reality. All of these describe what God does in and for the repentant, believing soul in the first moment of salvation. Here are some of the Bible terms and picture phrases:

1. Born again. John 3:3, 7; James 1:18.
2. Born of God. John 1:13; 1 John 5:4.
3. Born of the Spirit. John 3:5, 6.
4. Receiving or having the Holy Spirit. John 7:39; 14:17; 20:22; Rom. 8:9, 11; 1 Cor. 2:12.
5. The washing of rebirth. Titus 3:5.
6. Made alive. Rom. 6:11; 8:10; Eph.2:5; Col. 2:13.
7. New creation. 2 Cor. 5:17; Gal. 6:14-15; Eph. 2:10.
8. Crossing over from death to life. John 5:24; 1 John 3:14.
9. Salvation. (This is an all-inclusive word that may include primarily the new birth or may include all the saving acts of God in our life until our glorification in heaven.) Acts 4:12; 16:30-31; Rom. 1:16; 2 Cor. 6:2; Eph. 2:8; Heb. 2:3.
10. Forgiveness of sins. Matt. 9:6; Acts 10:43; 26:18; Eph. 1:7; 4:32.
11. Pardon. Isa. 55:7; Micah 7:18.
12. Purchased. Rev. 5:9; 14:4.
13. Redemption. Rom. 3:24; Eph. 1:7; Titus 2:14
14. Justification. Acts 13:39; Rom. 3:24, 28; 4:25; 5:1, 9.
15. Sins removed. Ps. 103:12.
16. Iniquities hurled into the depths of the sea. Micah 7:19.
17. Sins swept away. Isa. 44:22.
18. Sins put behind God's back. Isa. 38:17.
19. Sins wiped out. Acts 3:19; Isa. 43:25.
20. Sins blotted out. Psalm 51:1; Isa. 43:25.
21. Sins covered. Rom. 5:7.
22. Sins washed away. Ps. 51:7; Acts 22:16.

23. Freed from sins. Rev. 1:5.
24. Clean hands. Ps. 24:4; James 4:8.
25. Adoption. Rom. 8:15; Gal. 4:5; Eph. 1:5.
26. Delivered from darkness. Eph. 5:8; Col. 1:13; 1 Peter 2:9.
27. Baptized into the Body of Christ by the Holy Spirit. 1 Cor. 12:13.

DISTINCTIONS. The many Bible terms used to describe the first major experience of Christ's grace in our hearts indicate that the experience of God's salvation may be considered from various viewpoints.

1. From the standpoint of our sins in the sight of God it is: (a) forgiveness (pardon, remission); (b) sins blotted out, washed away, separated from us (Ps. 103:12), cast into the depths of the sea (Micah 7:19), covered (Rom. 4:7); (c) justification.

2. From the standpoint of sins in relation to ourselves, it is: (a) salvation, (b) redemption, (c) deliverance, (d) freedom.

3. From the standpoint of eternal life, it is: (a) a new birth (born again, born of God, born of the Spirit), (b) a new creation, (c) a passing from death to life (made alive), (d) regeneration.

4. From the standpoint of our relation to God, it is: (a) becoming a child of God, (b) adoption.

All these terms are useful in helping us understand all that God does for us in this first major work of God's saving grace. We can consider this holy experience from these four viewpoints. Yet they all describe what is received in one act of faith in one moment of time.

In discussing this first major work of God's grace theologically, we usually use these terms: justification, regeneration (new birth), adoption, initial sanctification, and the witness of the Spirit.

JUSTIFICATION

THE NATURE OF JUSTIFICATION. When we view human beings in relation to God, the primary fact to be noted is that we are morally responsible to God, the Moral Ruler of the universe. God has three primary roles toward us. As Moral Sovereign of the universe, He is (1) Ruler and (2) Judge. As God of all grace, He is (3) Father.

In the first major work of grace in the repentant, believing sinner God as Sovereign Ruler forgives, as Judge He justifies, and as Father He adopts. Justification and forgiveness are the same gracious act from two separate viewpoints. This is proved by Acts 13:38-39 and Romans 3:24-26; 4:5-8. Here justification, redemption, and forgiveness are associated together. To say that God justifies the wicked, crediting faith as righteousness, is the same thing as saying that transgressions are forgiven, sins covered, and sins not counted against the repentant sinner (Rom. 4:5-8).

God does not justify without forgiving. Neither does He forgive arbitrarily as an Absolute Sovereign. God in the same instant, on the basis of faith in the atonement of Christ by the repentant sinner, forgives and justifies that sinner. Pardon is an executive act by a ruler. Justification is a judicial act by a judge.

Judicial justification from the standpoint of the law alone requires innocence in the accused. A judge as judge cannot pardon. On the basis of the law alone justification of a guilty person is impossible (Rom. 3:20). The only possible justification of a guilty sinner has to be on another basis. Christ in the Atonement provides that basis.

Justification through the Atonement requires repentance and faith on the part of the sinner, after which God as Moral Sovereign can pardon and justify. Moral justification and forgiveness are inseparable (Rom. 4:7-8). They are only possible for a holy God because He has provided a way through Christ's atoning death as He, the Sinless One, took the punishment due the sinner (Rom. 3:26). Thank God for His amazing atoning, forgiving, and justifying grace.

Justification, when viewed negatively, is the forgiveness of sins. When viewed positively, it is the acceptance of the repentant believing sinner as righteous. It is a faith righteousness. It is by faith so it may be by grace (Rom. 4:16). Logically, forgiveness precedes justification, but actually they both occur in the same moment when the repentant sinner believes unto salvation (1 Peter 1:8-9).

Justification is God's gracious judicial act declaring the repentant sinner free from condemnation and the penalty for his sins, righteous through his faith in Christ as Savior, acceptable to God and entitled to heaven.

God as judge no longer counts him guilty for his sins, but counts him righteous because by faith in Christ the sinner accepts forgiveness through the atoning death of Christ, who took on Himself the full punishment of the sinner's sin. So the sinner who had no "works righteousness" before God receives "faith righteousness" by God's grace. God accepting his faith in Christ's atonement declares him righteous by faith and in the same instant regenerates him and adopts him into His family.

God's justifying act places the forgiven sinner in a justified, forgiven state. In heaven's records he is no longer in a guilty state before God, but in a forgiven, justified state. Thus moral justification and forgiveness are chronologically and spiritually inseparable.

God's declaration of His justification by faith or His new condition of faith righteousness introduces him into a new state of righteousness before God. The state of condemnation under which he lived as a sinner is replaced by a state of peace with God through Jesus Christ (Rom. 5:1). He is no longer in a state of guilt, but in a state of forgiveness. His guilt is canceled, his sinful record is blotted out (Ps. 51:1), his punishment is remitted, and he is accepted as a son (Heb. 12:6).

Justification, forgiveness, and adoption refer to the change in relation to God. Regeneration and sanctification refer to the change in the spiritual nature.

The act of justification is comprehensive--all the sins of the past are dealt with and the person is fully justified. It is personal--it must be personally appropriated by faith. It is instantaneous--it is received in an act of faith (John 3:36). There is a moment when the sinner has fulfilled God's condition of repentance and faith, and from that moment on he is no longer in a state of guilt but in a state of justification. From then on those sins will never be counted against him (Rom. 4:8). The state of justification is entered by an act of obedient faith and is maintained by obedient faith.

24

FAITH, THE GROUND
OF OUR JUSTIFICATION

The one and only ground of our justification is faith in the redemptive action of God in Christ through His shed blood on the cross as an atoning sacrifice for our sins. The meritorious ground is the blood of Christ; the efficient cause or agency is the Holy Spirit; the conditional cause and appropriating means is faith. Faith righteousness is dependent on both the atoning work of Christ and the person's personal trust in Christ his Savior.

Saving faith is not merely faith in God's Word and promise, but personal faith in and trusting commitment to Christ as Savior.

Thus the faith-justification is real, not legal fiction. The pardon accompanying the justification is real, and the initial sanctifying righteousness that accompanies the justification is real.

FALSE THEORIES OF JUSTIFICATION

1. *Justification by works.* It is impossible for a person to be justified by perfect obedience to God's perfect law. "A man is not justified by observing the law, but by faith in Jesus Christ. So we, too, have put our faith in Christ Jesus that we may be justified by faith in Christ and not by observing the law, because by observing the law no one will be justified" (Gal. 2:16). The law makes us more conscious of sin, but no one will be declared righteous in God's sight by observance of the law (Rom. 3:20).

No form of morality, good works, or attempt to serve Christ has any justifying value. No one is justified by repentance, or by Christian service. Justification and salvation by faith will be proved by appropriate good deeds after justification, but justification is not earned by good deeds. Good deeds are the fruit of the Spirit working in one's life after one becomes a child of God.

2. *Justification by faith and works.* A combination of faith and works does not save. Faith is internal. Works are external. Baptism is a commanded form of obedience and confession of our faith in Christ as Savior. Baptism is an outward testimony to God's inward grace, but there is no saving efficiency in anything another person can do to us. Christ is the only Savior. Baptism is a covenantal pledge, but it is in no sense a means to salvation.

Sometimes those who teach baptism as essential to salvation point to 1 Peter 3:21. But "Not the removal of the dirt from the body" makes it clear it is not the ritual of baptism that Peter refers to, but the resurrection of Christ that actually saves from sin. Baptism may save from a bad conscience, not from sin. Avoiding baptism to avoid persecution was a constant temptation in Peter's day, and for some believers in non-Christian nations today.

The believer makes a commitment to Christ with all his "good conscience" which he confesses at the time of baptism. The actual saving power, however, is in the death and resurrection of Christ.

The Roman Catholic doctrine is that we are justified by faith and good works. Our Protestant doctrine is that saving faith leads to justification and to good works.

3. *Justification by imputation of Christ's active obedience.* The Greek word for imputation means to count, consider, ascribe, credit. It is never used to credit one person's actions as having been performed by another. No person's sins are counted as having been done by another person. A person who sins is recognized by God as being the actual sinner. The sinner who does a righteous deed is recognized by God and counted as the one who did it (Ezek. 18:20).

There have been three theories of imputation in Protestant theology: Justification by imputation of Christ's active obedience, justification by imputation of the active and passive obedience of Christ, and justification by imputation of faith for righteousness.

The theory of justification by imputation of Christ's active obedience teaches that Christ's obedience was substitutionary. It makes a person righteous by proxy. It overemphasizes the "standing" of the believer and underemphasizes the "state," i.e., the actual impartation of righteousness in regeneration.

God is omniscient. He knows the truth of everything. He does not impute Christ's obedience to me and see me therefore as innocent of sin. Nor does He impute my sin to Christ and see Christ as guilty of my sin. Said John Wesley, "He can no more confound me with Christ than with David or Abraham."

If Christ's obedience to the law is counted mine, then in God's sight I have perfectly obeyed God's law and do not need any forgiveness of sin! How could I be justified from sins which God does not count my having committed? Against this theory we insist:

a. It is not supported by the Bible. Seven times Scripture refers to faith being counted for righteousness, and not once does it say Christ's righteousness is counted ours (imputed to us) or that our sins are counted His (imputed to Him). A verse like Jeremiah 33:16 refers to Christ being the source of our righteousness (Phil. 3:9).

b. If Christ's personal righteous acts are counted mine (imputed to me) and I am clothed in that righteousness, then I am clothed with a redeemer's righteousness, not the righteousness of an ordinary human being. In no sense can I ever be a redeemer.

c. This theory shifts the meritorious cause of justification from Christ's death to His life. If I am declared just (righteous) by reason of Christ's life, then I have no need of His death or His shed blood. Christ died for the unjust, not for the just. If His life was the basis of our justification, then Christ died in vain (Gal. 2:21). If I am declared just by reason of Christ's obedience, I am still under a covenant of works (Rom. 3:20), rather than of grace.

d. This theory lessens the sense of obligation to keep God's moral law and tends to carelessness in living. If Christ has already perfectly obeyed for me and nothing I do affects this fact, then I may tend to be careless in my obedience.

4. *Justification by the imputation of the active and passive obedience of Christ.* By the passive obedience we mean Christ's suffering. This would mean that Christ's life and death together are the basis of an imputed justification. This theory is open to objections a, b, and d under item 3. Furthermore, it is illogical. How could I be counted to have rendered perfect obedience in Christ and yet have suffered the penalty of sin in Christ? This would be unjust and absurd unless I myself were a redeemer.

Character is strictly personal. My father's character or my son's character are not mine. The character of one person can never be transferred or counted that of someone else. This is not what Scripture means when it says Christ died for us (Rom. 5:8).

JUSTIFICATION BY FAITH. The only imputation the Bible teaches is the imputation of faith for righteousness. This faith is saving faith and is necessarily preceded by repentance. The person who consciously and deliberately clings to sin cannot exercise saving faith. God at the same instant counts faith (imputes faith) for righteousness and forgives our sins and makes us righteous by His regeneration. Logically, repentance and saving faith enable God to forgive and hence to justify (Rom. 4:6-8). God does not declare a sinner to be just or not guilty, except as he is a pardoned sinner. In addition, in that same instant through the same saving faith, God grants initial sanctification. Thus the moment of justification is not only the moment the sinner is declared righteous; it is the moment he receives a God-given moral cleansing and righteousness.

What is saving faith?

a. It is a personal act of one who believes. Faith is only imputed for righteousness for the person who believes.

b. It is a condition of righteousness. Faith is not in itself righteousness (as Roman Catholics teach). Faith is counted by God as the basis for our righteousness.

c. It is not general faith. It is saving faith in Jesus' shed blood (Rom. 3:24-25).

These facts are proved by many Scriptures, including the following:

Romans 4:5--"His faith is credited as righteousness."

Romans 9:30--"A righteousness that is by faith."

Note also: Luke 7:50; John 1:12; 3:36; Acts 16:31; Rom. 3:26, 28; 4:3, 22; 5:1; 10:10; Gal. 3:6, 8, 26; Phil. 3:9; Eph. 2:8; 2 Tim. 3:15.

THE RESULTS OF JUSTIFICATION. Justification has these gracious results in the life of the believer: (1) The sense of condemnation for sins committed is removed (Rom. 8:1). (2) Peace with God is established (Rom. 5:1). (3) He is saved from the coming judicial wrath of God and will never face forgiven sins before the judgment throne of God (Rom. 5:9). (4) He becomes an heir of eternal life (Titus 3:7).

25

REGENERATION

DEFINITION. Regeneration is the work of the Holy Spirit in the heart of the sinner as he repents and turns to Christ for salvation. By regeneration his soul which had been dead in transgressions and sins is made alive by the Holy Spirit (Eph. 2:1, 5). In the same moment that he is forgiven and justified he is resurrected out of spiritual death. He is given new spiritual life and becomes a new creature in Christ Jesus.

This is a radical moral change. The one who had been consciously, willfully sinning is spiritually transformed and begins to participate in God's nature (2 Peter 1:4). He is delivered from the power of Satan (Acts 26:18). This is a change from the practice of sin to the practice of righteousness. It brings an instant radical change in character.

Regeneration is being born of God (John 1:13), born of the Spirit (John 3:8), born again (John 3:7), born from above (John 3:3-- alternate translation). It is becoming a new creation and everything becomes new (2 Cor. 5:17).

From the standpoint of God and the person, God gives birth and the person is born spiritually. God makes alive, and the person is spiritually resurrected, made alive (Col. 2:13), raised with Christ (Col. 2:12; 3:1). God creates the person anew spiritually and the person becomes a new creation (Eph. 2:10; 4:24; 2 Cor. 5:17).

The regenerated person is newborn. He has new life from God. He is now alive to God in Christ (Rom. 6:11). He has gone from darkness to light (Acts 26:18), and the eyes of his heart are enlightened (Eph. 1:18). He experiences an inner peace that transcends all understanding (Phil. 4:7) and an inexpressible and glorious joy (1 Peter 1:8). The love of God is poured into his heart by the Holy Spirit (Rom. 5:5). He lives in a new realm of understanding of spiritual things (1 Cor. 2:14).

The Spirit gives birth to spirit (John 3:6). The person lives a new resurrection life (Rom. 6:4). The old has gone, the new has come (1 Cor. 5:17). There is a new spiritual nature--a divine nature and disposition (2 Peter 1:4), a new victory over sin (1 John 3:6-10). There is a new spiritual appetite (1 Peter 2:2), a new love for fellow-believers (1 John 3:14), a new spiritual confidence before God (1 John 3:21). There is a new sense of the Spirit's presence witnessed to by the Holy Spirit Himself (Rom. 8:16; 1 John 4:13).

INADEQUATE SUBSTITUTES

1. *It is not reformation.* Reformation is the result of self-effort; regeneration is the result of the Holy Spirit's work in the heart. Reformation only changes outward conduct; regeneration changes the moral nature and the whole inner being becomes new. Reformation is a natural act or process; regeneration is a supernatural work of God's grace and power. Reformation may be progressive; regeneration is instantaneous. The Bible clearly states the complete impossibility of salvation by reformation. Note: Job 14:14; Jer. 13:23; Gal. 2:16; Titus 3:5.

2. *It is not baptism.* Baptism is God's ordained form of outward testimony to the inward work of God's grace in the heart of the new-born believer. It should follow regeneration. Such passages as John 3:5 and Titus 3:5 do not refer to water baptism but to the cleansing power of God's Word. Any spiritual cleansing or transformation is by the Holy Spirit applying the Word to the heart (John 15:3; 17:17; Eph. 5:26). There is no external ceremony that can transform spiritually and give spiritual birth, life, or cleansing.

In 1 Corinthians 4:15 Paul states that he became the spiritual father of the Corinthian Christians through the Gospel. But in 1 Corinthians 1:14 he plainly states he baptized almost none of them. They did not receive spiritual birth through baptism, though they were baptized. In Acts 11 Cornelius was saved before he was baptized, whereas, in Acts 8 Simon was not saved even though he was baptized. Simon's heart, even after baptism, was "not right before God" (v. 21), and he was "full of bitterness and captive to sin" (v. 23), and needed to repent of his wickedness (v. 22). David, the thief on the cross, and others went to heaven without baptism. The New Testament order, as shown in the preaching of John the Baptist, Philip, and Peter, was repent and believe, i.e., be regenerated and then be baptized.

Again and again individuals have received Christ as Savior but have not been able to confess Christ in public baptism before death. On the other hand, probably millions of people have depended on baptism and church membership for salvation and have not repented and been justified by faith. They have died unsaved in spite of a public ritual of baptism.

3. *It is not having Christian parents or living in a Christian community.* Christ told the people of Jerusalem that they would perish unless they repented (Luke 13:3). It makes no difference how rich a spiritual and Christian heritage a person may have had (Matt. 3:9), he still needs to repent and be born again. The new birth is from God only (John 1:12-13). Physical birth, no matter how godly the parent is, is not spiritual birth (John 3:6). It is wonderful to have a Christian home and heritage, but that does not give one salvation. Every person must for himself meet God's conditions and obtain personal forgiveness and regeneration.

4. *It is not a mere mental faith in Christ.* Simon "believed and was baptized" but was yet unsaved (Acts 8:13). A mental belief in Christ is the first step to true saving faith, but until the person has taken all three necessary steps of full saving faith, the person is not born of God and his spiritual death is not transformed into spiritual life. Saving faith is proved by obedience to God's command to repent and forsake sin, and by the inner witness of the Spirit (Rom. 8:16). For the full discussion see chapter 21, "Saving Faith."

5. *It is not Christian service.* God wants our full obedience, not just ceremonial sacrifice (1 Sam. 15:22). It is possible to have a reputation to be spiritually alive and yet to be dead in transgressions

and sins, even though good deeds are present (Rev. 3:1). Jesus tells us that many Christian workers and leaders will say to Him at the Judgment Day, "Lord, Lord, did we not prophesy in your name, and in your name drive out demons and perform many miracles? Then I will tell them plainly, 'I never knew you. Away from me, you evildoers!'" (Matt. 7:22-23).

It is possible to build a house that we consider to be a "Christian life," but to build it on sand instead of on the rock, Christ Jesus (Matt. 7:26-27; 2 Tim. 2:19; Eph. 2:20). It is possible to enter in by a gate and yet be on the wrong road (Matt. 7:13). It is possible to have all the outward appearances of a true Christian and yet be untransformed and unChristlike within our inner nature (Matt. 7:15).

THE NATURE OF THE NEW BIRTH

1. *The new birth is a supernatural work of God.* This is proved by the Scripture statements and Scripture illustrations. Only God can give us spiritual birth, causing us to be born of God (John 3:5; 1 John 3:4). Only God can give us a new heart and put His Holy Spirit within us (Ezek. 36:25-27). Only God can resurrect us from spiritual death (John 5:24; Eph. 2:1; Col. 2:13). Only God can adopt into His own family (John 1:12; Rom. 8:15; 1 John 3:4).

2. *Regeneration, or the new birth, is an instantaneous work of God.* This is proved by the manner in which it is received--by faith. Anything which is ours by faith is available to us whenever we believe, but is not ours until the moment we believe. In the instant of faith it is fully ours.

This is proved by the description of what happens--forgiveness is spoken by God. It is a word spoken, not a process. Adoption is an act, receiving citizenship in heaven is an act, having our name written in heaven is an act. Spiritual resurrection is a momentary act. None of these are processes. There may be preparatory steps leading to the moment of crisis--for the person must fulfill God's conditions first--but the act itself is instantaneous.

This is also proved by the symbols used in portraying the experience: birth and baptism. It is impossible to be both a child of

God and a child of the devil at the same time. There is no such thing as being partially a child of God and partially a child of Satan. At any given moment we are one or the other. Sin is a crisis or instant act; salvation is also a crisis, that is, an instant act.

3. *Regeneration, or the new birth, is a knowable work of God.* Jesus, speaking of the new birth, says that we know it and witness to what we know (John 3:11). In 1 John the word "know" is used 15 times. Is it possible for a dead person to become alive and well and not know it? Is it possible for a child to be born but there be no evidence of it? How could an adopted son make use of his rights as a son if he did not know for certain that he was a son? How could condemnation be gone if the person did not know he was forgiven (Rom. 8:1)? How could we have peace with God if we did not know we were justified and still felt guilty (Rom. 5:1)?

The salvation Christ died to provide for us is so noteworthy that any person can know if he has been saved or not. The Bible gives a number of clear evidences by which a person can know if he has experienced the new birth.

4. *Regeneration, or the new birth, is a wonderful work but not the only work of God at this moment.* While regeneration is received at the same moment with justification and adoption, it is a separate and distinct work of God. The one who is justified is completely justified. The one who is regenerated is immediately made fully alive. The person adopted immediately has the full rights of a son and heir.

The necessity for justification lies in the person's guilt. The necessity for his regeneration lies in his state of spiritual death and the deprivation or absence of God's indwelling Spirit. The necessity of adoption lies in the person's lack of any right as a child of God and a member of God's family. All three are distinct in nature, perfect in kind, and given by God at the same act of faith by the person in the instant he exercises that faith.

In addition, there is an initial sanctification which takes place at the moment of regeneration. Whatever pollution was incurred from the person's sinful acts before his salvation is cleared away at the same instant that the sinful thoughts, words, and deeds are forgiven.

The Word of God which regenerates (James 1:18; 1 Peter 1:23, 25; 1 Cor. 4:15) also cleanses (John 15:3).

However, although the acquired pollution from the person's sins is cleansed away at the moment of forgiveness and new birth, there is need for a deeper cleansing, an entire sanctification from the inherited pollution of original sin, the depravity he inherited from Adam. This entire sanctification is received in the second major work of God's grace known by various scriptural names. It will be discussed in a later section.

The gracious work of God in the first major work of His redemptive grace in regeneration and initial sanctification gives power to be victorious over sin and temptation, to live according to the Spirit instead of according to the sinful nature (Rom. 8:4), and to maintain a constant freedom from condemnation (Rom. 8:1). However, it does not completely deliver from the sinful nature.

The new birth brings salvation from the reigning power of original sin. It gives power for obedience. It delivers from sin's slavery. Thank God for regeneration and all the accompanying aspects of God's grace received in the same instant. Thank God also that there is a further work of God's redeeming grace that promises a still deeper work of the Spirit available for every believer.

THE NECESSITY OF REGENERATION. While much has already been said regarding the necessity of the regenerating work of God in our soul, let us add:

1. *Regeneration, or the new birth, is a universal necessity.*
   John 3:3--"Unless a man is born again, he cannot see the kingdom of God." Note also: John 3:5, 7; Gal. 6:15.
2. *Regeneration, or the new birth, is the only hope for the sinner.* God's holiness demands that the sinner be forgiven, washed from his sins, and made spiritually alive before he can have fellowship with God in this world or the world to come. Note: Jer. 17:9; John 3:6; Rev. 21:27.

26

THE EVIDENCES OF REGENERATION,
OR THE NEW BIRTH
(PART 1)

Assurance of salvation is the privilege of sonship. The witness of the Spirit and the evidences of saving grace are definite and discernible facts in the experience of sonship of the children of God. Some of the evidences of regeneration are only known in the heart. Others are known both in the heart and in evidence observable to other people.

1. *The witness of the Spirit.* This will be treated in a following section, so it is only mentioned here.

> **Romans 8:16**--"The Spirit himself testifies with our spirit that we are God's children."

2. *Holy love.* In the moment of the new birth you are given a new holy love for God and a love for all the other children of God. More than that, it also includes a love for all people.

Jesus is the supreme revelation of the love of God. He is the personification, the mediator, and the demonstration of the love of God. Love is not only the greatest attribute of God, more than that it is the very nature of God--God is love (1 John 4:8, 16). God's love is a love that flows out of God (1 John 4:7) and is poured into your heart by the Holy Spirit (Rom. 5:5).

It is impossible to be a Christian and not receive the love of God in your heart. Love is the first and primary fruit of the Spirit (Gal. 5:22). It is the supreme and most visible Christian grace (1 Cor. 13:13). Faith expresses itself through love (Gal. 5:6). Love is the law of Christ, the expression of Christ's Saviorhood in your life.

The love of Christ controls and compels the Christian (2 Cor. 5:14). The New Testament Greek word used for this love is *agape*. It is love that flows from the heart of God, its source, and makes you love like He loves. To love with agape love is to be like God. You love because He first loves you (1 John 4:19). It is His new commandment to you (John 13:34-35)--to love like He loves you.

This then is the public proof to God, to your own heart (1 John 3:14), and to the world that you are a child of God. "By this all men will know you that are my disciples, if you love one another" (John 13:35). "Whoever does not love does not know God, for God is love" (1 John 4:8; also vv. 20, 21). Love for your enemies proves you are a child of God, said Jesus (Matt. 5:44-45). The love of Christ puts you into such debt that you are obligated to love God and each human being (Matt. 10:8; Rom. 1:14; 13:8).

Love for God and love for your neighbor are not defined in Scripture, but both are illustrated again and again. Love is always active, always takes the initiative. Jesus was God's love in person, in action. He personalizes His love in you and expresses it through you. This is God's seal upon you, making your life as well as your words His witness to the world.

Galatians 5:22--"The fruit of the Spirit is love."

1 John 4:7-8--"Everyone who loves has been born of God and knows God. Whoever does not love does not know God, because God is love." Note also: Gal. 5:6; 1 John 2:9; 3:10, 14.

3. *Spiritual peace.* Spiritual peace is based on peace with God through our Lord Jesus Christ (Rom. 5:1). Pardon brings you the peace of forgiveness. There is no remaining guilt to make you fearful of God's justice or make you uneasy in His presence. Reconciliation brings you uninhibited peace in His presence. Adoption brings you the peace of a son in God's family.

Peace and reconciliation with God lead to peace and reconciliation with all in the family of God. You enjoy the peace of acceptance, brotherhood, and confidence of the love and caring relations within God's family.

Peace with God is based on spiritual reality, not mere holy emotion. Yet it is so glorious that it brings deeply satisfying emotional basking in God's loving care. Peace with God leads to "the peace of God which transcends all understanding" guarding your heart and mind in Christ Jesus (Phil. 4:7) and ruling in your heart (Col. 3:15).

Peace is one of the beautiful fruits of the Spirit (Gal. 5:22). It is the peace of loving fellowship in the Spirit. Jesus promised you as His follower that He would give you this peace, His peace (John 14:27). It combines hope, trust, confidence, and poise and quiet of soul.

This peace is yours in a hostile, broken world because it is not rooted in your circumstances, but in Jesus. The peace of the world depends on absence of warfare, tension, and problems. Spiritual peace is yours in Christ even though all around you is seemingly chaos.

John 14:27--"My peace I give you." Note also: Rom. 5:1; 8:6; 14:17; 15:13; Gal. 5:22; Phil. 4:7.

4. *Joy in the Holy Spirit.* Since joy is an eternal attribute in God, it is a vital and abiding characteristic of His children. God is the deep source of your joy as a believer. Joy is the second fruit of the Spirit (after love) which He brings to your heart (Gal. 5:22).

Happiness is joy in circumstances. The Christian is often happy, but joy in the Holy Spirit is an outflow from the nature of God into your nature. It rises above sufferings and circumstances. Though sorrowful, you always can be rejoicing (2 Cor. 6:10). Your sorrow turns to joy (John 16:20). No one can take your spiritual joy away from you (John 16:22).

Because your joy is grounded in God it is deeper, greater, and more abiding than any joy known by the unsaved person. The kingdom of God is joy in the Holy Spirit (Rom. 14:17). It becomes the characteristic mark of your close walk with God. It is God's spiritual gift--not just as emotion, but as an abiding attitude and lifestyle.

Holy joy becomes a repeated experience as you rejoice in God's presence, goodness, nearness, fellowship, blessings, providence, and answers to prayer. It is not static. The Holy Spirit makes it dynamic. As you look to Jesus in the liberty and freedom the Spirit gives, He fills you with His special victorious joy with which He Himself is specially anointed (Heb. 1:9). It is not surprising that the Bible uses more than 30 different Hebrew and Greek words for joy and rejoicing.

Romans 14:17--"The kingdom of God is . . . joy in the Holy Spirit." Note also: Neh. 8:10; Isa. 61:3; John 15:11; Rom. 15:13; Gal. 5:22; 1 Thess. 1:6.

5. *Absence of love for the world.* The term "world" can be used in various senses. The world of creation, of nature, was given by God to man for man to exercise stewardship over it and care for it. The "world" which God so loved that He gave His only Son to redeem (John 3:16) is the world of humanity. God loves everyone, even the most sinful person. He desires every human being to repent and be saved (2 Peter 3:9). You too should love all human beings, long and pray for their salvation, and seek to lead them to salvation in Christ.

The world we are not to love is the life and trend of human society in our age as it is manipulated and organized by Satan. It is the godless world, the world in its spiritual darkness, the world system and its self-centered priorities, ideals, and attractions which rival God and seek to entice you away from God and His holy will.

It is summed up by John (1 John 2:15-16): "Do not love the world or anything in the world. If anyone loves the world, the love of the Father is not in him. For everything in the world--the cravings of sinful man, the lust of his eyes and the boasting of what he has and does--comes not from the Father but from the world."

This command by John is an absolute prohibition based on two sound reasons given in verse 17: (a) Love for the world is completely incompatible with love for God the Father, and (b) the world is transitory and all it offers quickly passes away, but God's will, God's plan, and God's reward for the faithful Christian are eternal.

Now let us examine the threefold prohibitory command. Everything in the world that the Holy Spirit inspired John to condemn is included under one of these three. These combine to outline the pagan ways of life. They are materialistic and insidiously dangerous to every Christian.

a. *The cravings of sinful man.* These are the desires of our fallen and sinful nature. The literal Greek is "the strong desire of the flesh." It is the emotional pull of things which are not the will of God. They may not be base, immoral, or evil in themselves. Perhaps they are refined and seemingly desirable. But if they are contrary to the revealed will of God or the guidance and call of the Holy Spirit for you, they are evil for you. Anything not in the will of God for you is of the world as far as you are concerned.

"The craving of the flesh" is the attitude and lifestyle that is self-centered, which pursues its own interests and desires in self-sufficient independence of God's will. This can easily become the beginning of rebellion against God and His will. It includes all that is materialistic, selfish, and exploitive of others for personal advantage.

It is the cause of wrong attitudes to the poor, the weak and helpless, or those of another group, class of society, language, or race. It is the basis for prejudice, injustice, sexism, and racism. It can enjoy luxury while others are in need. It is pleasing the senses for personal enjoyment, rather than using self-discipline for good and moral purposes.

God gave us a body to enjoy food, rest, music, and pure human love, including sex. But any of these can be indulged to the point where they become temptation or sin. They can lead to sensuality. Love for the world in this sense is lust, not the love with which we love God.

b. *The lust of the eyes.* This is the tendency to be enticed by the outward show of things, to indulge in things attractive to the eyes. God made us so that our eyes can help us desire good and useful things. But it is easy for this to be perverted by Satan, to become greed, covetousness, or desire for seemingly attractive but actually sinful uses of things. Eve desired the forbidden tree and its fruit because it seemed delightful to the eyes. Achan saw the beautiful Babylonian robe and money and sinned. David saw lovely Bathsheba and fell into sin.

The lust of the eyes can cover any kind of lust, including sexual lust. In these days of constant sinful advertising, of unclean literature, movies, and entertainment, this is a tragic snare of Satan.

c. *The boasting of what he has and does.* This is an appeal to egotistical desire to obtain and display possessions, educational degrees. It is the passion to get ahead of others, to boast of attainments, to strive for positions in Christian organizations, to flaunt power over others. Desires for luxury, needless travel, and to outshine others are forms of this sin. It is the pride of reputation, status, and success.

> 1 John 2:15--"If anyone loves the world, the love of the Father is not in him." Note also: Gal. 1:4; 6:14; James 4:4.

The absence of love or desire for these three aspects of the world proves you are a child of God. You have had new spiritual birth and now have spiritual desires.

27

THE EVIDENCES OF REGENERATION, OR THE NEW BIRTH (PART 2)

6. *Obedience to God.* Positive obedience to the full will of God is characteristic of the born-again person. The Bible repeatedly teaches that obedience is an evidence of whether or not you are a child of God. Your life is a powerful witness to your commitment. Human experience also validates the old saying, "Your life speaks so loudly I can't hear what you say!" God and people expect your manner of life to be in harmony with your religious profession. If it is not, you are a hypocrite.

Obedience is the supreme test of your faith in God or love for God. Any faith which does not include obedience is not saving faith (James 2:17-20). Any claimed consecration which does not include obedience is hypocritical. Any professed love for Christ which does not result in obedience is a nominal love only; it is not sincere.

In the Old Testament the Hebrew word *sama* means both to hear and to obey. We must both hear and obey the voice of God. The equivalent Greek word in the New Testament is *akouo* and can have the same double meaning of to hear and to obey. The compound form is *hupakouo* (literally, to hear beneath), to hear one to whom obedience is owed.

Jesus says repeatedly, "He who has ears, let him hear" (Matt. 11:15; 13:9; Mark 4:9, 23; Luke 14:35. Compare Mark 8:18). Jesus said, "Blessed rather are those who hear the word of God and obey it" (Luke 11:28). "My sheep listen to my voice . . . they follow me" (John 10:27). Obeying is also described as remaining in the Vine

(John 15:4-10). "Remain in my love. If you obey my commands, you will remain in my love" (v. 10).

The spirit of obedience not only obeys a clearly spoken command of God but also whatever is in harmony with the general teaching of Scripture. The spirit of obedience not only walks in the light God gives but also welcomes any new light from God.

When you delight to do God's will, this is an evidence of saving grace, of regeneration. "I desire to do your will, O my God; your law is within my heart" (Ps. 40:8). "Direct me in the path of your commands, for there I find delight" (Ps. 119:35). "In my inner being I delight in God's law" (Rom. 7:22). Note also: Luke 6:46; John 14:15, 23; James 2:14; 1 John 2:3-6.

7. *Faith that overcomes the world.* The born-again believer has a victorious faith. God gives the power to overcome temptation by His living faith within you. Faith releases the almighty power of God within you. Faith sees temptation from the perspective of God. Faith makes you an overcomer. There may be temporary moments of discouragement, but the whole set of your soul as a born-again person is that of a victorious believer, and discouragements are soon swallowed up by faith.

1 John 5:4--"Everyone born of God overcomes the world. This is the victory that has overcome the world, even our faith." Note also: Rom. 8:37; 12:2; 1 John 2:13; 5:4; Rev. 12:11.

8. *Victory over sin.* As the Christian has the evidence of an attitude of obedience to God and an overcoming faith, he naturally experiences victory over sin. Sin, as we have seen, has various definitions. But the sin that brings guilt and separation from God is the committing of willful transgressions of God's understood law (1 John 3:4).

You are not saved beyond the possibility of sinning. Life is a probation where you make constant choices to obey or disobey God, to do what you know is right or to succumb to temptation and do what you know to be wrong. The longer you walk in victorious obedience, the stronger your character becomes and the easier it is to obey God when new choices arise. But salvation does not guarantee victory or sinlessness. You need not sin. A way to victory over temptation is always available (1 Cor. 10:13).

But what if you do sin? Thank God, the Bible gives clear instruction concerning the provision of God's grace. "My dear children, I write this to you so that you will not sin. But if anybody does sin, we have one who speaks to the Father in our defense--Jesus Christ the Righteous One. He is the atoning sacrifice for our sins" (1 John 2:1-2). This is not an excuse to sin, but it is God's gracious provision of atoning grace available if you do.

If in spite of God's saving grace, the Holy Spirit's guidance and restraint, and all God's past mercy--if in spite of all this you are suddenly snared and fall into sin, you must instantly flee to Jesus and His atoning blood, asking forgiveness and mercy. Instant repentance can bring instant forgiveness and restoration to God's favor. Thank God, Jesus is your Advocate before the Father. He knows you better than you know yourself. He is instantly ready to forgive, restore, and make you steadfast once more.

Regeneration saves from the practice of sin, from all habits of sin. No forgiven sinner is a second-class citizen of God's kingdom, but is by God's grace freed from condemnation (Rom. 8:1). Any sin brings guilt, but any sin humbly confessed in sincere repentance and determination to forsake that sin hereafter and to never again fall into it--any such sin can be instantly forgiven and the guilt will again be instantly removed.

Should you fail God and fall into sin after regeneration, never give up in despair. Don't go back to your former life of sin. Run to Jesus, run to the Cross. Instantly return to God's forgiveness and favor and determine by God's grace never to fall into that sin again. Walk more closely to God. Keep up your life of prayer and Bible reading. Be alert and watchful not to fall into Satan's trap in that way again.

But Scripture is very clear--a proof that you are God's child is the victory God gives you over the practice of sin. A regenerated believer will be distinguished from a sinner by the believer's victory over sin. His new life in Christ will be separated from his former sinful life by a consistent victory over sin.

> **1 John 1:6**--"If we claim to have fellowship with him and yet walk in darkness, we lie and do not live by the truth."
>
> **1 John 5:18**--"We know that anyone born of God does not continue to sin; the one who was born of God keeps him safe, and the evil one cannot harm him."
>
> **1 John 3:8**--"He who does what is right is righteous, just as he is righteous. He who does what is sinful is of the devil."

Yes, regeneration brings a changed life, a life of continuing victory over sin. The proof of salvation is victory over sin. If the devil trips you, get up instantly, claim Jesus' forgiveness, and go on following Jesus in a victorious walk day by day. Note these Scriptures: Matt. 7:16, 18; Rom. 6:14, 17-18; 1 John 3:6, 8, 9-10.

9. *The Holy Spirit within.* Every Christian from the moment he is regenerated and born of God has the Holy Spirit living in his inner nature. There is no Father-son relationship to you apart from the Holy Spirit. The Holy Spirit does not indwell the sinner, but at the moment of saving faith the Holy Spirit begins His indwelling ministry in you. The Spirit is the source of the new love, joy, and peace, for these are called the fruit of the Spirit (Gal. 5:22-23). The Spirit begins His witness in the innermost nature that sins have been forgiven and that God has accepted you as His own child (Rom. 6:16).

The Spirit develops a new freedom in God's presence, a spiritual liberty before God (2 Cor. 3:17). He develops the intimate Father-son relationship so that you call "Abba, Father" (Rom. 8:15). "Abba" is the most intimate way a small child in Christ's earth time could address its father. The Holy Spirit brings you into close childlike intimacy and freedom before God. This all assures you as a born-again person that your whole relationship to God has changed.

At the same time the Spirit begins His manifold ministry in your life. He begins to teach you (John 14:26), to reveal Christ to you more fully and wonderfully (John 15:26; 16:14-15), to guide you spiritually and in your practical living (John 16:15; Isa. 58:11), to give new holy desires (Rom. 8:5) and a whole new life orientation (Rom. 8:6) that results in peace with God and the peace of God blessing your whole being. Your entire outlook on life and every aspect of your inner life are blessed, transformed, and uplifted.

Not all of this is realized the instant of regeneration, but it is a realization that grows ever more meaningful and wonderful to you as a believer. God is made much more real by the indwelling Spirit. Christian familyhood and fellowship are made wonderfully significant, and life is blessedly transformed. A process of blessing has begun that evidences within your heart and life your new spiritual condition and relation to God.

Romans 8:9--"If anyone does not have the spirit of Christ, he does not belong to Christ."

1 John 3:24--"This is how we know that he lives in us. We know it by the Spirit he gave us."

Note also: John 14:6-17; 20:22; Rom. 8:16; 2 Cor. 1:22; Gal. 4:6; 1 John 4:13; 5:10.

10. *Guidance of the Spirit.* The new Christian has entered the whole new relation of privileged guidance through the Spirit. This was mentioned in the preceding paragraphs but must be specially emphasized. One of the evidences of salvation is that you begin to be led by the Spirit. "Those who are led by the Spirit of God are sons of God" (Rom. 8:14). Many Christians have not learned to avail themselves of this wonderful privilege as they should.

The newborn Christian becomes a Spirit-led person. The Spirit leads you in developing a prayer life and becomes your mighty Helper in prayer. "The Spirit helps us in our weakness. We do not know what we ought to pray for, but the Spirit himself intercedes for us. . . . The Spirit intercedes for the saints in accordance with God's will" (Rom. 8:26-27). The Spirit guides you in what to pray for and energizes you in your praying. There is no more important area of guidance than prayer.

The Spirit also guides you in your obedience to Christ and in how to do God's will more perfectly. He guides you in your growth in grace. He guides you to a place of total commitment so that He can cleanse and fill you.

The Spirit guides you in your witnessing for Christ and in leading other unsaved people to Christ. He guides you in giving loving service to others in the name of Christ. God wants you to glorify Him by good works that help and bless others (Eph. 2:10) and lead them to salvation (1 Peter 2:12).

The Spirit delights to guide you in all the practical details of your daily living so you can be a happy, wholesome Christian, a blessing to your family, to your church, to your nation, and to your world. So as you learn to sense and follow the guidance of the Spirit, this becomes a continuing assurance of your salvation.

Isaiah 58:11--"The Lord will guide you always." Note also: Isa. 9:6; 30:19-21; Rom. 8:14.

28

ADOPTION

Adoption is the gracious act of God the Father by which the repentant sinner is not only forgiven, justified, and regenerated (given new birth and life) but at the same moment is declared to be God's son. It is a declaratory act, just as justification is. Forgiveness and justification deal with the guilt and penalty of sin. Regeneration gives new life, and adoption gives status, position in the family with family rights, and inheritance.

Adoption was an ancient legal provision which became common among the Romans and Greeks, but was rather unknown among the Jews. Moses was adopted by Pharaoh's daughter and given royal privilege, education, and status. Jacob adopted Ephraim and Manasseh as his sons, and Esther may have been adopted by Mordecai.

The term adoption is not found in the Old Testament or in the Hebrew language. The Greek term found in the New Testament, *huiothesia*, means literally placing as a son. Adoption was an ancient way that a childless couple could adopt a slave or child of someone else as their own legal son and heir. The Romans usually adopted some free citizen. The adopted one came under the total authority of the adoptive father and received both duties and rights because of this.

Adoption is one phase of God's great eternal plan of salvation. "In love he predestined us to be adopted as his sons through Jesus Christ, in accordance with his pleasure and will--to the praise of his glorious grace, which he has freely given us in the One he loves" (Eph. 1:5-6). You who were separate from God, excluded from His presence and promises, "Without hope and without God in the world" (Eph. 2:12-13) have been brought near, brought into His family.

Adoption and its benefits and blessings are part of this great heritage God plans for you. "God sent his Son . . . that we might receive the full rights of sons" (Gal. 4:5).

BLESSED BENEFITS OF ADOPTION

1. *The Privilege of Sonship.* God's grace is always amazingly great. He makes you who were His enemy not only reconciled (Rom. 5:10), but brings you into His family. You could have no higher honor and privilege than that of being a member of God's royal family. In one sense this is the all-comprehensive benefit that includes all others. The blessedness of this is that it is not just a legality or symbol. You are truly given family privilege, blessings, and duties. You are treated henceforth as a son of God.

Christ is the eternal Son, you are only an adoptive son, yet Christ shares with you as if you were always a part of the family. Finite beings can never be infinite, but within the limits of your finite creaturehood Christ treats you as a full family member.

God is truly your Father. You approach Him as Father. Although He is your Creator, your Sovereign King, and you recognize, treasure, and worship His glorious majesty, yet your primary relation to Him is not that of being His creature or a subject in His kingdom, but of being His son in His family. His primary relation to you is a Father-son relationship. You belong to the family. You share the blessed family intimacy of God's household (Eph. 2:19). Note: John 1:12; Galatians 3:26.

2. *Brotherhood with Christ.* Jesus referred to His disciples as His brothers and sisters. "Whoever does the will of my father in heaven is my brother and sister and mother" (Matt. 12:50). Jesus is the Son of God in an eternal and unique sense. We are only adopted sons in God's family of redeemed creatures. Yet Jesus calls us His brothers and sisters! He considers us His family in the fullest sense, God's family.

"Both the one who makes men holy and those who are made holy are of the same family. So Jesus is not ashamed to call them brothers" (Heb. 2:11). "He says, 'I will declare your name to my brothers'" (v. 12).   After His resurrection, Jesus told the women as He met them, "Go and tell my brothers" (Matt. 28:10).

Jesus so fully considers you His true brother that whatever people do for you ("these brothers of mine"--Matt. 25:40) He considers done unto Him. He identifies with you before the whole world. God the Father considers you Jesus' own brother. He predestined you to be a brother of Jesus (Rom. 8:29).

Jesus became incarnate so He could be like us, His new brothers in God's special family (Heb. 2:17). So Jesus is not only your beloved Savior but your true Brother. This adds a dimension of blessedness to every prayer you pray, to your loyal love to Him, and to your life of loving fellowship and service with Him.

3. *Spirit-given Sonship.* The literal translation of Romans 8:15 is "You received the Spirit of adoption." The whole Trinity is involved. God the Father adopts you. Christ treats you as His brother. What more could you possibly need? You need somehow to enter into the fullness of the blessedness, privileges, and responsibilities of this position given by God's grace.

The Holy Spirit has been given to you not only to regenerate you and to witness to your salvation, He has been given to make you a true son. He enables you to realize and feel the blessedness of an adopted son. He teaches you how to act as a son of God and brother of Jesus. He develops in you the attitude of a son. He is, says God's Word, the Spirit of adoption, the Spirit of sonship.

He makes your new privileged position natural to you. He helps make you certain of your privileges in the glorious liberty of sonship (Rom. 8:21). He is your loving Counselor and Guide in bringing joy to God as He looks upon you as His child, and as you fulfill all the duties and responsibilities His loyal child should fulfill. This is part of the Spirit's specially assigned role. He delights to make your adoption ever more real, ever more meaningful and wonderful to you, and ever more meaningful and helpful to God in your doing His will.

4. *Familyhood.* Adoption not only brings you into new and special relations with each member of the Trinity, it gives you a new

host of redeemed people who become family to you. You are not a solitary adopted son. Jesus is bringing many sons to glory (Heb. 2:10). The Holy Spirit at the moment of your new birth baptizes you into the Body of Christ (1 Cor. 12:13). You are adopted into an ever multiplying family. You not only receive a heavenly Father, you receive a multitude of heaven-bound brothers and sisters.

God's children are called to be saints (Rom. 1:7), and they are repeatedly called saints. They are all forgiven sinners, transformed believers who also have been made alive in Christ, adopted by God as His very own. They include some of the choicest spiritual people this world has seen. They constantly are being given the fruit of the Spirit (Gal. 5:22-23). The Spirit is seeking to conform them more and more into Christ's own likeness (Rom. 8:29; 2 Cor. 3:18).

Nevertheless, every child of God has some areas of weakness, some aspects of personality needing more Christlikeness and the further work of the Spirit. God is not through transforming you or them yet. You must be patient and understanding with your family members, supportive of your brothers and sisters in Christ, and loyal to all the other family members. Nothing distresses Jesus more than disunity within His family. Nothing hinders revival and harvest more than these two great dangers--sin and disunity.

5. *Confident Access to God.* When you are adopted into God's family you are given a new right--freedom and confidence to approach God at any time. Whatever your need or concern, God is always available to you. The Greek word for this, *prosagoge*, means to lead or bring into the presence of someone. It can be translated as "introduction." It occurs three times in the New Testament.

The word presents the picture of a palace officer leading someone to the audience chamber of a monarch and introducing him to the ruler. In all three verses Christ is the One who gives you access-- who leads you to the throne and introduces you, giving you the freedom and the confidence to approach God directly. You need no priest or mediator on earth or in heaven apart from Christ. You have direct access yourself as much as any other child of God.

As an adopted child of God you have this wonderful right and privilege of instant access at any time in any situation. Through Christ the way is opened and you are introduced and endorsed by Christ your elder Brother and your Advocate (Heb. 10:19-20). Thus you have no hesitation or fear.

Galatians 4:6--"Because you are sons, God sent the Spirit of his Son into our hearts, the Spirit who calls out, 'Abba, Father.'" Note also: Luke 11:2; Rom. 5:2; 8:15; Eph. 2:18; 3:12; 1 John 3:21; 4:18.

Because of this access and confidence toward God, as a new believer you can quickly develop a strong prayer life. The Christian is born to pray. He is created in Christ Jesus to pray. This is specially illustrated by Romans 8:15 and Galatians 4:6 and the use of the Aramaic term "Abba" with Father.

Jesus set the example for us by praying, "Abba, Father" in the Garden (Mark 14:36). Apparently Jesus used this term constantly in prayer. So the early church did not hesitate to use it in their prayers. Jews did not regularly address God as Father, unless they added some such word as "in heaven." They would have been horrified at the intimacy suggested by the word "Abba."

"Abba" is the word that an Aramaic-speaking infant used when he first began to lisp words for his father. It is like saying "Daddy" to God. The new Christian has such intimate access to God that he can, as it were, lisp any form of prayer and it will be acceptable as well as heard by God.

"Abba" tells you that it is only the heart relationship to God that counts. Simple words can be powerfully prayed. No set forms or formal prayers are required. When God adopts you, He gives you the confidence, liberty, and intimacy of a little child with its father. A new believer can instantly pour out his love, worship, thanksgiving, and requests to God.

6. *The Privilege of God's House.* This is a further amplification of the privileges of sonship. This includes many blessings pictured for you in God's Word, such as:

a. *The Father's constant watching over you and care for you.* Note: 2 Chron. 16:9; Ps. 121:3-4; Isa. 49:15.

b. *The Father's constant will and delight to meet your needs.*
Note: Matt. 6:8; John 14:21, 23; 16:27; Phil. 4:19.

c. *The Father's diligent coordination of providence for your good.* Note: Jer. 29:11; Rom. 8:28; Phil. 3:20-21; Heb. 12:11.

d. *The Father's unending loving and gracious generosity to you.* Note: Deut. 31:6; Ps. 23:6; 46:1; Isa. 46:4; Heb. 13:5-6.

7. *Discipline.* In adoption, God takes upon Himself the responsibility to bring you to spiritual maturity. Positively, this involves God's instruction, guidance, and training. Negatively, this involves God's reproof, restraint, and punishment. He loves you so much that He takes time and effort to train you to be His worthy child. He wants to teach you how to live effectively for yourself, your loved ones, and for His kingdom. He is building quality character in you. He cares so much He patiently works with you, seeking to increase your likeness to Him and your eternal reward.

Deuteronomy 8:5--"As a man disciplines his son, so the Lord your God disciplines you."

Hebrews 12:5-8--"You have forgotten that word of encouragement that addresses you as sons: 'My son, do not make light of the Lord's discipline, and do not lose heart when he rebukes you, because the Lord disciplines those he loves, and he punishes everyone he accepts as a son.' Endure hardship as discipline; God is treating you as sons. For what son is not disciplined by his father? If you are not disciplined (and everyone undergoes discipline), then you are illegitimate children and not true sons."

Note also: Ps. 94:12; Prov. 3:12; 1 Cor. 11:32; Titus 2:11-12; Heb. 12:11; Rev. 3:19.

8. *An Eternal Inheritance.* The adopted child of God becomes the heir of God and the co-heir with Christ (Rom. 8:17). This inheritance is entirely of God's grace and is not merited or earned. The Holy Spirit enables you to experience and receive the inheritance. Therefore, it begins upon receiving the new birth and continues until its perfection when Christ comes again. The Holy Spirit is the Spirit of sonship (Rom. 8:15) and provides the experi-

ence of present inheritance along with the promise of future inheritance.

Your inheritance includes:

a. *The Kingdom of God* (Luke 12:32; James 2:5). In a truly blessed sense the kingdom begins with the new birth (Rom. 14:17). You are already a son of the kingdom (Matt. 13:38). The Father brings you into the kingdom of His beloved Son (Col. 1:13). In an ever more blessed sense, your inheriting the fullness of the kingdom is yet future (Matt. 13:43; 25:34; 2 Tim. 4:1; Heb. 12:28).

b. *Eternal Life.* Eternal life is the name for the life of the eternal God given you in the new birth. The term "eternal" refers initially and primarily to the quality of life, not to the duration. As you remain true to God, it continues on into eternity. Eternal life thus begins the moment the repentant sinner believes (John 3:36; 5:24; 17:3; Rom. 6:23). Yet in another sense, eternal life is yet future, when Christ returns (Matt. 25:46; Mark 10:30).

c. *God's Blessings.* You are called to inherit blessing from your Father (1 Peter 3:9). He gives you one blessing after another (John 1:16). You inherit blessing to the fullest (Rom. 15:29), for God blesses you with every spiritual blessing in Christ (Eph. 1:3). God's kingdom is righteousness, peace, and joy in the Holy Spirit (Rom. 14:17).

d. *Glory.* The foretaste of heaven's glory begins to transform the life of the person born of God. Christ gives His glory to you in its beginning stages (John 17:22). As inwardly the Spirit renews you day by day (2 Cor. 4:16), you reflect the Lord's glory as you behold Him in His Word and in prayer communion with Him. You are continually transformed into Christ's likeness with ever increasing glory by the Spirit's power (2 Cor. 3:18).

But the glory that awaits you when you receive your glorified body in the resurrection (2 Thess. 1:10; Phil. 3:21) far exceeds your glory here on earth and far outweighs your trials and sufferings for Jesus' sake during your earth life (2 Cor. 4:17). Then God's glory will be revealed in you (Rom. 8:17-18) in a likeness to Christ's glorious body (Phil. 3:21).

> **1 Corinthians 2:9-10**--"No eye has seen, no ear has heard. No mind has conceived what God has prepared for those who love him--but God has revealed it to us by his Spirit."

29

INITIAL SANCTIFICATION

God is a holy God and He desires His people to be a holy people. Fifty-one times the Bible calls God the Holy One. Holiness is more than an attribute of God. It is His very nature. Everything about God is holy--His name, His attributes, His throne, His works, His Word, and His truth. The Triune God is innately and infinitely holy. God is the Holy Father (John 17:11). Christ is the Holy One (Acts 3:14). And the Spirit is repeatedly called the Holy Spirit. "Holy, Holy, Holy is the Lord Almighty, the whole earth is full of His glory" (Isa. 6:3). God's heaven and God's angels are holy.

God desires that His people be holy. He says, "I am the Lord, who makes you holy" (Exod. 31:13; Lev. 20:8; 21:8). He commands, "Be holy, because I am holy" (Lev. 11:44-45; 19:2; 20:7-8; 1 Peter 1:15-16).

THE TERMS "HOLINESS" AND "SANCTIFICATION." The terms holiness and sanctification are very important in the experience and doctrine of salvation. Holiness is the primary term, and sanctification is the act or process by which something or someone is made holy. These words come from the same Hebrew and Greek words, as found in the Old and New Testaments.

No human language is adequate to describe God, so the Holy Spirit had to take the best words available in Hebrew and Greek and give them new meaning as He inspired Scripture. As God progressively revealed himself to Moses, to the Israelites and their history, and to the prophets, the true meaning of holiness and sanctify became ever more clear.

Whatever was related to God, whether thing or person, was holy. God's hand, God's word, God's throne, God's name, objects used in worship of God, people who served God--all were in some sense considered holy, set apart for God, dedicated to God, and separated to God and from surrounding things and people.

God's presence was a holy presence. As God's character was more and more revealed in His words and acts, and with His dealings with Israel, His holy character gave more and more meaning to the words. Israel learned ever more deeply the awesome holiness of God in all its ethical and moral content. By New Testament times, Jesus added more and more content to the meaning of holy, and the Holy Spirit brought out the whole spiritual significance. Thus, emphasis was not only upon holiness as separation, but also upon holiness as purity.

True holiness includes emphasis upon God's transcendence, His majesty, His deity, and His sovereignty and power. But above all, it is God's expression of His own personality. Positively, it is His infinitely pure, just, righteous being that is perfect in holiness and love. Negatively, it includes His abhorrence of all sin, evil, injustice, and unrighteousness. Holiness is the total moral perfection of God's personality. God's holiness is always moral, ethical, and expresses itself in sovereign love. Because God is holy He must save or judge when He is confronted with sin.

In the New Testament, the emphasis shifts from exalting the holiness of God to emphasis upon redeeming people and making them like God's holiness in their character and transformed personality. God's love must make everybody holy who will respond to His righteous provision of salvation, for God has created us to bear His holy image, share His holy fellowship, and live eternally in His holy heaven.

THE TERM "SAINTS." The most common term for Christians in the New Testament is saints, i.e., holy ones. It is the general term for all who have repented and believed in Christ for salvation and who thus comprise the Church. It is used in a general sense of being set apart by God's saving grace and thus devoted to Christ. It is used even for people in the local churches who manifest carnal, unsanctified character traits.

Positional sanctity as being a member of God's body, the Church, is expected to become true saintliness (or holiness) of life and character. The whole work of the Holy Spirit in bringing the sinner to repentance and initial salvation through the sanctifying ministry of the Spirit and the Spirit's transforming into the image and likeness of Christ in heaven is to make us truly saints. That involves both crisis and process, both divine elements and human responses.

Objectively, the saints are God's chosen people committed to Him and belonging to Him. Subjectively, they are separated from sin and purified by the Spirit who enables them to partake of God's holiness. The Bible constantly challenges God's saints to be what they are called, to be like God to whom they belong.

SANCTIFICATION AS CRISIS AND PROCESS. The sanctifying work of the Holy Spirit involves both crisis and process; that is, it is both instantaneous and gradual. It includes all the Spirit's transforming work in the Christian's heart, by which he is made morally and spiritually holy as God is holy. It includes the initial cleansing at the moment of the new birth, called initial sanctification. It includes the process of transformation from the new birth until the crisis moment of the sanctifying, infilling of the Spirit. And then it includes the process of positive transformation ever more and more into the likeness of Christ until glorification in heaven, when we see Christ as He is.

At this point we are specially concerned with the initial crisis and the initial process. A crisis is a transforming moment when the Spirit performs a major work in our moral being. The process consists in innumerable moments when we respond to new spiritual light, take new steps of obedience as we walk in God's light (1 John 1:7), and make new commitments of love and spiritual growth. Every aspect of growth in grace is a part of the sanctifying process. One biblical term for this sanctifying process is transfiguration (Greek: Rom. 12:2; 2 Cor. 3:18).

INITIAL SANCTIFICATION. Initial sanctification is a glorious aspect of the new birth. At the moment when the Spirit creates us a new creature in Christ Jesus, when we are justified, regenerated, adopted, and when our names are written in the Lamb's Book of Life (Luke 10:20; Rev. 20:12; 21:27), at that very moment we are cleansed from the depravity which we acquired by all our personal sinful acts from our birth until that moment. Every act of sin not only makes us guilty, but pollutes our spiritual being. Every act of sin depraves, debases, defiles, and perverts our spiritual nature to at least some degree. The Holy Spirit at the moment of our initial salvation cleanses us from this acquired depravity.

Initial sanctification is called "the washing of rebirth" (Titus 3:5). It cleanses from our past. "That is what some of you were. But you were washed, you were sanctified, you were justified in the name of the Lord Jesus Christ and by the Spirit of our God" (1 Cor. 6:11). Therefore Paul, addressing the church, could refer to them as "sanctified in Christ Jesus and called to be holy" (1 Cor. 1:2) even though the carnality of some in the church was deplorable. They were sanctified positionally and initially, but in many of them this holiness needed to be made entire, "through and through" (2 Thess. 5:23) or made "perfect" (2 Cor. 7:1).

This initial sanctification results in a life of holy love begun in the heart, a life of victory over the practice of sin, and a life cleansed from the pollution of the world. It is holiness begun, holy living initiated. The believer lives a life of separation from sin. The former sinner is now a new creature with new grace to live a new life. He is now able to say "no" to ungodliness and worldly passions and to live self-controlled, upright, and godly in the unholy environment that surrounds him (Titus 2:12). Believers are thus now "holy brethren" (Heb. 3:1).

The power of sin over the believer is broken and, instead, the power of the Spirit enables the person to live a holy life. Outwardly, his life must be a life of holiness. By the discipline of the Spirit, inner defeats are not to be enacted outwardly. The life of holiness has already begun. Sin has no reigning power. It is no longer master (Rom. 6:14). The cleansing from the sinful past is not partial; it is complete. The Holy Spirit does a complete work.

This initial sanctification inaugurates the process of sanctification in the believer. From now on the Word of God, as the believer reads and meditates on it, begins to cleanse him in new aspects of his living (Eph. 5:26). He is able to purify himself from contaminating ideas, influences, and surroundings by the help of the Holy Spirit (2 Cor. 7:1). In the words of Paul, he must now keep himself pure (1 Tim. 5:22).

Initial sanctification cleanses from the depravity of our forgiven sins, but does not cleanse us from our inherited depravity which we, in common with all humanity, have inherited from the sin of our foreparents, Adam and Eve. After a chapter on the witness of the Spirit, we will discuss that aspect of depravity and God's salvation from it.

30

THE WITNESS OF THE SPIRIT

Your assurance of salvation is based upon the objective witness of Scripture, the inner witness of the Holy Spirit, and the reproducing and affirming witness of your own spirit. God has not only planned your salvation, He has planned that you have full assurance and inward confidence of your salvation.

Spirit-given assurance is the complete opposite of self-confidence. It is assurance based on confidence in God, God's Word, and the faithful work of the Holy Spirit. It is confidence supported by spiritual transformation of life and the fruit of the Spirit in the life.

This is a blessed reality of tremendous importance to every believer. A life of spiritual doubt and uncertainty would rob you of the liberty of sonship (Rom. 8:21). Paul said, "I know . . . and am convinced" (2 Tim. 1:12), and 1 John is full of emphasis upon assured knowledge (1 John 2:3, 5, 13-14, 20; 3:10, 14, 19, 21, 24; 4:13, 16; 5:2, 10, 13, 19-20). In fact, this whole letter of 1 John is filled with truth about our assurance.

Thus assurance is not only a blessed doctrine, but a very practical gift of the Spirit to you. It moves you from fear to certainty, from self-centeredness to Scripture-centeredness and God-centeredness. It gives you the liberty to enjoy your spiritual relationship to each member of the Trinity--God the Father, Christ your Savior, and the Spirit, your Helper, Counselor, and Witness.

A. *The Witness of God's Word.* Both the Old Testament and the New Testament define faith as a state of God-given assurance. This truth is taught in many places without using the actual word assurance. In the New Testament, the Greek word *plerophoria* speaks of fullness, abundance, and wealth of conviction, confidence, and assurance. Thus there is a Spirit-given "much *plerophoria* (1 Thess. 1:5), full *plerophoria* of understanding (Col. 2:2), full *plerophoria* of hope (Heb. 6:11), and full *plerophoria* of faith (Heb. 10:20).

The Bible assures you of many aspects of your salvation:

1. Assurance of forgiveness of your sins (Prov. 28:13; Isa. 55:7; 1 John 1:9)

2. Assurance of freedom from condemnation (Rom. 8:1)

3. Assurance of acceptance by Christ (Matt. 11:28; John 6:37)

4. Assurance of salvation (Rom. 10:9-11, 13)

5. Assurance of sonship (John 1:12-13)

6. Assurance of eternal life (John 5:24; 1 John 5:9-13)

7. Assurance of eternal kindness and favor (Eph. 2:7)

The strong witness of God's Word is the solid foundation of your Christian assurance. God's Word is eternal, unchanging, and sure (Ps. 119:89). Its witness is not affected by your emotional changes and feelings at any given time.

B. *The Witness of the Holy Spirit.* The inner witness of the Spirit is always in harmony with the witness of God's Word. The Word is objective. The Spirit's witness is in some sense subjective, but it is based upon objective facts and objective truth. "This is how we know that he lives in us: We know it by the Spirit he gave us" (1 John 3:24). "We know that we live in him and he in us, because he has given us of his Spirit" (1 John 4:13).

The Bible gives you three illustrations of this role of the Spirit as a direct witness in assuring you of salvation.

1. *The Spirit is your divine witness.* He adds His personal testimony concerning your relation to God. "The Spirit himself testifies with our spirit that we are God's children" (Rom. 8:16). This is the inner assurance in your personal being that when you repented and confessed your sin to Jesus and asked His forgiveness He freely forgave you, accepted you into God's family, and that you are now a child of God. He witnesses to your new relation to God and your peace with God.

2. *He is your divine deposit and guarantee.* "It is God who . . . put his Spirit in our hearts as a deposit, guaranteeing what is to come" (2 Cor. 1:21-22). As you sense the Spirit's working in your life, you know that this is only the beginning. It is God's guarantee of further action of the Spirit in your life. He now has come to make His home there, to live in you permanently.

"Having believed . . . the promised Holy Spirit . . . is a deposit guaranteeing our inheritance" (Eph. 1:13-14). The Spirit's guarantee is reliable, for the Spirit is truth (1 John 5:6).

3. *He is God's seal upon your heart.* "He anointed us, set his seal of ownership on us, and put his Spirit in our hearts" (2 Cor. 1:21-22). "You were marked in him with a seal, the promised Holy Spirit" (Eph. 1:13).

The Holy Spirit stamps His imprint upon your submissive heart, the seal of a new Christlikeness. As you walk with God in close fellowship, the image of this seal will become ever clearer--the image of Christlikeness. It will be visible to you; even more so, it will be visible to other Christians. It will even be discernible to the world. It also will be visible to God's holy angels and to God Himself, giving Him holy joy as He sees Christ's nature increasingly evident in you.

THE NATURE OF THE SPIRIT'S WITNESS. This witness of the Spirit immediately gives you freedom of access to God. You no longer approach God as a guilty enemy of God, but as a forgiven child of God. "Because you are sons, God sent the Spirit of his Son into our hearts, the Spirit who calls out, 'Abba, Father'" (Gal. 4:6).

Just as a child learning to say his first words says in simple trust, "Papa" to his father, so the same beautiful attitude of trust in the forgiven sinner further witnesses to his spiritual sonship to God. You cannot have this loving, trusting, childlike freedom before God without the Spirit's inner witness, just as you cannot truly call Jesus your Lord without the Holy Spirit's work in your soul (1 Cor. 12:3).

Anyone can repeat those words like a parrot, but no one can say them with inner conviction and assurance but by the aid of the Holy Spirit. The Spirit assures you that not only have you come to Christ and accepted Him as Savior, but that He has accepted you and come into your life savingly.

This inner testimony of the Spirit immediately assures you of your peace with God (Rom. 5:1). This Spirit-given peace so assures and delights you that you then experience the joy of sins forgiven, the Spirit's joy as a child of God (Rom. 15:13; Gal. 5:22; 1 Peter 1:8), for the kingdom of God is righteousness, peace, and joy in the Holy Spirit (Rom. 14:17).

This testimony within you becomes God's testimony to you, and in your heart it is a testimony with you--with the testimony of your own spirit.

C. *The witness of your human spirit.* The Bible teaches that you have a witness in yourself apart from the witness of the Holy Spirit. This is your personal consciousness, including the testimony of your own conscience that your spirit has been made new. "If anyone is in Christ, he is a new creation; the old has gone, the new has come" (2 Cor. 5:17). In contrast to the direct witness of the Spirit, this is the indirect witness of your own spirit. Thus each supports the other, the Holy Spirit reinforcing our spirit, and our spirit endorsing the Holy Spirit. "The Spirit himself testifies with our spirit that we are God's children" (Rom. 8:16).

The direct witness of the Spirit joins with the indirect witness of your own spirit of what God's grace has done in your life. You become aware in your heart that condemnation has gone and you have peace with God (Rom. 5:1). Fear is gone and in its place abides a childlike loving trust in God. Slavery to sin is gone, and you have a freedom in Christ as you triumph over sin (1 John 3:9-10).

You know you have passed from death to life because you love your fellow-Christians (1 John 3:14). You have a clear conscience because Christ has forgiven your sin. "We know that we have come to know him if we obey his commands" (1 John 2:3). You recognize the new fruit of the Spirit in your life (Gal. 5:22-23).

The moral witness of a transformed life, a life fully in accord with Bible standards, is the all-essential evidence of the new birth and Bible salvation. Every believer has the privilege of the full assurance of salvation based on the fulfillment of scriptural conditions. This involves (1) the inner witness of the Spirit, (2) the spirit and conscience of the person confirming the transformation of life, and (3) the witness of the person's spirit and conscience that he is fully obeying God's will. The first work of grace which we have been studying includes this final work of the Spirit in the succession of justification, regeneration, adoption, initial sanctification, and assurance.

LIVING BY FAITH. In this threefold witness, the witness of the Word is primary and foundational. In the new birth and in entire sanctification, God's Word is unchanging as the foundation of our experience. When you have met God's conditions as outlined in His Word, you are on the Eternal Rock. You can stand on that word unshaken at the judgment throne of Christ at the last day.

Whether you are aware of the Spirit's witness or not, you can know you have fulfilled God's Word. In the moment of believing God's Word for your salvation or usually within a matter of a few more moments, occasionally perhaps several hours of standing on pure faith on the Word, the Spirit's witness confirms to your soul or even floods your soul with the assurance that Christ has met your need. Then as you walk with God the assurance of your own spirit confirms and reconfirms with the witness of the Holy Spirit that you are indeed a new creature in Christ Jesus. Thank God for this threefold witness.

God may permit occasions in your Christian life when for a time God's presence does not seem as near or consciously real. These are times when you walk by "naked faith." As long as you know you have been obedient to God, just hold steady. The Spirit's assurance will again become as strong and as real as before. These are sometimes referred to as "dry times," "faith times," or even "the dark night of the soul." Satan will be there to accuse you. He is a liar.

Just hold steady. God holds your hand even when you do not sense His doing so. God's Word is still true. You are on the Solid Rock. Stand!

At such times your own spirit, your indirect witness, may assure you that you have indeed remained grounded on God's Word, that your life is indeed changed by God's grace. And as you hold steady, the direct witness of the Spirit will again become real and strong. Such times of walking by faith build strength and solidness of character in your soul. We receive Christ by faith, and we must live by faith.

The Spirit's witness is real. It is God's divine seal. It is God's gracious gift to every Christian. You will not sense it every moment of every day. But if God permits times of testing and walking by faith, just keep walking. As surely as God is in heaven, the witness will return in all its fullness.

THE NECESSITY OF ASSURANCE. Nothing is more important to any person than the clear knowledge that his sins are forgiven and that God has accepted him as His child and he is now entitled to all the privileges of a child of God. Nothing is more urgent than that you know your name is written in heaven (Luke 10:20; Rev. 20:15), and that should death come at any time your eternal salvation and home in heaven are sure.

Is it possible to be subjectively deceived about your salvation? to place your hope on a false understanding? Yes. Millions will experience this at the judgment seat of Christ.

> **Matthew 7:21-23**--"Not everyone who says to me, 'Lord, Lord!' will enter the kingdom of heaven, but only he who does the will of my Father who is in heaven. Many will say to me on that day, 'Lord, Lord, did we not prophesy in your name, and in your name drive out demons and perform many miracles?' Then I will tell them plainly, 'I never knew you. Away from me, you evildoers!'"

From this it is clear that many Christian workers are deceived and will be shut out of heaven. Why? They still have unrepented sin in their lives. Salvation is not the result of taking the name of a

Christian, of joining a church and being baptized, of taking the Lord's Supper, or of reading the Bible (James 1:22).

God's Word is clear. Sin must be repented of, confessed, and forsaken. The changed life must prove the salvation in the heart. A person can do all the forms of Christianity outwardly yet never experience God's saving grace in his heart. It is possible to work up religious emotions but have an unchanged heart and life.

Pastors, you have a tremendous responsibility to preach salvation so clearly, scripturally, and fully that no one will miss heaven because of lack of clear preaching (Ezek. 33:7-9). Paul was very much aware of this responsibility for the blood of those to whom he preached and had this Scripture in Ezekiel in mind when he said farewell to the Ephesian church elders (Acts 20:26-28, 31).

31

THE TWOFOLD
NATURE OF SIN

Any study of humankind and sin soon must recognize that sinful acts which curse our human relationships, society, and civilization spring from, are rooted in, and are motivated by a sinful nature. Human beings are not merely sinners; they are sinful. This leads us to explain the twofold nature of sin.

Sin's twofoldness began in Eden. Our holy God has never created sinful beings. All beings He created were created for fellowship with Him and for serving Him. Sin perverts and destroys fellowship, and sin impairs and hinders service. All that God created is good and perfect for its intended role. Adam and Eve were created good and holy.

Adam and Eve's holiness. Adam and Eve were created in the likeness of God (Gen. 1:26-27). This included full personality like God's--intelligence, affections, will, and conscience; a spirit nature like God's; and a moral nature like God's--holiness. Theirs was a created holiness; to become holy in character they would need to be tested and make right choices. Character is developed by our choices.

God gave Adam and Eve every opportunity for holy living and the development of holy character. They were created innocent--they had never sinned. They began to develop righteousness--which is righteous character developed by right choices. Because they were personal like God, they had choice, but God made right choice easy and their testing simple, with every possibility of developing personal righteousness and holy character.

The Ideal Probation. God in His grace and love made every provision for Adam and Eve to remain holy and grow in holy character. As we discussed in chapter 7:

1. *The environment was ideal.*
2. *They had regular daily fellowship with God.*
3. *They had holy hearts.*
4. *The indwelling Holy Spirit was available to guide them,* strengthen them in right choices, and to bless them spiritually, helping them to grow in grace and in holy character.
5. *They had the simplest, most easy form of testing.*

The Sinful Act. In spite of such ideal circumstances, Eve and Adam chose to disregard God's clear instruction and assert their own independence, rather than accept their ultimate dependence on God. They listened to the tempter rather than to God. Their one act of sin had tremendous significance.

1. They doubted and denied the wisdom and love of the God who created them and fellowshiped with them.
2. They rejected God's lordship and chose to be, as they thought, their own lord, and do their own will.
3. They refused to obey and thus rejected God's government and sovereign role.
4. They disbelieved and dishonored God, were disloyal and knowingly disobedient.

Adam and Eve were no longer innocent. They were now guilty. But there was a second, even more tragic consequence.

The Sinful Nature. The sinful act brought a sinful nature. Sin always pollutes. Our foreparents entered a sinful state. From a state of innocence, they were now guilty. From a state of impurity, they had become impure. They had gone from obedience to disobedience, willful rebellion. They had revolted against God's command, government, and lordship.

They had been in a state of fellowship with God. That fellowship was now broken and they were in a state of hostility. The spiritual unity and social harmony with God were broken. The state of confidence was replaced by a state of doubt and fear. The state of inner peace of heart and innocence of conscience was replaced by a state of condemnation.

The fullness of the Holy Spirit who filled their personalities imparting holiness was replaced by spiritual emptiness. They were no longer filled or even indwelt by the Holy Spirit. Rebellion had driven Him away. Losing Him, they lost their purity, for He was their only source of holiness. Their human nature was now polluted by rebellious sin. Their purity was now replaced by sinfulness. Sin's stain, sin's pollution, sin's perversion, sin's hardening, sin's enslaving-- all these had begun.

The tragic fall of Adam and Eve was twofold. Outwardly they became sinners in act. Inwardly they became sinful, indwelt by a sin principle. They now had a sinful nature.

Sin as a Condition of the Heart. Adam and Eve became sinners and sinful by their own act. Their misuse of their freedom to choose, their sinful willing resulted in a sinful condition of heart. Sin (in the singular) is a heart condition. It is a sinful source from which come all kinds of sinful thoughts, words, and deeds.

Sin as a nature is the root from which grows sinful fruit in the life. It is a state of sin which expresses itself in acts of sin. It is a defiled fountain from which impure streams flow. It is a sinful will from which come many sinful choices. It is a sinful nature from which come "the acts of the sinful nature" (Gal. 5:19-21). This sinful nature has been called the carnal nature, inbred sin, original sin, Adamic sin, and "the old man."

For all humankind, sin has become an inherited inward quality, a unitary principle of evil. Sinful acts are many and diverse, but they come from one interior source (Mark 7:20-23). They come from a polluted nature, and they further pollute the nature. It is an inherited inclination and tendency to sin. Every human being has this sinful nature from birth on.

This depravity or disposition to sin affects the whole human being. All humankind is affected by the fall into sin, and the entire being is affected by the Fall.

a. Mind and conscience are corrupted (Titus 1:15). Every inclination of the thoughts is constantly evil (Gen. 6:5).

b. The understanding is darkened (Eph. 4:18). Spiritual things are not readily understood (1 Cor. 2:14).

c. The heart and conscience are hardened (Eph. 4:18; Heb. 3:13; 1 Tim. 4:2) and corrupted (Titus 2:15).

d. The will is enslaved (Rom. 7:18-23).

e. The heart is deceitful (Jer. 17:9).

f. The whole person is enslaved (John 8:34; Rom. 6:16-17, 19-20; Heb. 2:15).

The Chronology of Sin. Each human infant is born with a sinful nature. Salvation is not inherited; each person must personally choose Christ as Savior. At some point in the child's life he reaches a state where he sufficiently understands right from wrong and becomes personally accountable for his choices. A sinful choice thereafter is a personal sin for which he will be judged unless he repents.

Only God knows the age when the child is fully accountable in God's sight. It may be earlier in some than in others. It is at that age when the child sins by his own volition. It often seems possible to help a child understand Jesus' love at an earlier age than he fully understands the full aspects of sin. How much better it is to lead a child to Christ before the child experiences full hardening and depraving results of sin.

The act of sin is the manifestation and yielding to the inner state. The Bible gives various definitions of sin, but the definition we must be concerned about in regard to our salvation is 1 John 3:4: "Everyone who sins breaks the law; in fact, sin is lawlessness." It is this act of sin, a willful transgression of a known and understood law of God that makes us personally guilty before God. All have thus sinned (Rom. 3:23).

Sinful acts are committed in the form of sinful thoughts, words, and deeds. These acts are related to the sinful nature as fruit is related to root. Almost always in the Bible when the source, the sinful nature, is referred to, "sin" or "iniquity" is used in the singular.

When the sinful acts are referred to, the plural is usually used: "sins" or "iniquities."

32

HUMANITY'S SINFUL NATURE

TERMS FOR THE SINFUL NATURE. In order to give a more complete understanding of the nature of the sinful condition of each person's heart, the Bible uses a variety of terms, each of which adds to our understanding of the subject. Terms which follow are words or phrases which biblically describe the sin nature remaining in the heart of a born-again person until he is cleansed in entire sanctification through the infilling of the Holy Spirit.

1. *The Sinful Nature.* Note: Ps. 51:5; Rom. 8:8, 13; Gal. 5:17; Col. 2:11.

2. *The Sinful Mind* (the mind of sinful man, the mind set on the flesh, the carnal mind).

Romans 8:5-7--"Those who live according to the sinful nature have their minds set on what that nature desires; but those who live in accordance with the Spirit have their minds set on what the Spirit desires. The mind of sinful man is death, but the mind controlled by the Spirit is life and peace; the sinful mind is hostile to God. It does not submit to God's law nor can it do so."

This term refers to a mind-set which is the opposite of the mind of Christ. Unless cleansed away by the sanctifying work of the Spirit, this mind-set is typical of or present in every human being, whether unsaved or saved.

The Greek word *phronema* used here includes aspects of thinking and willing. Thus it describes an attitude, a mind-set. It is a bias toward the values, aspirations, desires, and appetites of "the flesh."

The sinful mind-set is hostile to God (Rom. 8:7). It is more dominated by self than by God, except as the person is aided by the

Spirit to be victorious. The person controlled by the sinful mind cannot please God (Rom. 8:8). It has a spiritually deadening influence (v. 6). It resists God's will.

The sinful mind is not a separate mind but a spiritual mind-set which influences the whole of the person's life. It is a pervasive power which operates like a dominating law of sin (Rom. 7:23, 25), of sin and death (Rom. 8:2). It is a mind set on the flesh (Rom. 6:7, Greek).

3. *The Old Self* (Rom. 6:6). Our old self was crucified with Him. Note: Eph. 4:22; Col. 3:9.

4. *The Body of Sin.* Note: Rom. 6:6.

5. *This Body of Death.* Note Rom. 7:24.

6. *The Sinful Law.* The sinful nature is described as a law seeking to prevent our obedience to God's will (Rom. 7:21), a law "at work" in the body, "waging war against the law of my mind" (i.e., God's law written in my conscience) (v. 23). This law of sin enslaves (v. 25). The sin nature is called a law because: (1) It acts in a predictable, uniform way. (2) It is beyond human power to control or eliminate. (3) It is natural for the person to sin. It is not an enacted code of law. Thus the law of sin may be called the inherited bias or impulse to sin.

Romans 7:21--"So I find this law at work: when I want to do good, evil is right there with me."

7. *The Law of Sin and Death.* Paul repeatedly shows that sin produces death (Rom. 5: 15, 17, 21; 6:16, 21, 23; 7:10-11; 8:6, 10, 13). This is another way to state the law of sin. Just as the law of God is synonymous with God, so the law of sin and death is synonymous with the sin nature. Note also: Rom. 8:2.

8. *Sin Living in Me.* Note: Rom. 7:17.

9. *Sin* (in singular). "Sins" in the plural form always refers to the acts of sin which can be forgiven in the new birth. "Sin" in the singular usually refers to the sin nature. Note: Rom. 6:11-13, 22.

The term "sin" occurs 28 times between Romans 5:12 and Romans 8:10. It is used in the sense of a hostile, deadly nature that lives in the heart, exerting its deadly power against all that is spiritual and holy.

10. *Flesh.* The term "flesh" is often used in Scripture to refer to the human body. Thus Jesus' flesh and bones, after His resurrection, proved the reality of His body (Luke 24:39). "All flesh" is a way of saying all humanity (Gen. 6:12; 1 Peter 1:24).

In the New Testament, especially in Paul's writings, "flesh" or "sinful flesh" often becomes a term for the sinful nature. Sinners live "according to the sinful nature" [Greek: sinful flesh] (Rom. 8:5). This sinful flesh has sinful passions and desires (Gal. 5:24). These sinful passions bear fruit for death (Rom. 7:5). The sinful nature [Greek: flesh] desires what is contrary to the Spirit, and the Spirit what is contrary to the sinful nature [Greek: flesh] (Gal. 5:17). This flesh produces sinful acts (Gal. 5:19-21), which are contrasted with the fruit of the Spirit (vv. 22-23). The sinner sows to please the flesh (Gal. 6:8). So the term "flesh" is a prominent term for the sinful nature and is often translated sinful nature. The unsaved person is con-trolled by it and its sinful pressures do their deadly work (Rom. 7:5).

11. *Contamination of Spirit.* Note: 2 Cor. 7:1.

12. *Worldly* (unspiritual). Note: Rom. 7:19; 1 Cor. 3:1, 3.

13. *Iniquity* (singular). Iniquity in the singular, like sin in the singular, usually refers to the sin nature. Note: Ps. 51:2; Isa. 53:6.

14. *Unrighteousness.* Note: 1 John 1:9.

15. *The Stony Heart.* Note: Ezek. 36:26.

16. *Sin which so easily entangles us.* Note: Heb. 12:1.

17. *Double-mindedness.* Note: James 4:8.

The Strength of the Sinful Nature. This sinful nature is so strong in the unsaved person that apart from God's prevenient grace he would never choose to come to Christ (John 6:44, 65). The unsaved person is morally impotent to meet God's demands.

Just as created holiness in Adam and Eve contained a natural inclination to God and God's will through the indwelling Spirit and fellowship with God, so the sinful nature of Adam and Eve after the fall into sin was an inner inclination to sin. Like produces like. So all of Adam and Eve's descendants, since they were born after the fall into sin, are born with the inherited inclination to sin. They are born without the indwelling presence of the Holy Spirit, and they are born separated from fellowship with God.

However, man's condition is not helpless or hopeless. Christ was the Lamb who in the mind and purpose of God was slain from the creation of the world (Rev. 13:8). Therefore, God's prevenient grace which has been available even before Adam and Eve's sin became available to them after their sin. God's prevenient grace from that time on has been available to anyone whenever he of his free will turns to God. Wherever sin increases, God's available grace increases all the more (Rom. 5:20).

THE SINFUL NATURE AND THE WORLD. The sinful nature is an active principle of evil that works within the person. It is appealed to and tends to relate to what the Bible calls "the world." This is the spirit, the culture, the value system, and the attitudes of society as darkened by sin operating on non-Christian principles. So the sinful nature is attracted and easily drawn into the spirit of the world. It is easily misled by Satan's deceptions, entangled by cravings and lusts suggested by him, and is easily molded by the whole world's system as coordinated by Satan, the god of this age (2 Cor. 4:4).

Thus the world, the flesh, and the devil are a complex of darkness, of which the Christian must be constantly aware and which he must constantly resist and overcome (1 John 2:15-16). He must not succumb to the temptation to love any part of it. As the sinful nature confronts the world and Satan, its manifestations assert themselves and demonstrate the need of Christ's atonement and transforming grace.

The world and Satan seek to shape the sinful nature in conformity with their sinful characteristics, spirit, desires, and goals (Rom. 12:2; 1 Peter 1:14). The unsaved person does not have the Spirit's help to withstand the pull and the pressure of these foes of the soul. People with a good moral heritage and a sensitive conscience may have less difficulty in resisting the grosser enticements of Satan and the world. But often the world's allurements are so subtle and pervasive that the person is influenced far more than he realizes.

OUR SINFUL NATURE AND GOD'S ANSWER. The new birth is God's answer for the guilt of sin. But the Bible nowhere teaches that it cleanses us from the sinful nature. There is a purifying and a perfecting of holiness that needs to follow the new birth (2 Cor. 7:1). Paul prayed that the Thessalonian Christians be sanctified through and through (1 Thess. 5:23). This is a clear expression of a need after the new birth. When Jesus prayed His high priestly prayer for His disciples, He prayed for their sanctification (John 17:17), although earlier in the prayer He testifies to their salvation.

We have pointed out that sin is twofold--it is a nature and it is the act that results from the sinful nature and expresses that nature. In salvation, God first meets the need of our personal sins. He forgives us, declares us righteous in His sight (justifies us). This is logical. Since sins have caused our spiritual death, God does a manifold work in our hearts in the new birth, as we have seen. Let us review. He gives us spiritual life and regenerates us and cleanses us from the defilement of our personally committed sins. He makes us His child, officially adopts us, and makes us an heir of blessings and heaven. He gives us the Holy Spirit to indwell us, witness to our salvation, guide us, help us pray, and give us strength to serve Him.

But we are still unholy in nature. We have an inherited sinful nature, as has every human being since Adam. Adam is not only our ultimate source of genes and chromosomes, he is also the one ultimately responsible for our being born without the Holy Spirit living and indwelling us, as Adam and Eve were created. Thus we were not born holy.

You are not guilty for having an unholy nature. You were born that way. You are not guilty for not being indwelt by the Spirit. You were born that way. Therefore, you cannot be forgiven for these aspects of your condition. You can be forgiven only for those things for which you are personally responsible. What you need is a cleansing of the nature which you inherited from Adam.

You were cleansed from the defilement in your personality and nature resulting from your own sins. That was initial sanctification. That was the first installment in the life of holiness. What you now need is a cleansing from the nature you inherited. That is full cleansing, entire sanctification. It is the second major event in your experience of God's holiness, the holiness you derive from God the Holy Spirit.

As you go on in the life of holiness, you may realize repeatedly that you have made a mistake, have fallen short of what you intended to be or do. Repeatedly, God will show you new light on how to live a more holy life. The Holy Spirit is the One who will give you this increasing light, for He leads you in the life of holiness.

You must continue to walk in the light God gives you. "If we walk in the light, as he is in the light, we have fellowship with one another, and the blood of Jesus, his Son, purifies us from all sin" (1 John 1:7). In the Greek, the present tense is used in this verse. This means you could translate it, "If we **continue** to walk in the light, we **continue** to have fellowship, and the blood of Jesus, his Son, **continues** to purify us from all sin."

This is progressive holiness, an ever more saintly godliness, a constant cleansing from the experiences of life as you live it. Note John 13:10. Cleansing is the negative part of the life of holiness. Growth in grace is the positive part of the life of holiness. There is some growth in grace between the time when your sins are forgiven and the time when you are cleansed by the sanctifying fullness of the Spirit. However, the most significant and rapid growth in grace begins when you are thus fully cleansed and filled with the Spirit.

The progression in the life of holiness can become ever more blessed, more precious, and more marked by positive transfiguring grace, until you reach the third major event in the life of holiness-- the glorification of your body in the heavenly world. "He who began a good work in you will carry it on to completion until the day of Christ Jesus" (Phil. 1:6).

In the first major work of grace (justification), Christ declares you free from your sinful past. In the second major work of God's grace (entire sanctification), He delivers you from your sinful nature. And in the third major work of God's grace (glorification), He delivers you from the presence of sin and the unintentional failures of your humanity.

33

GOD'S GLORIOUS STANDARD
FOR BELIEVERS

GOD'S REQUIREMENT OF HOLINESS. God has one requirement and glorious standard for all believers who are saved by God's transforming grace. The standard does not change from the moment of the new birth until the believer passes from this world to God's glory world. God's standard is Spirit-filled holiness manifested in a righteous and holy life.

God's standard is expressed clearly from the time of Moses right through the New Testament. "The Lord said to Moses, 'Speak to the entire assembly of Israel and say to them: "Be holy because I, the Lord your God, am holy"'" (Lev. 19:1-2). Peter reaffirmed this standard by saying, "Just as he who called you is holy, so be holy in all you do; for it is written: 'Be holy, because I am holy'" (1 Peter 1:15-16).

God's unchanging requirement and standard is a heart holiness ("Be holy") expressed in a holy life "in all you do." Note that it is not enough to avoid sin in your actions. You are to do holy actions from a holy nature. God wants not only holy doing but holy being. Doing holiness is another way of saying holy obedience. God is the only Lord. If He is Lord, He has absolute, sovereign right and duty to demand obedience. God can have no other standard for His creatures then obedience.

Obedience is the law that underlies all expressions of God's law. It was the one simple requirement for Adam and Eve when they were created. God progressively increased His moral light and increasingly clarified His will over the centuries. The law underlying God's revealed will to the patriarchs (Adam, Seth, Noah, Abraham,

Isaac, Jacob, Joseph, and his brothers) was the law of obedience to
the light received up to that time.

The law underlying the law of Moses was obedience. God
wanted Israel to be a holy nation, separated to Him but also separated from the sins of their age (Exod. 19:6). The law underlying
God's treatment of the pagan nations is the law of obedience to the
light they have received as monitored by their conscience (Rom. 2:14-
16). The law underlying this gospel dispensation of grace is still the
law of obedience. Obedience to God results in more or less holiness
of life according to the light the person has received.

The life of every Christian should be characterized by holy living.
Every human being lives his life in a body more or less impaired by
the Fall. Everyone is liable to forget, make an inadvertent mistake,
or to misunderstand others and thus respond imperfectly. No human
being has mental, emotional, or social perfection. But every Christian
is saved from willful, intentional breaking of God's known and
recognized law.

Salvation is salvation from sin. Jesus came to save people from
their sins (Matt. 1:21). To be a Christian means to be saved from the
habit and practice of willful transgressions of God's law.

1 John 3:9-10--"No one who is born of God will continue to sin. . . .
He cannot go on sinning, because he has been born of God. This is
how we know who the children of God are and who the children of
the devil are: Anyone who does not do what is right is not a child of
God; nor is anyone who does not love his brother."

A holy life is God's normal standard for all Christians. It is
possible for anyone to be ensnared and yield to temptation; and if so,
he has instant access to Christ for forgiveness if he instantly repents
and resolves not to yield to that temptation again (1 John 2:1-2).

However, until he has been cleansed by the infilling of the Holy
Spirit no human being has a holy nature. You retain your unholy
nature until you confess your heart's uncleanness, surrender your
total being in a vow of total and permanent committal, asking the
Spirit to cleanse your inner nature and fill you completely with His
holiness.

Is there such a full and powerful inner cleansing and infilling which can make us holy within? Is it possible to obtain on earth the inner holiness you will need when you are in God's holy presence, in His holy heaven? If the pure in heart can see God, can I have the blessing of that purity now (Matt. 5:8)? If without holiness no one will see the Lord, can I obtain that necessary holiness now while I am living my Christian life on earth (Heb. 12:14)? If Jesus came so I could live without fear in righteousness and holiness all my days (Luke 1:72), does God really fulfill His Word before my death?

Thank God, the unequivocal answer is yes, a glorious yes. God does not require an impossible standard from you. God will fulfill all His will in your life if you fulfill His clear conditions. God is not a deceiver. He means what He says. His love does not cause Him to lower His standard of holiness for you. He cannot. He must be true to the infinite holiness of His nature. But He can and did provide a redemption adequate for your need.

We become sanctified through and through in the crisis of entire sanctification (1 Thess. 5:23, Greek aorist) when our cleansing is made complete and through the process of growth in positive holiness, the transformation of Romans 12:2 and 2 Corinthians 3:18. The Greek word for this is the word used for Christ's transfiguration.

GOD PLANS FOR YOUR SANCTIFICATION NOW ON EARTH. If salvation is from sin, salvation can never be complete until you are saved from your sinful nature. Since sin is a moral problem, it must be dealt with before death. Mistakes and infirmities arise from your psychological, mental, and physical nature. Deliverance from them must await the glorification of your body. Glorification is salvation of the body, not of the soul. Glorification does not deal with your moral condition.

If entering heaven saved you and cleansed you from sin, Christ did not need to come to earth to die. Every sinner could have been saved by transporting him to heaven when he died. If glorification did not require justification, regeneration, and sanctification beforehand, resulting in moral transformation before death, God could have provided automatic salvation through glorification at death.

It was for earth life that Adam and Eve were created holy and continued in holiness for a period of time. It was during earth life that they sinned and became sinful. It is on earth that people have lived in sin. Christ's atonement for sin was provided while He was on earth, and it is provided for us who continue to live on earth. All the provisions in God's Word--commands, exhortations, and promises--are for us while we live on earth. Christ's triumph is incomplete and His salvation from sin is incomplete unless salvation from both the guilt and the nature of sin is available for us during earth life.

The provision of God for you is a righteousness and holiness available to you in Christ for all the remaining days of your life on earth (Luke 1:74-75). Then you will be enabled to live a self-controlled, upright, and godly life in this present age (Titus 2:11), because your great God and Savior, Jesus Christ, gave Himself for you to redeem you from all wickedness and to purify you for Himself as His very own, eager to do what is good (vv. 13-14) right here on earth.

The prayer of Jesus for the sanctification of His disciples was because "I will remain in the world no longer, but they are still in the world" (John 17:11). So Jesus wanted them to be sanctified (John 17:17) while they were living on earth. How complete is this sanctification which God has provided for His children while they are on earth? Paul's inspired prayer answers that. "May God himself, the God of peace, sanctify you through and through" (1 Thess. 5:23). Then the rest of the verse can be fulfilled: "May your whole spirit, soul, and body be kept blameless at the coming of our Lord Jesus Christ."

Don't reprove Paul by saying, "But, Paul, that is just a beautiful ideal we can only hope to strive for but never attain." Paul's next verse is God's promise for you! "The one who calls you (to this holiness) is faithful and he will do it" (v. 24).

God's will is that you be sanctified and live a morally holy life (1 Thess. 4:3). If sanctification is not till death, you cannot live a life of full holiness on earth.

When Paul said farewell to the Ephesian elders at Miletus, he said, "Now I commit you to God and to the word of his grace, which can build you up and give you an inheritance among all those who are sanctified" (Acts 20:32). This building up in sanctification is the same concern for which Jesus prayed, "Sanctify them by the truth; your word is truth" (John 17:17). This was a sanctification to be done here on earth.

Paul's commission from God was to bring his Gentile converts to experience on earth a twofold salvation--the forgiveness of sins and sanctification by faith (Acts 26:18). This would happen on earth for them just as it did for the 120 at Pentecost and for those at the house of Cornelius in Caesarea, as reported by Peter. "God, who knows the heart, showed that he accepted them by giving the Holy Spirit to them, just as he did to us. He made no distinction between us and them, for he purified their hearts by faith" (Acts 15:8-9).

The only ministry of the Holy Spirit described in the Bible is on earth. It is always available to us while we are alive on earth. The making of the church holy by the washing with water through the Word (Eph. 5:26) is done while the members of the church are alive on earth in order that they may be prepared and ready for the time Christ comes to get them and present them to Himself in full radiant holiness as His bride.

Heaven is nowhere described as the moral answer to sin. Death is nowhere described as God's moral answer for sin. Scripture nowhere exhorts us not to worry because our salvation from sin will be completed when we die. Death is our last enemy (1 Cor. 15:26).

Death is not an ideal time to deal with the great issues of salvation and sanctification. Salvation must be understood, accepted, and God's conditions met while you are in the full use of your personhood. Death often is not a time of full alertness and the full exercise of your personhood.

You are sanctified by the Holy Spirit using God's truth which you must appropriate (John 17:17; Eph. 5:26). You are sanctified by faith (Acts 15:9; 26:18). Sanctification and faith in the truth are associated together (2 Thess. 2:13). Death is not an ideal time for such important moral transactions with God or for faith to be exercised. Thank God that at times He condescends to meet great spiritual needs just before death. But this is not God's normal or standard procedure. Salvation, including full sanctification, is God's provision of grace for living.

You are sanctified for obedience to Jesus Christ (1 Peter 1:2). This obedience is obedience for earth life. The promises of God are given you for claiming in this life. There is no scriptural proof that when you get to heaven you will claim these promises in order to complete your salvation. There is no scriptural proof that in heaven faith is exercised for salvation or that we need to do so then. Heaven is a place of sight, not a place for faith.

Thank God, salvation is real, it is available now by faith, it is experienceable now, knowable now, witnessed to by the Holy Spirit now. We rejoice in it and thank God for it now. Thank God that salvation can be completed now. God has made full provision for full salvation by faith. Since it is by faith, it is available to whoever will, and since it is by faith, it is available now.

34

SANCTIFICATION
FOR HOLY LIVING

Thank God, every person who has been born of God can and should live a holy life. Holy living begins the moment you are born of the Spirit. Every Christian is indwelt by the Spirit (Rom. 8:9; 2 Tim. 1:14). Your body becomes the temple of the Holy Spirit who resides in you (1 Cor. 6:19).

Until the sinful nature is cleansed, however, you at times find inner resistance to God's will. You need not yield to this resistance. "You, however, are controlled, not by the sinful nature, but by the Spirit, if the Spirit of God lives in you" (Rom. 8:9). Romans 7:7-25 pictures a life of struggle with the sin principle. Some commentators consider this to be the life of an awakened Jew under the Mosaic law. However, many believe that this accurately portrays the experience and heart-cry of a born-again Christian as he becomes more sensitive to the sin nature struggling against his spiritual desires.

Many a truly regenerated believer in his most honest moments confesses that Romans 7 is all too vivid a description of his own struggle, seeking to be all God calls him to be, and yet sensing an inner bondage, an inner drag, an inner opposition and rebelling against part of God's will.

Paul verbalized for us this struggle which once characterized his own experience and described how he came to the end of himself, exclaiming, "What a wretched man I am! Who will rescue me from this body of death?" (Rom. 7:24).

Thank God, Paul gave the answer God gave him in the next verse. "Thanks be to God--through Jesus Christ our Lord!" And then Paul plunges into Romans 8, the wonderful chapter of victory through the Holy Spirit. How much easier it is to live the holy life in the victory the Holy Spirit gives when He cleanses fully and fills us completely with His empowering presence!

SANCTIFIED FOR LOVING GOD. Jesus summarized Old Testament righteousness and religion in two related commandments which are still God's will for you today. "Love the Lord your God with all your heart and with all your soul and with all your mind and with all your strength" (Mark 12:30). This is the heart and essence of holiness as it relates to God. It expresses the wholeness of total commitment.

The command "love" is a verb, an action word. Love is not a passive relaxing. It is positive action, and Jesus says that every aspect of your personality must be actively involved in this action of loving God. All of your inner self, including all of your will, all of your affection, all of your mind, and all of your energies, are to be mobilized.

Love is a flame that is always to be kept burning in your innermost nature, a longing that constantly reaches out to God, a constant mental focus, an attentiveness to God, and a constant volitional commitment to God. Every aspect of your being is reaching out to God, delighting in God, and eagerly willing God's will. No unsanctified, un-Spirit-filled heart can love God this totally, this constantly, and this committedly and unreservedly. The Holy Spirit makes this love the deepest reality of the sanctified person's being. It is only as your heart is cleansed by the Spirit and filled with the fruit of the Spirit--the first two of these being love and joy--that you can truly love God according to Mark 12:30.

SANCTIFIED FOR LOVING OTHERS. The second and insepparable aspect of Bible righteousness, holiness, and religion is "Love your neighbor as yourself" (Mark 12:31). You are not loving God as Jesus said unless you are loving your neighbor as Jesus said. "Anyone who does not love his brother, whom he has seen, cannot love God, who he has not seen" (1 John 4:20). "Whoever loves God must also love his brother" (v. 21).

The love for others which the Bible teaches is not just a theoretical love. It must be a practical love, the love of 1 Corinthians 13:4-7. It is a love that is patient with others, kind to others, does not envy others, does not boast, is not proud (because these are always attitudes in comparison with others), is not rude to others, is not self-seeking, is not angry with others, and keeps no record of the wrongs received from others. It does not delight in the misfortune of others, but rejoices in good truth about others. It always protects others, always tends to believe the best of others, and continues to hope for the best about others. It perseveres in all these good attitudes to others.

There is no more searching passage in Scripture than the picture presented in these verses. No person with a nature uncleansed from sin and not enabled and empowered by the fullness of the Spirit can live up to this standard. It takes sanctification through and through to enable you to love others according to 1 Corinthians 13.

SANCTIFIED FOR HOLY RADIANCE. God desires you to be so filled with His Spirit that you are radiant with His presence. God wants to beautify your personality and character by His holiness and by His sweetness in your disposition. Moses prayed, "May the beauty of the Lord our God rest upon us" (Ps. 90:17, margin). God wants to bestow on you "a crown of beauty instead of ashes" (Isa. 61:3). When God shines forth from Zion, God considers her "perfect in beauty" (Ps. 50:2). This beauty is the beauty of Christlikeness, of your joy in the Holy Spirit, and of the glory which the Spirit places within and upon you.

The sin nature tends to make one unChristlike and carnal, instead of like Jesus; irritated, impatient, and unhappy, instead of joyful with holy inner joy; and earthy, worldly, and strained looking, instead of touched by God's glory. To be really radiant continuously with Christ's presence, you need the cleansing and fullness of the Holy Spirit through a sanctified, Spirit-filled life.

The Spirit, when He really floods your soul with the fullness of His presence, conforms you to the likeness of Jesus (Rom. 8:29), brings you ever nearer "the whole measure of the fullness of Christ" (Eph. 4:13), and you "are being transformed into His likeness" (2 Cor. 3:18).

As the Spirit floods and fills you, He makes you radiant with the joy of the Lord. This does not depend on outward circumstances, but the Spirit fills you with this joy from His inner spring of living water within you.

Jesus prayed for your sanctification (John 17:17) so that you might have the full measure of His joy (v. 13). When the Holy Spirit fills you, He fills you with joy (Acts 13:52), for joy is given by the Spirit (1 Thess. 1:6). The kingdom of God filling you means joy in the Holy Spirit (Rom. 14:17). One of the main forms of the fruit of the Spirit is joy (Gal. 5:22), a joy which Peter describes as "inexpressible and glorious" (1 Peter 1:8).

Added to this Christlikeness and joy supplied by the Holy Spirit is the special touch of God's radiant glory. Usually this consists in general radiance of spirit which others recognize in some sense as heavenly, attributable to a special sense of God with you, God's grace and touch upon you, and God's nearness with you. It is hard to describe but beautiful to recognize.

Such spiritual radiance may not be apparent constantly every day, but it definitely will be perceivable again and again, specially so when you are really communing with Jesus as you go about your work. Spiritual people sometimes sense it in you after you are thus Spirit-filled, and often God uses it to speak to the unsaved. It was something like this which caused the woman of Shunem to recognize Elisha as "a holy man of God" (2 Kings 4:9).

Sometimes for a brief time some of God's people have seemed to be touched temporarily with a visible glory from God's presence within. Moses experienced this (Exod. 34:29). Christian history has on occasions recorded this of others also. But whether or not you ever experience a touch of God's glory visible to others, at least you are to be so Spirit-filled that your face from time to time reflects the inner glory.

2 Corinthians 3:17-18--"Where the Spirit of the Lord is, there is freedom. And we who with unveiled faces all reflect the Lord's glory, are being transformed into His likeness with ever-increasing glory, which comes from the Lord, who is the Spirit."

A life sanctified through the fullness of the Holy Spirit is the all-essential foundation for this kind of spiritual radiance which is to be Christ's testimony to others.

SANCTIFIED FOR EFFECTIVE PRAYING. You are saved to pray. A new Christian does not need to be taught to pray. He prays as naturally spiritually as he breathes physically. There is great blessing in teaching new Christians more fully the liberty of praying, the elements of prayer, and the joy of taking everything to God in prayer. Often God gives new Christians beautiful answers to prayer shortly after their spiritual birth. Nothing is more spiritually natural.

Nevertheless, the Christian soon learns that there are many longstanding needs, resistant situations, even urgent needs where special power in prayer is required. God knows this, and so built into your Christian life is the special role of the Holy Spirit to help you in your prayer weaknesses.

Romans 8:26--"The Spirit helps us in our weakness. We do not know what we ought to pray for, but the Spirit himself intercedes for us with groans that words cannot express."

The more completely you are filled with the Spirit, the more fruitfully and powerfully the Spirit can pray within you.

An unsanctified, sinful nature often shrinks and hesitates to undertake prevailing prayer. It often senses a vague tendency to draw back from prayer. Satan fears mighty praying so greatly that he makes use of the vulnerability of the sinful nature to hinder your praying.

The sinful nature can mislead you with wrong desires, can poison your praying with self-centered and wrong motives, and can inject doubt to weaken your faith. One of the main causes of problems in prayer is an unsanctified heart that is not completely filled with the Spirit.

On the other hand, spiritual liberty, delight, and power in prayer are an outstanding seal of the Spirit on a Spirit-filled life. The Holy Spirit can pray much more powerfully through a Spirit-filled person. He much more easily can guide a Spirit-filled person in his praying. He so possesses the inner nature of a sanctified person that He repeatedly draws him to prayer at times when God and others specially need that prayer.

Communion in prayer should be a delight to every Christian. There are few joys that equal or surpass the joy of prayer, and mighty prevailing intercession is the need of the church and of our world. There is absolutely no way that communion and mighty intercession can be all God plans them to be in your life and in the extension of His kingdom apart from a vibrant experience of the Spirit's fullness. And for those in Christian service, this is, if possible, even more essential.

SANCTIFIED FOR EFFECTIVE WITNESSING AND SOUL-WINNING. The work of witnessing for Christ and of winning people to Christ is constantly dependent on the Holy Spirit. Without the Holy Spirit, your witness is nothing but words. True words, perhaps, but not saving, life-giving words. It takes more than truth to convict and convert. Only the Holy Spirit convicts. But He does use the truth to convict us of sin, righteousness, and judgment (John 16:8-11).

The external letter of the law, apart from the work of the Spirit, is not saving--it can be even spiritually deadly (2 Cor. 3:6). Witnessing to unsaved people without the Spirit's guidance, without the Spirit's anointing, and without the Spirit's power does not necessarily lead people to Christ.

Many people have wondered why their witness was so ineffective. It may well be that they had so little of God's Spirit in them and on them that their effort, though well intended, was all on the human level. Salvation is a work of God; it is not a mere matter of human witness.

There is such power in the Word of God that God has at times used His Word printed in a Gospel tract or in a portion of Scripture, even though given by a non-Christian, to bring a person to Christ. However, it is far more effective and fruitful in salvation when accompanied by the personal testimony of a Spirit-filled, Spirit-anointed person.

Paul knew he ministered with the help of God (1 Thess. 2:2). He was keenly conscious of the power of the Spirit upon him as he ministered and spoke. "Our gospel came to you not simply with words, but also with power, with the Holy Spirit and with deep conviction" (1 Thess. 1:5). Is your ministry only words, or words empowered by the Spirit?

Jesus urged His apostles who had been trained by Him for three years not to begin their witness and ministry until they had the sanctifying fullness of the Spirit. "Repentance and forgiveness of sins will be preached. . . . You are witnesses of these things. I am going to send you what my Father has promised; but stay in the city until you have been clothed with power from on high" (Luke 24:47-49).

Jesus promised, "You will receive power when the Holy Spirit comes on you; and you will be my witnesses" (Acts 1:8). Jesus had already assured them, "You know him, for he lives with you and will be in you" (John 14:17). Their relation to the Spirit, though real, was insufficient. But when at Pentecost they were filled with the Spirit (Acts 2:4), their witness and ministry took on a whole new divine dimension. Within days thousands were saved.

We read further of their witness, "With great power the apostles continued to testify . . . and great grace was upon them all" (Acts 4:33). This is what we need in our secularized age today. It is possible only as we also are cleansed, filled, and empowered by the Holy Spirit. Sanctification by the infilling of the Holy Spirit is all-essential for your holy living and service.

35

GOD'S TWOFOLD SALVATION

We have noted the twofold nature of sin. Sins are acts--in thought, word, or deed. Sin is also a nature which is unlike God, is a spiritual hindrance to the Christian, and which becomes a source of our sinful acts. It motivates, expresses its desires, and inclines toward sinful deeds.

These two aspects of sin are expressed in two repeated heart-cries common among people of all nations.

1. *The cry, "I have sinned."* While chronologically each one of us is born with the sin nature and later reaches the age of accountability, yet in returning to God and receiving His salvation each of us first realizes the need of forgiveness and usually only later realizes the need of cleansing.

Our cry as a guilty sinner convicted by the Holy Spirit and repenting sincerely before God is, "I have sinned," "I did," "I spoke," "I thought." We ask ourselves, "Why did I do it?" "Why did I say that?" "Why did I think that way?" So the heart-cry of the sinner is, "Alas, I have sinned."

2. *The cry, "I am unclean!"* Even sinners may at times realize that they are very sinful, unclean in nature, and unholy. However, until a person repents, the Spirit chiefly convicts of sinful, committed acts.

After the person has repented and been wonderfully forgiven by God's grace and has received new life in Christ, he often is so full of joy from his assurance of God's forgiveness and his new relation with Christ that he may not sense any further spiritual need for some time.

However, as he continues in his Christian life, he sooner or later becomes aware of a remaining sinfulness in his nature that was not cleansed away at the time of the new birth. He knows that he is a child of God and he loves the Lord. He may be perplexed or even dismayed to find something within that tends at times to draw back from doing God's will. By the Spirit's help, he is able to subdue the inner tendency, but sometimes he finds a real inner struggle.

He now at times feels the Holy Spirit's conviction--not mainly because of committed acts, but because of his inner sinfulness, inner resistance and rebelliousness. He realizes that part of his nature is not holy in the sight of God. His cry now is not, "I did," but "I am."

"I am not holy," "I am unclean," "I am so spiritually weak I need more power," "I am so helpless in myself," "I am defeated within even though I may not show it from my actions." This is conviction of the sinful nature, the realization that more of the Spirit's cleansing, more of the Spirit's power is truly needed.

THE TWO MAJOR MOMENTS OR CRISES IN SALVATION

How the Crises May Come. The Holy Spirit in His patient love and faithfulness may repeatedly knock on the sinner's heart's door or reprove and convict of sins. This may continue over a period of days, months, or even years before the sinner truly repents of his sins and experiences full, clear, assured forgiveness of sins.

Sometimes the primary struggle is not one of obedience but, rather, of faith. This is specially true in those who have not come from a Christian home or who were followers of another religion or sect. In those cases, it may require considerable time before Christ's truth is understood and all doubts answered by Scripture.

It may be that as God's light and God's truth were received the person accepted one aspect after another--it was a series of steps of faith before full faith was received, or perhaps a series of steps of obedience before the last sin was confessed or the last act of restitution was taken. In such cases, the person may hardly be aware of the exact moment of the new birth because he was receiving and walking in one aspect of God's light after another.

However, usually persons are very aware of the time when the burden of sin was gone and they knew their sins were forgiven and they were now children of God. In either case, there is always a definite moment, a crisis moment, when the new birth becomes real. Many a person records and remembers that exact day or occasion when faith and obedience touched God. Thank God, it is knowable and real.

In a similar way, a born-again Christian may feel the Holy Spirit's conviction of need for inner cleansing and may come repeatedly and partially respond on various occasions before the time comes when his consecration and surrender becomes total, or before he actually by faith claims full cleansing through the infilling of the Holy Spirit. This is particularly true when the person has not had clear teaching on the experience of entire sanctification through the infilling of the Holy Spirit.

Multitudes of true Christians who love the Lord and have a vague awareness that God surely has a deeper victory for them than they have ever received, as yet have not understood or believed that this definite experience of full cleansing and true fullness of the Spirit is biblical, obtainable, and knowable in this life. They are loyal to the Lord and to the doctrine they have been taught, but they are still aware of inner defeat. They cannot help but long for something deeper, higher, more complete, and more victorious.

That inner longing and sense of partial dissatisfaction is God's gift. We were created to be filled with the Spirit. We are never spiritually all God wants us to be, and until we are fully cleansed and filled by the Spirit, the Spirit lovingly reminds us of this. God does not want us to be totally satisfied until we have experienced all for which Christ died on the cross. "Jesus also suffered outside the gate to make the people holy through His own blood" (Heb. 13:12).

1 Thessalonians 5:23-24--"May God himself, the God of peace, sanctify you through and through. May your whole spirit, soul, and body be kept blameless at the coming of our Lord Jesus Christ. The one who calls you is faithful and he will do it."

On the other hand, there are wonderful Christians who have never clearly understood God's provision for their cleansing and infilling. But after the new birth they have hungered for more of God's purity and power, have yielded themselves to God--perhaps repeatedly. They have sensed God's meeting them as they have reached out to Him, and God has met their heart-cry as He faithfully responded to their longing and walking in His light.

They may not have been aware that they had a definite new, deeper experience with God. They may have felt they had a series of deeper experiences. But the time did come in their walk with the Lord when their surrender in love and faith became total, and God met their need. Now as they receive clearer teaching they may say, "Why that is exactly what God did for me! Now I recognize how it is described by God's Word. Now I know what to call it. Praise God! That experience is already real in my life!"

The Second Major Work of God's Grace in the Soul. The second major work in salvation by the grace of God is this work of the Holy Spirit in cleansing the innermost nature, and then taking complete possession of our cleansed temple and filling it with His holy being, His love, and His power (1 Cor. 3:16).

In one sense, your body is the temple of the Holy Spirit (1 Cor. 6:19), for the body is indwelt by your personality, your spirit nature. Actually, God's Spirit does not indwell your flesh and bones but indwells your spirit, which of course inhabits your body as a part of your total personality. As the Jewish temple had a holy place, so you are to keep your body pure. There was also an inner room of the temple called the Most Holy Place, where the Holy Spirit resided, as symbolized by God's Shekinah glory over the Ark of the Covenant. Even so, within your body your spirit resides, and God's Spirit lives in your spirit as the Shekinah indwelt the Most Holy Place.

The second major work of God's redemptive grace in us may be called entire sanctification, for that is the basis of all the Holy Spirit does at this time--He cleanses completely. Thus the first work of grace is often called justification, or the forgiveness of sins, for that is the basis of all that God does in the new birth. Or instead of entire sanctification, the second major crisis experience may be called the fullness of the Spirit, since all the cleansing and the infilling and the empowering is done by the Holy Spirit. When He cleanses away the extraneous hindrances, He can now fill you completely.

The Spirit then makes and keeps you holy as you live for God and walk obediently in His light (1 John 1:7). Holiness is not a substance which you receive. It is a quality of the Holy Spirit's nature which He imparts to you as He fills you. Holiness is not an "it" which God gives you. It is a spiritual state of your nature which results from the Spirit's filling you. It is not merely cleansing from sin (the negative aspect). It is all the Spirit's presence, power, and fruit filling you (the positive aspect). See Gal. 5:22-23.

36

TERMINOLOGY FOR
ENTIRE SANCTIFICATION

All human languages are inadequate to express spiritual realities. When we attempt to fully describe God and His wonderful holy being fully we have to use many words. All of these help us understand God better by describing some different aspect of His being. For example, we speak of God's grace, mercy, goodness, love, and compassion. Each word adds some depth of meaning, but there is also overlapping. God's love includes God's compassion, mercy, and goodness. God's goodness includes God's love, mercy, and compassion. Yet each of these terms helps us understand God better. Each adds its own special meaning.

But not one of these is a material substance. God is not a mixture of these or a compound of these. God is a glorious personal being, who is infinite and perfect in all of these. We define love from what God is. God is a Being who loves. We define goodness from what God is. He is a being who is infinitely good. We learn the meaning of all these terms as we see Jesus.

The realm of spirit can never be perfectly understood by terms, word pictures, and illustrations taken from the physical and material realm. Yet we live in a material world and have a physical body. Hence, to describe spiritual realities, such as sin and salvation, we have to use a variety of words, each of which adds to our understanding.

TERMS FOR ENTIRE SANCTIFICATION. The following terms are Bible descriptions of that second major work of God's grace in which our spirit is cleansed from the sinful nature which remains in the believer even after the new birth, and in which we are filled by the Spirit's presence and power.

1. *Sanctify, sanctification.*

   John 17:17-19--"Sanctify them by the truth; your word is truth. . . . for them I sanctify myself, that they too may be truly sanctified." (Since Jesus had no sinful nature, He needed no cleansing, and for Him sanctification was only setting himself apart and submitting himself to God's will. For us it must necessarily include a moral cleansing.)

   1 Thessalonians 5:23-24--"May God himself, the God of peace, sanctify you through and through. May your whole spirit, soul, and body be kept blameless. . . . The one who calls you is faithful and he will do it."

   Note also: Acts 20:32; 1 Thess. 4:3; Heb. 10:10; 13:12.

2. *Holiness, holy.*

   Luke 1:74-75--"To enable us to serve him without fear in holiness and righteousness before him all our days."

   Hebrews 12:14--"Make every effort to live in peace with all men and to be holy; without holiness no one will see the Lord."

   Note also 2 Cor. 7:1; Eph. 4:24; 1 Thess. 4:7; 1 Peter 1:15-16.

3. *Clean heart.*

   Psalm 51:7--"Cleanse me with hyssop, and I will be clean; wash me and I will be whiter than snow." (Hyssop was used in applying the blood of the sacrifice.) In Psalm 51:10 and 73:1 the Hebrew can be translated either clean heart or pure heart. Note also: Ezek. 36:25.

4. *Pure heart.*

   Psalm 24:3-4--"Who may stand in his holy place? He who has clean hands and a pure heart." (Clean hands point to freedom from external sins through Christ's forgiveness, and a pure heart refers to cleansing of the sinful nature.) Note also: Matt. 5:8; Acts 15:9; 1 Peter 1:22.

5. *Baptized with the Holy Spirit.*

   Mark 1:8--"He will baptize you with the Holy Spirit." Note also: John 1:33; Acts 1:5; 11:16.

Perhaps it is wise at this point to clarify that the term "baptism" is used in two senses in relation to the Holy Spirit. At the moment of the new birth every Christian receives the Holy Spirit. If anyone does not have the Spirit of Christ he does not belong to Christ (Rom. 8:9). At that same moment the Spirit baptizes each into the body of Christ--the true Church consisting of those whose sins are forgiven (1 Cor. 12:13). So you are a member of Christ's true Church the moment you are born again, even though you may not become the member of a local church on earth until later. This baptism by the Holy Spirit inducts us into the Church. It is not the baptism John promised. John foretold the baptism Christ gives.

John promised the baptism which Christ would give. Christ baptizes with the Holy Spirit (Mark 1:8). God the Father told John that the one on whom the Holy Spirit descended at the time of His baptism was the one who would baptize with the Holy Spirit (John 1:33). Jesus promised His disciples that He would baptize them with the Holy Spirit (Acts 11:16). This is what happened at the Day of Pentecost (Acts 1:5), though it was described in Acts 2:4 as their being filled with the Holy Spirit. Filling with the Spirit and being baptized with the Holy Spirit are two terms for the same experience. Furthermore, Peter refers to this same moment or experience as being purified by faith (Acts 15:9). So one major result of the baptism with the Spirit or the filling with the Spirit is being purified or sanctified in heart. This is further emphasized by the expression in Matthew 3:11--"He will baptize you with the Holy Spirit and with fire," the fire emphasizing the cleansing.

The Holy Spirit baptizes the sinner at the moment of his conversion into the body of Christ (1 Cor. 12:13). In a completely different experience, Christ baptizes the born-again believer with the Holy Spirit, purifying and filling the believer. It is this experience which is called "the" promise of the Father (Luke 24:49; Acts 1:4)-- the great promise for the Church. It is also called "the" gift of the Spirit from God (Acts 2:38; 10:45; 11:17). This is to distinguish it from the plural "gifts of the Spirit" which the Holy Spirit gives to believers whenever He sees fit (Rom. 12:6; 1 Cor. 12-14; Heb. 2:4).

"The" gift of the Spirit is the same as "the" promise of the Father, which is the purification of the heart by the sanctifying, baptizing, infilling of the Holy Spirit.

6. *Baptized with the Holy Spirit and with fire.* Matthew 3:11. (Fire symbolizes the cleansing, purifying work of the Spirit. Compare Isa. 6:1-7.)

7. *Filled with the Holy Spirit.* Note: Acts 2:4; 6:5; 9:17; 11:24.

8. *Fullness.* Note: Rom. 15:29; Eph. 3:19; 4:13; Col. 2:10.

9. *Circumcision of the heart.* Deut. 30:6. (An unsanctified nature prevents us from loving God in such totality.) Note also: Col. 2:11.

10. *Perfection.* Note: Gen. 17:1; Matt. 5:48; 2 Cor. 13:9; Col. 1:28.

11. *Perfect love.*

> 1 John 4:17-18--"Love is made complete (Greek can also be translated perfect) among us so that we will have confidence on the day of judgment, because in this world we are like him. There is no fear in love. But perfect love drives out fear. . . . The one who fears is not made perfect in love."

12. *Crucified.* Note: Rom. 6:6; Gal. 2:20; 6:14.

13. *Saved completely.* Heb. 7:25. (Greek: wholly, to the uttermost).

14. *Rest.* Note: Heb. 4:1, 3, 9, 11.

Other names, although not found in the Bible, have been used also to describe this second major work of God's grace in the heart of the Christian: the higher life, the deeper life, the quiet life, the rest of faith, the life of absolute surrender, the victorious life, the second blessing, the fullness of power, Christian perfection. The important thing is not the name, but that you know in your own spiritual experience the wonderful reality of this cleansing, filling, empowering work of the Holy Spirit.

DISTINCTIONS IN THE TWO WORKS OF GOD'S GRACE.

The following comparisons may prove helpful in understanding more fully the differences in the new birth and in entire sanctification by the infilling of the Holy Spirit.

In the First Work (New Birth)	In the Second Work (Entire Sanctification)
1. The birth of the Spirit (John 3:5)	1. The baptism of the Spirit (Acts 1:5)
2. Pardon (Matt. 9:6)	2. Purity (Acts 15:8-9)
3. Regeneration, i.e., new life (Titus 3:5)	3. Crucifixion, i.e., death of sinful self (Gal. 2:20)
4. Justification for sinners (Acts 13:39)	4. Sanctification for born-again Christians (John 17; Acts 20:32; 2 Tim. 2:21)
5. Guilt of sin removed (Ps. 103:12)	5. Pollution of sin removed (2 Cor. 7:1)
6. Right to heaven obtained (John 1:12; Rev. 21:27)	6. Fitness for heaven obtained (Heb. 12:14)
7. Adoption, as child of God (Gal. 4:5; Eph. 1:5)	7. Anointing for service (1 Cor. 1:21-22; 1 John 2:20) (Available for all believers but mainly for the Spirit-filled)
8. Restoration to the favor of God (Eph. 2:12-13)	8. Restoration to holiness (the moral image of God) (2 Cor. 3:17-18; Eph. 4:24)
9. Preceded by repentance and faith (Mark 1:5)	9. Preceded by consecration and faith (Rom. 12:1)
10. Freedom from committed sins (in plural) (Eph. 1:7; Rev. 1:5)	10. Cleansing from sin nature (sin in singular) (Rom. 6:6; 1 John 1:7)
11. Death and destruction of personal sins (Rom. 8:13; Col. 3:5-6)	11. Death and destruction of sin nature (Rom. 6:6)
12. Change from darkness to light (Eph. 5:8; 1 Peter 2:9)	12. Change from Spirit's indwelling presence to indwelling fullness (Acts 2:4; 6:3; 9:17; 11:24; Col. 2:10)

13. Peace with God and people (Rom. 5:1; Heb. 12:14)

13. Inner rest of soul from strivings of self (Heb. 4:1, 11)

14. Symbolized by clean hands (outward cleansing) (Ps. 24:8; James 4:8)

14. Called a pure heart (Ps. 24:8; James 4:8; Acts 15:8-9)

15. Compared with cleansing by water, i.e., for externals-- words, deeds (Titus 3:5)

15. Compared with purifying by fire i.e., for inner nature (Ps. 24:4; James 4:8; Acts 15:8-9)

16. Creation of what did not exist--spiritual life (2 Cor. 5:17)

16. Perfection of what was received through new birth (Matt. 5:48; Heb. 6:1-2; 1 John 4:17-18)

17. Forgiveness through Christ's blood (Matt. 26:28; Heb. 9:22)

17. Cleansing through Christ's blood (Heb. 13:12; 1 John 1:7)

Thus, there is clearly a continuity of the salvation which Christ begins in the new birth and makes complete in entire sanctification. Yet there is a special and separate role for each. Each is complete in itself--forgiveness is a total and complete forgiveness; cleansing of the sin nature and the receiving of the fullness of the Spirit is a complete work of God's grace in itself. As we shall see, both are clearly pictured in God's Word.

Could not God have done both at the same time at the moment of the new birth? It is not for us to state what God can or cannot do. It is the clear testimony of the Church over the centuries and the repeated experience of God's children that there remains a sinful nature in believers even after the Spirit has transformed them in the new birth, and after receiving a clear witness of the Spirit that they are now a child of God. But there is also a clear testimony in multitudes of Christians that God brought them to a second moment of spiritual crisis when God did a deeper, fuller work of cleansing and empowering, just as the Bible teaches.

37

BIBLE EXAMPLES OF A
SECOND CRISIS EXPERIENCE

The twofold work of the Holy Spirit is taught and illustrated in the Bible. Regeneration, the imparting of spiritual life in the new birth, is a definite and knowable work of the Spirit available to whoever will accept God's invitation (Matt. 11:28; Rev. 22:17) and provision of salvation (John 3:5-6, 8; Titus 3:5).

Entire sanctification through the infilling of the Holy Spirit is also a definite and knowable work of the Spirit available to every born-again child of God (Acts 2:29-30; 2 Thess. 2:13; 2 Peter 1:2). The book of Acts gives five examples of this.

THE APOSTLES AND DISCIPLES. The whole trend of the Gospels is a witness that Christ's disciples--both the apostles and others, including a number of women--were truly saved. We know this from Jesus' own testimony and words.

1. Jesus repeatedly called God their Father, especially during the Sermon on the Mount, two years before the Cross.

2. Jesus called them the salt of the earth (Matt. 5:13).

3. Jesus called them the light of the world (Matt. 5:14).

4. Jesus sent them out and gave them authority to preach, heal, and cast out demons (Matt. 10:1).

5. Jesus said whoever received them received Him (Matt. 10:40).

6. Jesus testified that they were doing the Father's will (Matt. 12:49-50).

7. Jesus said their names were written in heaven (Luke 10:20).

8. Jesus said the Holy Spirit was with them (John 14:17). (In the high priestly prayer of Jesus for His apostles in the Upper Room, Jesus gave clear testimony about them to the Father. He prayed for their sanctification--which they had not yet received. However, they were clearly born again and thus were eligible to be sanctified.)

9. They had obeyed God's Word (John 17:6).

10. They had accepted Christ's Word (John 17:8).

11. They had believed (John 17:8).

12. They were a distinct group from the "world," i.e., the unsaved (John 17:9, 23; 15:19).

13. Christ was glorified in them (John 17:10).

14. They were God's and Christ's (John 17:9-10).

15. They were given to Christ by God and now needed to be kept, rather than to be forgiven or born again (John 17:6, 11-12, 24).

16. They had been kept by Christ (John 17:12).

17. Only one of the Twelve (Judas) was in an unsaved or lost condition (John 17:12).

18. They were not "of the world" (John 17:14, 16).

19. They had received Christ's glory (John 17:22).

20. Christ entrusted to them the ministry of making His forgiveness available (John 20:23).

However, the apostles were not sanctified. Hence, Christ prayed for this (John 17:17, 19), promised a second crisis experience (Luke 24:49; Acts 1:5, 8), and commanded them to receive it (Luke 24:49; Acts 1:4). It is recorded in Acts 2:4 that they received this experience, and it is said to be the fulfillment of Christ's promise, "Exalted to the right hand of God, He has received from the Father the promised Holy Spirit and has poured out what you now see and hear" (Acts 2:33).

This second experience is said to be for all believers down to our day, not just for the apostles (Acts 2:38-39). It is interpreted by the Bible to be the fiery baptism of the Holy Spirit which was promised (11:15-17), and the result is said to be a purified heart (15:8-9).

THE APOSTLE PAUL. Saul (later called Paul after his conversion) was a fanatical opponent of the Church. He started to Damascus to persecute the church there. He was angry against Christ and had rebellion in his heart. Probably he was struggling in his heart with deep conviction from the Holy Spirit and could not forget the radiant face (Acts 6:15) and victorious, Christlike spirit and words of Stephen (7:55-60). What took place when the Holy Spirit struck him down on the Damascus road?

Jesus proved to Saul that He was the Sovereign God by striking him to the ground and blinding him by the intense light of His glory. The Holy Spirit used this to convict Saul deeply. So overwhelming was the experience that Saul knew it was God dealing with him. When asked, "Why do you persecute me?", Saul asked in amazement, "Who are you, Lord?" "I am Jesus," came the answer.

The proof that Paul became born again immediately there on the Damascus road is clear:

1. He was instantly so convicted that he was humble and ready to obey Jesus.

2. As soon as Paul knew it was Jesus, he called Him, " Lord" (Acts 22:10).

3. Jesus commanded him to stand on his feet after Saul called Him, "Lord" (i.e., accepted Jesus immediately as his Lord) (Acts 22:10). This symbolized that he was now a converted person eligible for Jesus to use.

4. Jesus specifically told him He had an assignment for him (Acts 22:10). Jesus would not have told him he had an assignment if he had not already been transformed by saving grace.

5. Jesus told Ananias that Saul "is my chosen instrument" (not "will become my chosen instrument after his conversion").

6. Jesus testified to Ananias that Saul was praying. Prayer was instantly a major characteristic of Paul's life, as it was throughout the rest of his ministry.

7. Ananias recognized Jesus' testimony to Saul's salvation by calling Saul "Brother Saul" (Acts 9:17), and placing his hands on Saul's head (obviously Saul was praying when Ananias found him).

8. Ananias told Saul, "Jesus . . . sent me so that you may . . . be filled with the Spirit" (Acts 9:17). Saul was healed instantly and obviously was filled instantly with the Spirit, for the Holy Spirit was tremendously at work in Saul's life from then on.

Paul immediately began to preach with God's power resting on him. Repeatedly in his epistles he refers to the presence of the Spirit in his ministry. Paul testified to the "fullness" which abided in him (Rom. 15:29), i.e., the fullness of the Spirit. Acts 13:9 asserts that Paul was filled with the Spirit. Paul wanted others to receive this experience of the Spirit (Acts 19:2) and commanded his converts, "Be filled with the Spirit" (Eph. 5:18).

THE SAMARITAN CHURCH. Philip went to Samaria and preached, healed the sick, and cast out demons. There was a mighty revival, and so many were converted that the Bible describes it, "Samaria had accepted the word of God" (Acts 8:14). The apostles in Jerusalem immediately sent the two leaders of their group, Peter and John, to Samaria. What was the spiritual condition of these Samaritan converts?

Note: 1. They all paid close attention (Acts 8:6). 2. They believed (v. 12). 3. They accepted the Word of God (v. 14). 4. They received great joy (obviously spiritual joy) (v. 8). 5. They were baptized in the name of Jesus (vv. 12, 16). This proves that Philip believed they had been born again.

Peter and John praised God for the revival, but they realized that the converts needed to be filled with the Holy Spirit to establish them in victorious Christian living. They believed that all believers should be Spirit-filled. As soon as Peter and John arrived, they prayed for the new believers to be filled with the Spirit. They did receive this experience, just as the 120 had at Pentecost (Acts 8:17) as a second definite experience.

THE ROMANS AT CAESAREA. This is the first account of Gentiles being saved. It obviously was very significant to God and He prepared Peter by a vision repeated three times. It was important to the early church, for they investigated carefully Peter's actions on this trip. This was the opening of the door of the Gospel to the Gentiles.

God worked through Cornelius, a Roman officer, and his friends, who were probably fellow officers or soldiers. The Roman army was composed of soldiers from many nations within the Roman Empire.

What was the spiritual condition of Cornelius and his family? They were clearly accepted by God as His children; they were born again.

1. He and all his family were devout. His life and witness had influenced his family and probably his soldiers, who served in his household in typical military fashion (Acts 10:2).

2. He and his family were God-fearing. This technical term indicates that in spite of being Gentiles they went to the synagogue regularly to worship Jehovah. This proved they had real commitment to God regardless of what the army officers thought.

3. The Bible testifies to his prayer life, including his prayer habits at home (Acts 10:2, 4, 30, 31). In the vision God gave him, the angel told him God was listening to his prayer and observing his generous gifts to the poor.

4. He was so righteous that the public recognized it (Acts 10:22), and Peter testified he recognized God had accepted Cornelius (v. 35).

While Peter was still preaching, before he could even pray with Cornelius, the Holy Spirit "came on them" (Acts 10:44). The Bible says "the gift of the Holy Spirit" was "poured out" on them (v. 45).

Peter later testified that they had received the identical infilling of the Spirit the 120 had received at Pentecost (Acts 15:8). The main result of this outpouring of the Spirit, said Peter, was this: God "made no distinction between us and them, for he purified their hearts by faith" (v. 9).

THE GREEKS AT EPHESUS. Here is another example of great importance. Not only is it an example of how the infilling of the Spirit is a second experience, but also of how Paul and the early church put priority on all believers receiving the fullness of the Spirit. The apostles sent Peter and John to Samaria as soon as God sent revival there, to be sure the new converts were also filled with the Spirit. Even so, Paul's first question when he found the new converts at Ephesus was, "Did you receive the Holy Spirit?" (Acts 19:2).

That the Ephesian group was truly born again is proved by:

1. They were disciples (Acts 19:1). This term was used by Paul and the early church only for true believers.

2. They had repented and been baptized (v. 4). Had they not received the new birth, Paul would have begun to preach repentance and faith in Christ for the forgiveness of their sins. Paul's spiritual concern was that since they were believers--disciples--they also be filled with the Spirit in a second crisis experience.

When Paul prayed for them, the Holy Spirit came on them. Thus, we see four examples after Pentecost of other people receiving the same sanctifying, heart-purifying, infilling of the Holy Spirit after having received the new birth. This was in fulfillment of God's promise as proclaimed by Peter at Pentecost (Acts 2:38-39). The Gospel and the sanctifying infilling of the Spirit had now reached the three main civilizations of that day--the Jews, the Romans, and the Greeks.

The promise was fulfilled in wider and wider circles: (a) Paul, the former Pharisee, (b) the Samaritans, (c) the Romans, and (d) the Greeks. Peter's testimony would be applicable to all four situations: God "made no distinction between us and them, for he purified their hearts by faith." This experience of heart purity, entire sanctification, the baptism of the Holy Spirit, or the infilling of the Holy Spirit-- whatever term you choose to use--is not just for the apostles. It is, as Peter said, "For you and your children and all who are far off (even to our century)--for all whom the Lord our God will call" (Acts 2:39).

38

HEART PURITY--
GOD'S WILL FOR US

Though all evangelical Christians agree that the sinful nature remains in the heart of the believer after the new birth, many have not realized that it is God's good will for us to be cleansed from the sinful nature. They have not realized that the Spirit will purify our hearts through our faith by the experience of entire sanctification, or the fullness of the Spirit.

A. HEART PURITY IS PROBABLE AND BIBLICALLY LOGICAL

1. *If God is holy, He will require us to have pure hearts* in order to be holy as He is holy. If He fills our hearts with Himself, surely He will not permit sin to coexist with His fullness. He can permit no unholy one to live in heaven (Rev. 20:6; 21:27), but Christ is preparing heaven for us. He will surely require us to be holy.

2. *If God is holy, He will desire us to be holy.* He is served by holy angels. He lives in a holy heaven. He desires even closer fellowship with us than with the angels since He has made us His children. He loves us too much not to provide a salvation by which we can be made holy as He is holy.

3. *If God is omnipotent, He is able to purify our hearts.* If God is our Creator and is all powerful, He has adequate power to cleanse our heart. If God is God, He is greater than the power of sin and can cleanse from all sin.

4. *If God is omniscient, He will know how to purify our hearts from sin.* Satan is not wiser than God. Satan cannot cause a problem for which God has no answer. God can purify us from any

defilement from Satan. God knows how to accomplish His holy will in us through the atonement He provided in Christ.

5. *If God is perfect, He will not provide an incomplete salvation.* He will not plan a salvation which saves from the guilt of sin but not from its power. He will not leave a sinful nature in us without providing salvation from it. If He is perfect, He will not permit the Holy Spirit to give us a longing for salvation from the sin nature but make no provision to meet that longing and our need. If He is perfect, He will not command us to be holy if it is impossible for us to be holy.

6. *If God is just, He will make the same provision of grace for whoever will.* He will not provide a cleansing, infilling of the Spirit for the apostles or prophets or the early church and not provide the same blessed experience for you and me. Since God requires holiness, He cannot be just unless He provides the way for anyone to be made holy.

7. *Since God is all this, He is sure to make heart purity possible.* God is holy, and He longs for us to be holy. He has all power and all wisdom. He is perfect and just. He is sure to make an adequate salvation available according to His essential conditions. The blood of Christ will be able to cleanse from all sin if it is able to cleanse from any sin. If this is not true, the whole message of the Bible is insincere and our condition is helpless and hopeless.

B. GOD COMMANDS HEART PURITY

Leviticus 11:44--"I am the Lord your God; consecrate yourselves and be holy; because I am holy."

Leviticus 19:2--"Be holy because I, the Lord your God, am holy."

Deuteronomy 6:5--"Love the Lord your God with all your heart and with all your soul and with all your strength." See Luke 10:27.

Matthew 5:48--"Be perfect, therefore, as your heavenly Father is perfect."

Hebrews 12:14--"Be holy; without holiness no one will see the Lord."

1 Peter 1:15-16--"As he who called you is holy, so be holy in all you do; for it is written: 'Be holy, because I am holy.'"

God would not command the impossible. If God commands us to be holy, it is proof we can be holy.

C. GOD PROMISES HEART PURITY

Deuteronomy 30:6--"The Lord your God will circumcise your heart. . . . so that you may love him with all your heart and with all your soul."

Ezekiel 36:25-29--"I will cleanse you from all your impurities. . . . I will remove from you your heart of stone and give you a heart of flesh. And I will put a new spirit in you and move you to follow my decrees. . . .I will save you from all your uncleanness."

Matthew 5:6--"Blessed are those who hunger and thirst for righteousness, for they will be filled." (A new-born soul instinctively longs for holiness of heart.)

Acts 2:38-39--"You will receive the gift of the Holy Spirit. The promise is for you and your children and for all who are far off--for all whom the Lord our God will call." (This was the promise of the Father (Luke 24:49), the enduement of power (Luke 24:49; Acts 1:8), the filling of the Holy Spirit (Acts 2:4), or the baptism with the Holy Spirit and fire (Matt. 3:11).)

1 Thessalonians 5:23-24--"The God of peace, sanctify you through and through. . . . The one who calls you is faithful and he will do it."

D. GOD WILLS HEART PURITY

1 Thessalonians 4:3--"It is God's will that you should be holy."

2 Thessalonians 2:13--"From the beginning God chose you to be saved through the sanctifying work of the Spirit."

Ephesians 1:4--"He chose us . . . to be holy and blameless in his sight."

Hebrews 10:10--"By that will, we have been made holy through the sacrifice of the body of Jesus Christ once for all."

E. GOD CALLS US TO HEART PURITY

1 Thessalonians 4:7-8--"God did not call us to be impure, but to live a holy life. Therefore, he who rejects . . . does not reject man but God, who gives you his Holy Spirit."

1 Thessalonians 5:23-24--"The God of peace, sanctify you through and through. . . . The one who calls you is faithful and he will do it."

F. CHRIST DIED FOR OUR HEART PURITY

Ephesians 5:25-27--"Christ loved the church and gave himself up for her to make her holy, cleansing her . . . to present her to himself as a radiant church, without stain or wrinkle or any other blemish, but holy and blameless."

Colossians 1:21-22--"He has reconciled you by Christ's physical body through death to present you holy in his sight, without blemish and free from accusation."

Titus 2:14--"Who gave himself for us to redeem us from all wickedness and to purify for himself a people that are his very own."

Hebrews 13:12--"Jesus also suffered outside the city gate to make the people holy through his own blood."

1 John 1:7--"The blood of Jesus, his Son, purifies us from all sin."

G. INSPIRED MEN PRAYED THAT THE BELIEVERS MIGHT RECEIVE HEART PURITY

John 17:17--"Sanctify them."

John 17:20--"My prayer is not for those alone. . . . I pray also for those who will believe in me through their message."

Ephesians 3:14-19--"For this reason I kneel . . . that you might be filled to the measure of all the fullness of God."

Colossians 4:12--"Epaphras . . . always wrestling in prayer for you, that you may stand firm in all the will of God, mature" (NASB, perfect).

1 Thessalonians 5:23--"The God of peace sanctify you through and through."

1 Peter 5:10--"The God of all grace . . . make you strong, firm and steadfast" (NASB, perfect).

(If God did not want to answer these prayers, He would not have inspired the Bible writers to record them.)

H. THE BIBLE EXHORTS US TO OBTAIN HEART PURITY AND LIVE A HOLY LIFE

Romans 12:1--"Therefore, I urge you, brothers, in view of God's mercy, to offer your bodies as living sacrifices, holy and pleasing to God-- which is your spiritual worship."

2 Corinthians 7:1--"Since we have these promises, dear friends, let us purify ourselves from everything that contaminates body and spirit, perfecting holiness out of reverence for God."

James 1:4--"Perseverance must finish its work so that you may be mature and complete" (Greek also means perfect).

James 4:8--"Purify your hearts, you double-minded."

2 Peter 3:11--"What kind of people ought you to be? You ought to live holy and godly lives."

I. THE BIBLE GIVES EXAMPLES OF PEOPLE PRAYING FOR HEART PURITY

Psalm 51:2, 7--"Wash away all my iniquity and cleanse me from my sin. . . . Cleanse me with hyssop, and I will be clean; wash me, and I will be whiter than snow."

Psalm 51:10--"Create in me a clean heart, O God."

J. THE BIBLE GIVES EXAMPLES OF PEOPLE WHO WERE PURE

Genesis 6:9--"Noah was a righteous man, blameless (Hebrew: perfect) among the people of his time, and he walked with God."

Acts 2:4--"All of them were filled with the Holy Spirit."

Acts 11:24--"He was a good man (Barnabas), full of the Holy Spirit."

Romans 6:6--"We know that our old self was crucified with him so that the body of sin might be rendered powerless." (Do you know that your old self is crucified?)

Romans 15:19--"I know that . . . I will come in the full measure of the blessing of Christ."

Galatians 2:20--"I have been crucified with Christ and I no longer live, but Christ lives in me."

Galatians 6:14--"The cross of our Lord Jesus Christ, through which the world has been crucified to me, and I to the world."

Philippians 3:15--"All of us who are mature should take such a view of things" (Paul).

1 Thessalonians 2:10--"You are witnesses, and so is God, of how holy, righteous and blameless we were among you who believed."

1 John 4:17--"Love is made complete (Greek: perfect) . . . because in this world we are like him."

K. HEART PURITY IS THE OBJECT OF ALL GOD'S DEALINGS WITH US

1. *The object of Christ's mediatorial work.*

    Luke 1:74-75--"To enable us to serve him without fear in holiness and righteousness before him all our days."

    Ephesians 5:25-27--"Christ loved the church and gave himself up for her to make her holy, cleansing her . . . to present her to himself as a radiant church, without stain or wrinkle or any other blemish, but holy and blameless."

    Titus 2:14--"Who gave himself for us to redeem us from all wickedness and to purify for himself a people that are his very own."

    1 John 3:8--"The reason the Son of God appeared was to destroy the devil's work."

2. *The object of the giving of divine promises.*

    2 Peter 1:4--"Through these he has given us his very great and precious promises, so that through them you may participate in the divine nature" (His is a holy nature).

3. *The object of the institution of the Christian ministry.*

    Ephesians 4:11-13--". . . He who gave some to be apostles, some to be evangelists, and some to be pastors and teachers, to prepare God's people for works of service, so that the body of Christ may be built up until we all reach unity in the faith and in the knowledge of the Son of God and become mature, attaining to the whole measure of the fullness of Christ."

    Colossians 1:28--"We proclaim him . . . so that we may present everyone perfect in Christ."

L. THE NECESSITY OF A PURE HEART

1. *It is necessary because God is holy.* 1 Peter 1:15-16.
2. *It is necessary because Christ died to make us holy.* Titus 2:14; Heb. 13:12. We dishonor Christ's blood if we disregard it.
3. *It is necessary because God commands it.* See B.
4. *It is necessary if we would live a holy life.* Matt. 7:18. Our lives tend to be what our hearts are.
5. *It is necessary to fulfill Christ's purpose for us.* We can never be fruitful as we should, witness as we should, or glorify God as we should without it.

   1 Peter 2:9--"You are . . . a holy nation . . . that you may declare the praises of him who called you."

   John 15:2--"He cuts off every branch in me that bears no fruit, while every branch that does bear fruit he trims clean so that it will be even more fruitful."

   Acts 1:8--"You will receive power when the Holy Spirit comes on you; and you will be my witnesses."

   2 Timothy 2:21--"If a man cleanses himself from the latter, he will be an instrument for noble purposes, made holy, useful to the Master and prepared to do any good work."

6. *It is necessary to enter heaven.*

   Matthew 5:8--"Blessed are the pure in heart, for they will see God."

   Hebrews 12:14--"Be holy . . . without holiness no one will see the Lord."

   Revelation 20:6--"Blessed and holy are those who have part in the first resurrection."

   Revelation 21:27--"Nothing impure will ever enter it, nor will anyone who does what is shameful or deceitful."

39

THE NATURE OF
ENTIRE SANCTIFICATION

To be cleansed and filled with the Spirit, to be clothed with power from on high, and to be sanctified through and through is a God-given new experience to the born-again Christian. It is more than being merely interested in spiritual things, more than faithfulness in prayer and the reading of God's Word. It is more than avoiding willful yielding to temptation.

Every Christian should live a life of separation from sins in all their external forms. The outer life of the born-again Christian who has not been Spirit-filled should be just as holy as that of an entirely sanctified person. It is in the inner life, unseen by others, that the cleansing, the fullness, and the empowering of the Spirit are realized. The newness in a person who has been crucified with Christ and sanctified through and through is an inner newness of love, cleansing, victory, and power.

A. IT IS A KNOWABLE, DEFINITE EXPERIENCE

The sanctifying infilling of the Spirit is a definite, knowable transforming work of the Holy Spirit in the life of the believer. God wants us to know and understand what He has done for us and in us (1 Cor. 2:12). It is the special work of the Spirit to give us a clear witness, a full assurance as to our spiritual state in God's sight.

The Spirit uses our whole personality--our mind, our conscience, our memory, and our emotions--to convict us of our sins. But when we repent of our sins and trust God for the forgiveness of our sins, we know that God has heard our prayer. We know our sins are forgiven, the guilt is removed, the burden of sins is gone, peace has come, spiritual darkness has changed to spiritual light, and we have new life in Christ. Know it? Of course we know it!

Similarly, when a Christian experiences the sanctifying, infilling of the Holy Spirit, it is real and testified to by the same Holy Spirit. The Spirit makes us aware of an inner cleanness. Whatever the form of defilement of our hearts before, it is now cleansed away. Sinful pride is cleansed away, and it becomes spiritually natural to be humble. Sinful stubbornness and willfulness is cleansed away, and it becomes spiritually natural to have yieldedness, and to be eager to obey God. Again and again in prayer, in testimony, in loving service the person becomes aware of an inner power of God.

"I did not know the Christian life could be like this," "I did not know this is what is meant by the Spirit-filled life"--these are the kinds of new awareness and testimonies in the heart of the believer when he has been entirely sanctified. It is when strong temptation or strong provocation comes that the Spirit-filled person suddenly recognizes the blessed reality--"Why I don't feel that inner reaction, that sinfulness waiting to express itself through me! The Spirit keeps me pure within!"

B. IT IS AN INSTANTANEOUS WORK OF THE SPIRIT

There is an instant difference between the before and the after, the time when the Spirit was present but had not filled your soul, and the time when you became aware that He had filled you by God's grace and power. Spiritual growth is God's gracious privilege for the Christian. This is more than growth. There comes a moment when the Christian has totally surrendered self, self-will, possessions, the future, and all--surrendered totally to God and by faith claimed God's promise. In that instant the Holy Spirit fills with His cleansing and power.

1. *Christ's prayer was instantly fulfilled.* Christ prayed that His apostles might be sanctified, and at Pentecost this was suddenly and instantly fulfilled (Acts 2:1-6). Before this they were cowardly and fearful. They all forsook Jesus at the Cross. They hid behind closed doors. Now, instantly, they were empowered by the Spirit.

Immediately they were bold witnesses to the Jerusalem people. Before this they were jealous of each other, arguing who was the greatest. Now, instantly, they were cleansed, and we never see that envy or argument about who is greatest again.

James and John, the sons of thunder, had been ready to call fire down from heaven and destroy the opposing Samaritans (Luke 9:54). Now instantly, God's holy love purified their hearts by faith, and you never see that defensive anger and spirit of revenge again. Before long God sent a revival to Samaria and John went to pray for them, that they too be cleansed and filled with the Spirit. The son of thunder was now the apostle of love.

Something happened that moment in the Upper Room when that Shekinah glory of God which Israel had once known came down and visibly touched each of the praying, waiting, believing disciples, and all of them that moment were filled with the Spirit. The essential thing that happened at Pentecost was that their hearts were purified by faith (Acts 15:8-9). The other things were outward evidences to call attention to God's power and to inaugurate this new dispensation of the Holy Spirit.

The sound of the mighty rushing wind has been only heard a few times in church history since that occasion. A visible presence of the Shekinah of God occasionally has been beautifully or faintly seen on the radiant faces of some of God's children, but this is not normal or necessary as an accompaniment of the fullness of the Spirit. The gift of tongues was repeated as an outward validation on the first occasion when the Romans were filled with the Spirit and when the Greeks were filled with the Spirit. It is not the normal accompaniment of the infilling of the Spirit today.

Gifts of the Spirit are for ministry, with different gifts to different people apportioned only as God wills. The new birth and the sanctifying infilling of the Spirit are for every believer, and their evidence is not external gifts but the fullness of the Spirit Himself as evidenced by His fruit in the life of the believer. The Spirit is the supreme witness Himself to the Christian. You need no special miracle gifts of the Spirit or outward signs to show you your spiritual condition. The Holy Spirit Himself is the witness to your soul. Please note Appendix C.

2. *Sanctification is by faith and hence it is instantaneous.* If sanctification were by works then you might expect people to gradually become more and more holy. Then bit by bit they would be made pure within. If sanctification were by growth in grace, then you could expect sanctification to be a life-long process.

But Scripture says they were purified by faith. The moment they met God's conditions of total consecration and surrender and by faith claimed the promise of the Father (Luke 24:49; Acts 2:33), they were instantly cleansed and filled.

We are justified by faith at the new birth in a moment of time (Rom. 5:1). At that moment our sins are forgiven. We have peace with God. We are made alive in Christ Jesus. It is instant and complete.

So also, sanctification is by faith (Acts 15:8-9; 26:16-18). At that moment we are sanctified through and through (1 Thess. 5:23), filled with the Spirit (Acts 2:4), baptized with the Spirit and with fire (Matt. 3:11), and clothed with power from on high (Luke 24:49).

Sanctification is not a gradual process. It is not a life-long growth. It is an instantaneous experience which the Holy Spirit gives in answer to our faith. We do not earn it or deserve it. It is by grace. It is by faith so that we receive it and then live in the freedom and fullness of that cleansing, infilling, and empowering. There should be growth as long as we are on earth walking in God's light. But entire sanctification is something completely different from growth. We will speak about progressive sanctification at a later point. The cleansing, infilling of the Holy Spirit, in a moment of entire sanctification, is a one-time experience.

3. *The New Testament Greek uses the aorist tense to describe this instantaneous experience.* The aorist tense describes an action as an event, as finished, completed. It is something that has happened, or a possible event, not a possible process. It indicates a point of time, a decisive action. It is a crisis that is completed, or can be used in a prayer for a decisive act that will be completed.

If the Greek refers to an act which will occur repeatedly, it uses the imperfect tense. If it refers to an act that occurs continuously, the present tense is used.

The aorist tense, for example, is used for the healing of the leper in Matthew 8:2-3, the healing of Peter's mother-in-law in Matthew 8:15, and the healing of the paralyzed man in Mark 2:4. In other words, the healings were completed, they were not in process.

This aorist tense of the verb is the tense the Holy Spirit chose to use to describe the sanctifying work in the soul. It is this tense Jesus used in praying for our sanctification (John 17:17), and it is used for the purifying by faith that took place at Pentecost and at the house of Cornelius (Acts 15:9). It is used for the crucifixion of our old self in Romans 6:6, for the cleansing of 2 Corinthians 7:1, for the "put off," "put on" and "created" in Ephesians 4:22-24, for "sanctify you through and through" in 1 Thessalonians 5:23, and in other such places. Entire sanctification is a decisive experience of the soul completed in one act of God at the moment of faith. It is a transforming experience that is available to the believer now.

4. *Bible commands and promises indicate you may obtain this experience now.* Zechariah, father of John the Baptist, prophesied that through Jesus you would be able to serve God in holiness and righteousness all your days (Luke 1:75). Ezekiel promised that God would take away your heart of stone, give you a heart of flesh, and put His Spirit within you, "move" you to follow His commands, and that this would accompany His cleansing work within you (Ezek. 36:25-27).

Paul exhorts you to experience it now (2 Cor. 7:1), prays that you receive it now and promises God will do it for you now (1 Thess. 5:23-24). The writer to the Hebrews commands you to experience holiness now before you see the Lord (Heb. 12:14). Peter reiterates God's command to be holy now (1 Peter 1:15-16), and John assures you if you walk in God's light you will have fellowship and cleansing now (1 John 1:7). So this is not a gradual process that is never complete till you get to heaven. It is a momentary act of God's Spirit available to you now.

5. *The sin nature is a condition of the human spirit and cannot be cleansed in parts.* Our whole nature is influenced by sin until it is cleansed by the Spirit. The Spirit does a complete work in whatever He does. Forgiveness is a forgiveness from all of your sins. Justification is a declaration that God makes you completely righteous and you have no condemnation. Adoption is a complete adoption. The cleansing from the depravity of your personal sins in initial sanctification at the time of the new birth is a complete cleansing. Now sanctification of your inner nature is a complete sanctification through and through (1 Thess. 5:23).

God does not cleanse you bit by bit. Your personality is a whole personality, and what God does in it He does the moment He does it. He does not deal with sins gradually or fill with the Holy Spirit gradually. He cleanses you completely and fills you with His Spirit completely. Of course once having been filled with the Spirit, you can be refilled again and again. This will be discussed later.

6. *Christians testify to receiving this experience at a definite time.* Christians use many different words as they testify to their inner experience. Yet Christian testimony and biography over the ages repeatedly tell of how God met this need of their soul for an inner cleansing and empowering at a definite point and time subsequent to their receiving Christ as Savior. This is always a transforming experience.

C. IT IS A SECOND WORK OF THE SPIRIT EXPERI-ENCED AFTER THE NEW BIRTH

God blesses the Christian's life with many touches of His grace and power. Spiritual growth should be continuous from the moment of your new birth until you reach heaven. However, you have two major moral needs to prepare you to live a victorious, holy life on earth and to prepare you to live in heaven: (1) you need the forgiveness of personal sins and to receive spiritual life in the new birth, and (2) you need the cleansing of the inherited sinful nature and the fullness of the Spirit in all God's grace and power. Of necessity, forgiveness must precede cleansing. New life must precede the Spirit's full possession and control.

1. *Sanctification is for the Christian--not for the sinner, for the church--not for the world.* When Jesus prayed His high priestly prayer for sanctification and unity of His followers, He specifically stated, "I am not praying for the world, but for those you have given me, for they are yours" (John 17:9). Jesus adds in verses 17 and 18 that He wants them to be sanctified, for they are His sent ones "into the world." The ones He sanctifies are already a separate group from the world (vv. 14-16).

Paul's exhortation, "Be filled with the Spirit" (Eph. 5:18), is obviously addressed to Christians, not to the unsaved. His prayer in 1 Thessalonians 5:23 was for the members of the church to be sanctified through and through, not for people of the world. Unsaved people must first come to Christ and receive Him as Savior.

2. *Logically, this must be a second experience.* The sinner is in no position to consecrate himself. He is in rebellion against God. He is under the death penalty (Rom. 6:23). He must cease his hostility to God and repent. Only after he is pardoned is he free to approach God for other purposes. Only after peace with God has been established through the new birth can he give himself in loving consecration and holy surrender to God. Such consecration is the essential preparation before the Spirit will sanctify. When the person makes this surrender to God, it must be as a living sacrifice (Rom. 12:1). He must be made spiritually alive in the first major work of the Spirit in his soul before he can take this step, giving himself totally to God.

3. *Psychologically, this must be a second experience.* The mind can take care of but one major issue at a time. The whole issue in the new birth is guilt and forgiveness. The sinner is under condemnation for sin. The issue in entire sanctification is completely different. The concern here is consecration based on the debt to Christ for the forgiveness and salvation already received, and love for Christ from a forgiven child of God.

The sinner cannot fully realize the sinfulness of his nature when he is practicing sin. It is condemnation for his committed sins which convicts him, so the sinner is unaware of the full sinfulness of his sinful nature. Only after he has been born of God is the Spirit able to reveal to him that there is an inner deeper need for purity. And the Spirit is not able to purify him until that person is born again and receives the Holy Spirit. Consecration is the act of a forgiven, transformed person who is now a child of God. The Holy Spirit now indwells him and is able to show him his inner need of cleansing from the sinful nature.

4. *There is no specific amount of time that must elapse between the first and second major works of the Spirit in your soul.* The natural response of your personality in the new birth is joy, peace, a sense of newness of life, and a desire to share this newfound reality with others. The natural reaction is rejoicing, witnessing, loving God, and loving others. The new birth is not simply an emotional experience, yet it is so profoundly transforming that there comes great emotional release and deep emotional response. In this deeply significant transformation with all its holy thrill, you are usually not aware of any further spiritual need or any inner sinfulness of nature.

Sooner or later, however, you realize that even though the new birth was a tremendously transforming experience that there are elements of unholiness and spiritual resistance which you at times sense within. By God's grace and the Spirit's help, you maintain victory over the sinful nature. But you begin to feel the Spirit's conviction over this residue of inner sinfulness.

Praise God, the Spirit is available to lead you immediately into a full surrender and God's sanctifying infilling of the Spirit if you will walk in the light (1 John 1:7). The time between the new birth and entire sanctification may be very brief, or it may be longer, according to how soon you sense your need and meet God's conditions of consecration and faith.

In the case of people who, before they are born of the Spirit, have been well taught in Scripture, including this doctrine, the time between the new birth and being filled with the Holy Spirit may be very brief. When this doctrine has not been understood or heard of before, it may take a longer time before the person fully recognizes his need and finds God's wonderful provision for this need.

40

THE RESULTS OF
ENTIRE SANCTIFICATION

Entire sanctification results in a new fullness of God's presence and work in the life of the believer. The Christian who has been walking in the light after the new birth is already manifesting a holy life outwardly. The awareness of the need for entire sanctification is an inner awareness. The primary results are in the inner nature. The Spirit gives inner cleansing, inner empowering, inner fullness of love, the fruit of the Spirit, and spiritual rest.

Naturally, as the Spirit multiplies these results in the inner nature those observing the Spirit-filled believer will be conscious of the abundance of the victory the Spirit gives and the overflowing of godliness in the person. Christlikeness will be ever more apparent. Spiritual radiance and effectiveness will be more constant. Thus often those who knew the Spirit-filled Christian best will notice the deeper, more Spirit-controlled dimension of spiritual life. Note some of these results:

A. ENTIRE SANCTIFICATION BRINGS CLEANSING

The first essential result of entire sanctification is the purifying of the heart from indwelling sin or inherited depravity. This work of purification is the basis of all else. The sinful nature must be cleansed from the heart. Webster's Third New International Dictionary (unabridged edition) defines sanctification:

1. Act of sanctifying or state of being sanctified; esp. Theol., the act or process of God's grace by which the affections of men are purified, or alienated from sin, and exalted to a supreme love to

God and righteousness; also the state of being thus purified. 2. Act of consecrating, 'consecration.'

In the Old Testament, "sanctify" was primarily used in relation to things and meant to be set apart to and for God. This use is also found in a few places in the New Testament. But in the New Testament the main concept is transformed into an ethical one, and sanctification becomes the making holy and pure of the character. The idea of consecration remains, but it is more than that--it is a consecration that leads to heart purity. The central emphasis for the Christian is the making holy of life by God's act within the soul.

Among the Greek terms used in the New Testament for sanctify are:

>   *katharizo*--to cleanse, to free from defilement
>   *ekkathairo*--to cleanse out thoroughly or purge
>   *luo*--to loose, free from, destroy
>   *stauroo*--to crucify with, utterly destroy the power of
>   *katargeo*--to abolish, cause to cease

These and other similar words clearly teach the putting to death of the sin nature, the destruction of the sin nature, the cleansing from the sin nature, the purifying from the sin nature. It is the cleansing of the soul from sin. If this is not the clear meaning of the New Testament then sanctification has no meaning.

Sanctification is accomplished by God's act after the Christian has met God's conditions. The meritorious or procuring cause is the blood of Christ (1 John 1:7; Heb. 13:12); the efficient cause or agency is the Holy Spirit (1 Peter 1:2; 2 Thess. 2:13); the instrumental cause is truth (John 17:17; 1 Peter 1:22); and the conditional cause is faith (Acts 15:9; 26:18).

Christ's wounds provide perfect healing from sin; His cross provides perfect destruction of sin; His blood provides perfect cleansing from sin. This is the negative aspect of sanctification which is basic to the positive aspect. Both the negative and the positive aspects are vital. It is a mistake to emphasize either without the other.

PURITY AND SPIRITUAL HEALTH. The purifying work of the Holy Spirit cleanses away the sinfulness of your nature, which always tended to diminish your spiritual health and to express itself in symptoms and acts. Among these carnal tendencies were impure thoughts and desires, idolatry of self and personal goals, criticalness and contentiousness, stubbornness, jealousy and envy, selfish ambitions, anger with people, suspicions of all but your own little group, unforgiveness and holding grudges, impatience, pride, touchiness.

In the place of these negative emotions and attitudes which the Spirit cleanses away, He fills you with His positive fruit--love, joy, peace, patience, kindness, goodness, faithfulness, gentleness, and self-control (Gal. 5:22-23). These are the fruit of the Spirit, and the Spirit multiplies these within the sanctified believer, replacing the negative with the positive.

The power which the Spirit imparts to you in entire sanctification gives you the spiritual strength which helps keep you spiritually healthy and vigorous. All of the sanctifying work of the Spirit within you makes for spiritual wholeness and wholeness of personality.

PURITY AND SINGLENESS OF HEART. God promised through Jeremiah, "I will give them singleness of heart and action" (Jer. 32:39). This is basic to spiritual wholeness and is the opposite of a divided heart or double-mindedness. David prayed, "Give me an undivided heart that I may fear your name" (Ps. 86:11). This corresponds to God's greatest command--to love Him with all your heart and being (Deut. 13:3). Only the entirely sanctified person can in the fullest sense love God with all the heart, soul, mind, and strength (Mark 12:30).

God promised to give His people a heart to know Him (Jer. 24:7). God said that circumcision of the heart (another figure of speech that means cleansing) was necessary to love Him with "all" the heart (Deut. 30:6).

James' call to holiness is worded, "Wash your hands, you sinners, and purify your hearts, you double-minded" (James 4:8). James said that double-mindedness causes spiritual instability, another way of saying spiritual ill health (James 1:8).

Spiritual life can be yours in its fullness or abundance (John 10:10) only when your heart is cleansed from the negative sinful nature and filled with the positive fruit and fullness of the Spirit.

B.   ENTIRE SANCTIFICATION BRINGS EMPOWERING

The negative cleansing of the Spirit must not be emphasized to the exclusion of the positive empowering of the Spirit. In the same instant that the Spirit cleanses a believer in entire sanctification, He floods the inner being with His holy and abundant power.

The power of the Spirit has manifold purposes, for it meets a number of your spiritual needs.

1. *Power for a holy life.* God's command to you is to be holy as He is holy (1 Peter 1:16). Being is primary. Doing is the outflow. You are to be holy in all you do (1 Peter 1:15) because you are holy in your innermost nature. It is a greater miracle to be holy in your innermost being than to be holy and righteous in your acts.

The fruit of the Spirit is yours through the Spirit's power (Gal. 5:22-23). The Spirit's power fills you with joy, peace, and hope (Rom. 15:13). You are filled with power in the inner being by the Holy Spirit (Eph. 3:16). This fullness of power gives ability to obey and walk in the light (1 John 1:7), for sanctification is for the purpose of obedience (1 Peter 1:2), and for constant cleansing to maintain the sanctified life (1 John 1:7).

It is out of your innermost being that the streams of living water must flow and be manifest in your life. What is the source of the streams from within? The unlimited supply furnished by the Holy Spirit, said Jesus (John 7:38-39). It is out of the overflow of your heart that your mouth speaks (Matt. 12:34).

The Spirit-filled Christian is conscious of an inner power beyond what he knew before he was Spirit-filled. It is not power for you to use at will. You do not use the Spirit. It is power to be, power that lives in you and flows through you and is manifest through you as the Spirit chooses.

2. *Power for effective witness and service.* Any Christian can witness, but the power for witnessing comes from the Holy Spirit. Witnessing and power are associated together in the New Testament. "You are witnesses . . . I am going to send you what my Father has promised; but stay in the city until you have been clothed with power from on high" (Luke 24:48-49). "You will receive power when the Holy Spirit comes on you; and you will be my witnesses" (Acts 1:8).

Peter was filled with the Spirit as he witnessed to the Sanhedrin (Acts 4:8). It was as the Christian group "were all filled with the Holy Spirit" that they "spoke the word of God boldly" (4:31). Peter confessed, "We are witnesses . . . and so is the Holy Spirit" (5:32). Stephen was filled with the Holy Spirit (6:5) and spoke with empowering by the Spirit (6:10). It was the power of the Spirit that used Philip (8:29, 39). In fact, it was the power of the Spirit that equipped Jesus in His humanity for His service for God (Acts 10:38).

Paul was forthright in telling that what Christ accomplished through him was "through the power of the Spirit" (Rom. 15:18-19). He testified, "My message and my preaching were . . . with a demonstration of the Spirit's power" (1 Cor. 2:4). "This all-surpassing power is from God and not from us" (2 Cor. 4:7).

Paul's whole desire was for this power to rest upon him (2 Cor. 12:9). He became a servant of the Gospel by the working of God's power (Eph. 3:7). He confessed his ministry was "with all his energy, which so powerfully works in me" (Col. 1:29). He assures Timothy that God gave us "a spirit of power" (2 Tim. 1:7), "for the kingdom of God is not a matter of talk but of power" (1 Cor. 4:20). Every Christian has an anointing from God (the Holy Spirit) (2 Cor. 1:21; 1 John 2:20, 27), but that anointing in all its power is only on the Spirit-filled.

3. *Power in Prayer.* There is an inseparable relationship between the fullness of the Spirit and power in prayer. God's plan is for every believer to be an intercessor-priest (1 Peter 2:5, 9; Rev. 1:6). Any Christian, even a child, can pray and receive answers from God. But it often requires special power to prevail in resistant situations.

The Lord's prayer teaches us to pray constantly for God's kingdom to come (Matt. 6:10). Christ is reigning on heaven's throne by His intercession as our High Priest-King (Heb. 2:17; 3:1). We are to come near in prayer through Christ our Great High Priest (Heb. 10:21-22). As High Priest-King, He is enthroned at the right hand of God the Father (Eph. 1:20; Col. 3:1), but He depends on our prayer as priests of God to join with His in extending His kingdom.

The Holy Spirit is given in His fullness to make you mighty in prayer. You do not know God's priority except as the Spirit teaches you.

> **Romans 8:26**--"The Spirit helps us in our weakness. We do not know what we ought to pray for, but the Spirit himself intercedes for us with groans that words cannot express."

The Spirit gives you power in believing as you pray (Rom. 15:13). Faith is a fruit of the Spirit. Faith and the fullness of the Spirit are associated together (Acts 6:5; 11:24). In fact, special faith can be the gift of the Spirit (1 Cor. 12:9).

Your spiritual wrestling and warfare is to be primarily a warfare by prayer (Eph. 6:10-18. Note specially v. 18). To be mighty in prayer warfare you need the fullness of the Spirit in all His empowering. In fact, all prayer should be in the Holy Spirit (Eph. 6:18). "Pray in the Spirit" (Jude 20). Often the measure of mighty prevailing prayer in the life of a Christian is according to the measure of the Spirit's fullness and power.

C. ENTIRE SANCTIFICATION BRINGS PERFECT LOVE

Christ almost shocks us when He commands, "Be perfect, therefore, as your heavenly Father is perfect" (Matt. 5:48). But note, this is the last verse of a section on love. The only human perfection that the Bible teaches is the perfection of our love.

Jesus had just told the rich young man to love his neighbor as himself. Then Jesus added, "If you want to be perfect, go, sell your possessions, and give to the poor. . . . Then come, follow me" (Matt. 19:21). John speaks three times about being perfect in love (1 John 4:12, 17-18).

You will never, before you reach heaven, be perfect in mind, in understanding, in speech, or in performance. The only perfection available is perfection in love. This does not mean a perfection in quantity so that you can never grow any more in love. Nor does it mean a perfection in the expression of your love. The only possible meaning is perfection of quality in the sense that your love is unmixed with any sinful attitude or sinful intention.

The New Testament uses the Greek word *agapao* (to love) and *agape* (love) for the love given by the Holy Spirit. This is the love with which Christ loved you, the love referred to as your spiritual standard. This word is called the characteristic word of Christianity. It is the only love that can be perfect. What is agape love? It is the word used for the love of God, the love of Christ, Christian love to God, to other Christians, and to the other people of our world. Agape love is self-giving love. It is love regardless of the merits of the one loved.

Agape love is both a holy affection and a dominating principle. Both repeatedly manifest themselves in the devotion, commitment, and character of the Spirit-filled Christian. As affection, perfect love fully rejoices in the Person of God, His welfare, interests, and work. Secondarily, it refers to love to others. It eagerly welcomes every opportunity to experience the nearness and presence of God and the opportunity to show the resulting love to people.

As a principle, agape love actively motivates and governs all expressions of love. Perfection of agape love means that it is untainted by any mixture of self and self-interest, prejudice, or ulterior motive. Love is a basic law of Christ (Gal. 5:14; 6:2). It is the very nature of love to express itself.

Perfect love is primarily perfect love to God. It is manifest in the holy affections, ardent emotion, undivided loving of God above all others and all else. It is the commitment and desire to be as constantly and fully loving to God as is humanly possible.

Perfect love is secondarily the genuine love of 1 Corinthians 13 shown to others by giving itself in serving others, in every way that is suitable and possible in the situation. You are to love others with the love the Holy Spirit pours into your being. As you pour out, He pours in. You are to love others as He loves you (John 13:34) and as you love yourself (Matt. 22:39).

The fullness of the Spirit in entire sanctification is the fullness of love, baptisms of love, streams of outflowing love. Love is to be the hallmark of the Spirit-filled Christian. Each person has his or her own personality. Some are more expressive than others, but each in his or in her own way will be transformed by agape love.

Yet, remember, love is a governing principle. This means that at times love is of necessity lovingly firm, lovingly frank, lovingly faithful to the best interests of the one loved. Love has high standards. Love is ethical. Love must sometimes oppose wrong attitudes or actions. Love must abstain from unworthy forms of fellowship. Love cannot agree with what is wrong. Love must be true to what is highest and best.

D. ENTIRE SANCTIFICATION BRINGS FULLNESS

Abundance is characteristic of the fullness of the Spirit. God gives the Spirit without limit (John 3:34). Paul says God pours His Spirit on us generously (Titus 3:6). Knowing that he was filled with the Spirit, Paul knew that when he came to minister he would come with the fullness of God's blessing (Rom. 15:29).

When the Spirit fills you, He multiplies His fruit within you. So while every Christian is to show the fruit of the Spirit (Gal. 5:22-23), yet the Spirit-filled person can be expected to have an abundance of love, joy, peace, patience, kindness, goodness, faithfulness, gentleness, and self-control. The Holy Spirit will fill you and then flow out from your innermost being with these streams of living water (John 7:38-39).

This does not mean that the sanctified person will always be having a "mountaintop" experience of abundance of evident blessings. It is normal for every sanctified person to have occasional "dry times" when God's Spirit is not specially sensed. But thank God, when you once have been filled with the Spirit you can be refilled again and again as you wait upon God and as long as you let no disobedience bring a spiritual cloud over your experience. The sanctified person lives by faith as much as any person, but the sanctified person will again and again be flooded with the Spirit's fullness as he keeps obeying the Spirit. This is repeatedly illustrated in the Acts of the Apostles.

The Holy Spirit helps you share Christ's life to the full (John 10:10). He plans for you to be "filled to the measure of all the fullness of God" (Eph. 3:19). He desires you to "become mature, attaining to the whole measure of the fullness of Christ" (Eph. 4:13). Maturity is an ever increasing experience attained as you grow in grace. However, being filled with the Spirit speeds the whole maturing process.

The fullness of the Spirit not only brings fullness to His fruit within you, but also brings fullness to His ministry within you. Thus you can expect a new fullness of the anointing of the Spirit after you are sanctified (2 Cor. 1:21; 1 John 2:20, 27). This is available in many ways. There also will be a new fullness of the guidance of the Spirit if you learn to be sensitive to the Spirit, developing a listening ear.

The fullness of the Spirit will bring a fullness of the Spirit's help in prayer, for He delights to help you in your natural prayer weakness (Rom. 8:26). Of course, the Spirit depends on your cooperation by your putting priority on prayer and giving time to prayer.

The fullness of the Spirit will add a new degree of guidance and blessing in your witness, for the fullness of the Spirit is specifically associated with witnessing (Luke 24:48-49; Acts 1:8; 5:32), and the Spirit's fullness will bring a new dimension of guidance into the whole life of the person who is entirely sanctified.

E. ENTIRE SANCTIFICATION BRINGS REST

In Hebrews 4:1, 3, 9, 11 we have described a spiritual rest of which God's rest from His works of creation is a type. Israel never entered into this rest because of unbelief. It was more than the rest of Canaan after Egyptian bondage. It is a Sabbath rest, a state or life of rest like God's (Gen. 1:31-2:2).

Hebrews 4:9 says that this special Sabbath rest still remains for us to receive. Note:

a. It is for the people of God (not for the unsaved).

b. It must be entered into by faith (v. 2). The act of faith leads to a state of faith in which you rest in God. To not enter by faith is to disobey (v. 6) and to harden your heart (v. 7).

c. It is a rest from sin. Since you cease willful transgressions in the new birth, this rest that remains must be a rest from the struggle of the sin nature. God's Word is living and powerful and performs a spiritual surgery in your innermost nature (v. 12).

d. It is a rest available to you. Jesus is your Great High Priest (v. 14). He is touched by your need, yet He Himself was without sin (v. 15). Therefore, you should come in boldness of faith to God's throne of grace and find the help (the cleansing) you need.

e. It is rest you enter into at a definite point (the Greek uses the aorist tense), and this results in an abiding state of soul rest (v. 11).

This is the spiritual rest Paul longed for in Romans 7. It is a rest where the sinful nature no longer opposes your spiritual desires. The inner antagonism to the will of God is cleansed away. It is a blessed state of soul rest, a rest of faith, a knowable experience and life of inner spiritual leisure. It brings poise and calmness of soul and the undisturbed filling presence of the Holy Spirit.

The inner double-mindedness of soul is gone. Your personality is united, integrated in the will of God. The freedom from inner conflict enables you to delight in the will of God. "I desire to do your will, O my God; your law is within my heart" (Ps. 40:8). This is the fulfillment of God's new covenant as promised, "I will put my law in their minds and write it on their hearts" (Jer. 31:33; Heb. 8:10).

The great spiritual struggles of your soul with the will of God are now past. The total surrender of your life, your future, your will, and your all to the will of God is the necessary precondition for sanctifying faith. With that commitment to God's will eternally sealed, all you now need is to learn the will of God and you at once are gladly ready to do it. There may be some apprehension of the new and unknown--that is human, but there is no inner struggle with the known will of God. All sinful resistance, all stubborn self-will as opposed to God's will--all is cleansed away. Your soul is at rest, delighting in the unfolding will of God.

41

STEPS TO
ENTIRE SANCTIFICATION

Perhaps you personally have the clear and definite assurance that you have received the Holy Spirit's ministry in entire sanctification, or perhaps you are now realizing your own personal need of this second major experience of God's wonderful salvation. This chapter is written to help lead you into the clear experience of God's sanctifying infilling of the Holy Spirit in your own heart. On the other hand, if you are personally rejoicing in God's sanctifying power, this chapter illustrates how you can lead others into this clear experience and victory which God has provided through the Holy Spirit.

The Christian wishing to be entirely sanctified must be living in the assurance that he has been born of God. You cannot be cleansed in your inner nature until you know that your sins are forgiven and that you are walking obediently in all the light God has given you. It is good to search your heart to be sure there is nothing hindering God's answering your prayer.

1. *Prayerfully search your heart to be sure you are walking in all the light God has given you.*

Is there any unforgiveness in my heart against anyone? (Matt. 6:14; Eph. 4:32; Col. 3:13).

Is there any unconfessed sin in my heart? (Ps. 66:18).

Is there a problem between me and any other person about which I have not taken the biblical step (Matt. 5:23-24)? Note that you are responsible to act regardless of who is to blame. You are responsible to go. Be sure you go in a humble spirit.

Is there any step of obedience the Lord has asked of me and I have thus far been unwilling to obey?

2. *Open your heart to the Spirit's revelation of your need.* You will not realize how impure your heart is in the sight of God until the Spirit shows you the fullness of your need. Peter did not think there was anything in his heart which could ever deny Jesus. Yet Jesus saw it, and Peter denied his Lord three times (Luke 22:31-34). The disciples did not realize how offensive to Jesus their jealousy and vengeance were (Luke 9:54-55), or how carnal their rivalry really was. Again and again they, in their pride, argued who was the greatest. Even on Jesus' last night with them, before Jesus instituted the Lord's Supper, they were disputing again (Luke 22:24-27). Often you do not realize how unwholesome your carnal attitudes appear to others.

Isaiah did not see his full spiritual need. He was already a prophet of the Lord, but when he had his transforming vision of the awesome holiness of God he saw his own uncleanness as he had never before realized it. He called out, "Woe to me! . . . I am ruined! For I am a man of unclean lips . . . for my eyes have seen the king, the Lord almighty" (Isa. 6:5). Remember Matt. 5:6 and Heb. 12:14.

Ask God to give you a new vision of how your heart's need appears in His sight. Examine your heart in the light of 1 Corinthians 13 with prayerful heart searching. Take time to let God speak to you. Confessing every need He shows you, rejoice in His power to meet all your need.

Perhaps also you are convicted at the comparative meagerness of the Spirit's working within you and through you. You read how Jesus plans for streams of blessing to flow out of your inner nature as the Spirit fills you, and you must confess that you are far from being filled and overflowing with the Spirit's presence and power (John 7:37-39).

3. *Hunger and thirst for the Spirit's cleansing, empowering fullness.* No two persons' experience and testimony are exactly the same, so do not seek an exact duplicate of someone else's testimony. God has a personal experience for you that will exactly meet your need. It will be real, practical, and deeply satisfying to you as the Spirit

cleanses and fills you. Has your soul been longing for a deeper cleansing? a more mighty infilling of the Holy Spirit? As you read the accounts of the early church in the book of Acts, or as you read Paul's testimony in his letters of how powerfully the Spirit worked in his life, do you long for an experience more like the Bible describes?

That deep longing and hunger is God's gift to you. It shows how personally God loves you. He does not want you to be satisfied with anything less than His fullest salvation, His entire sanctification of your inner nature, His mighty empowering abiding and filling you day by day. The Holy Spirit gives you that heart hunger to lead you into God's satisfying, sanctifying fullness.

Just let your spiritual hunger deepen. Let your heart feast on the Bible descriptions of the Spirit's working in the lives of the early church. God is no respecter of persons. This is a new day and you have your own unique personal need, but God's grace is available to you. God does not give you hunger to mock you but to lead you to His fullness.

Do not hunger for the seemingly spectacular outward details in the testimonies of others. These vary from person to person. Hunger for the deep inner reality that is the essential ongoing basis of all your future spiritual victoriousness and all God's presence and working in and through you.

Matthew 5:6--"Blessed are those who hunger and thirst for righteousness, for they will be filled."

Psalm 107:9--"He satisfies the thirsty, and fills the hungry with good things."

John 7:37-39--"'If anyone is thirsty, let him come to me and drink. Whoever believes in me, as the Scripture has said, streams of living water will flow from within him.' By this he meant the Spirit."

Isaiah 55:1-2--"Come, all you who are thirsty, come to the waters. . . . Come. . . . Come . . . your soul will delight in the richest of fare."

4. *Prayerfully seek the Spirit's cleansing.* It is true that as a child of God you already have the Holy Spirit indwelling you. This indwelling is real. You do not have only part of the Spirit. He is a holy Person and cannot be divided. When you speak of desiring

more of the Spirit, it would be more accurate to speak of desiring Him to have more of you, to possess and fill you more totally. The limitation is not on God's part; it is on your part.

Some have questioned why you should ask for the Spirit when you have the Spirit already within you. The Bible clearly instructs you to ask. Ask because you hunger to experience more of His presence, more of His holy working in and through you. Your asking is part of your hungering and yielding. Jesus says if you are thirsty you are to come, drink, and believe (John 7:37-38). This means asking and seeking. Jesus assures you how eager the Father is to give you the Spirit if you ask (Luke 11:13). This is addressed to Christians, so you as His child are to ask specifically for this fuller need of the Spirit's work within you.

To seek means to strive earnestly. It is not that you earn this experience by your seeking effort. No! It is that as you seek you search your heart to be sure there is no hindrance. You search to see if there is any aspect of obedience you have not fulfilled. You seek to be sure that you have yielded and consecrated every aspect of your being, your future as well as your present.

God's Word is very clear. God the Father gives the Spirit to those who ask and also to those who obey. "The Holy Spirit whom God has given to those who obey him" (Acts 5:32). To say it in another way, "If we walk in the light, as he is in the light . . . the blood of Jesus His Son, purifies us from all sin" (1 John 1:7). Note, this is sin in the singular--it refers to your sin nature, not to your committed sins, which are cleansed away in the new birth. This is a promise to you as a Christian for the inner purification of your sinful nature.

5. *Consecrate yourself totally and forever.* Do you realize how God has been longing for you to take this step of total consecration? If your heavenly Father, when you were a prodigal son, longed for your return so He could forgive you, how much more He longs now that you as His obedient child present yourself as a love gift in total consecration.

Consecration is an act, and consecration is a state of being. Only a child of God can consecrate himself as a living sacrifice. Do it now. "Offer yourselves to God, as those who have been brought from death to life; and offer the parts of your body to him as instruments of righteousness" (Rom. 6:13). Place yourself in God's hands unreservedly.

There must be this initial act of total yielding of yourself to God. You must purposefully give yourself absolutely to God in total yieldedness for time and for eternity. Having made this initial act, you must then maintain your yieldedness to God by loving obedience which affirms your once-for-all consecration. Thus, when the Spirit accepts your giving of yourself and fills and sanctifies you, you now live in a state of continuous consecration.

Romans 6:13 suggests how detailed this act of consecration should be. You are commanded to offer yourself and "the parts of your body." You are in danger of rushing a verbal commitment which is rather superficial. Rather, Paul seems to say, take your whole body and life, part by part, and deliberately place it all in God's hands. The verb in this verse is in the aorist tense. This means it is a one-time, once-for-all commitment. It refers to the specific act of total yielding as you present yourself to the Spirit to be filled and sanctified "through and through" (1 Thess. 5:23). Here, too, the aorist tense is used. This "through and through" sanctification is to be done in one completed act.

Consecration, in one sense, can be done in a moment of time. But it is spiritually wholesome to be very deliberate in your act of consecration. Place your whole life, your present, your future, your plans and ambitions, your fears, your desires--all you know and all you don't know--into God's hands. The most difficult part of this careful and complete consecration is the unknown future. But trust it all to God in one eternal surrender to His will. Say your eternal yes to God.

Romans 12:1-2--"I urge you, brothers, in view of God's mercy, to offer your bodies as living sacrifices, wholly and pleasing to God--this is your spiritual act of worship. Do not conform any longer to the pattern of this world, but be transformed by the renewing of your mind. Then you will be able to test and approve what God's will is--his good, pleasing and perfect will."

Place your family, your possessions, your work, your relationships--place them one by one in God's hand in deliberate commitment. From now on you will have no question about doing God's will. Your only concern will be to know God's will. Your eternal yes to the will of God has already been said.

The responsibility for your whole life is now in God's hand. He holds you and the future in His loving hands. You cannot make a mistake when you let God decide for you. How blessed! God willingly takes the full responsibility for your life from now on.

6. *Appropriate the Spirit's cleansing and fullness by faith.* As with all of salvation, entire sanctification is by faith. All is by God's grace. All must be accepted by your appropriating faith. Just as the 120 in the Upper Room at Pentecost were cleansed and filled with the Holy Spirit by faith (Acts 15:8-9), so you too are sanctified by faith.

You are unworthy, but He waits to cleanse and fill you. When you have consecrated your all, you need delay no longer. What more can you do but rush into God's loving arms? If a human father delights to give good things to His children, how much more your God, your loving Father, delights to give the Holy Spirit (Luke 11:13). Jesus Himself told us that this was the promise of the Father (Luke 24:49). Among the last things Jesus said on Mount Olivet just before He ascended was to remind His disciples of this promise (Acts 1:4). It is Christ's priority for you in this dispensation. That promise is just as surely for you as it was for the apostles (Acts 2:38-39).

God has made many promises, but this is the promise of all promises. It is "the" promise of the Father (Acts 2:39). The Father finds great joy in fulfilling this promise for you.

Believe Him. Receive His love gift to you. What more could He give than His fullest measure of His Holy Spirit? What greater gift could you ever receive? The Holy Spirit gives wonderful gifts, but the gift of the Holy Spirit Himself in all His fullness is the greatest gift of all--the gift given by the Father as He promised--"the gift of the Holy Spirit" (Acts 2:38).

Receive Him in His fullness by faith. This was Jesus' plea after His resurrection. They already had the Spirit indwelling them, but they needed to receive Him in His sanctifying fullness. So Jesus said, "Receive the Holy Spirit" (John 20:22). Stretch out your hand by faith and receive Him just now.

Remember, faith is not sight; it is faith. It is not feeling or emotion; it is faith. Emotions may or may not be profoundly stirred at the moment of faith. You can be sure they will come in due time as you live in the fullness of the Spirit. But you are purified, sanctified by faith, just as you are justified by faith.

You believe it because God commanded it, promised it, and sent His Holy Spirit to make it real in your life. You believe it because when you have fulfilled God's condition you know that God is true to His Word. Satan may try to get you to doubt it, but God's Word is your anchor. You stand by faith (Rom. 5:2; 2 Cor. 1:24). Your whole journey of salvation until you get to heaven is by faith. You live by faith (Rom. 1:17; Heb. 10:38). It is all by grace through faith (Rom. 4:16; Eph. 2:8).

God the Father gave His one and only Son that you might have a complete and perfect redemption. He promised the Spirit's baptizing work to cleanse you. Would He hesitate to fulfill His promise when you have met His conditions?

Jesus suffered outside Jerusalem's gate to make you holy through His blood (Heb. 13:12). "Christ loved the church and gave himself up for her to make her holy" and "to present her to himself as a radiant church without stain or wrinkle or any other blemish, but holy and blameless" (Eph. 5:25-27). Would He hesitate to cleanse you and fill you with His Spirit whom He promised to send (Luke 24:49)?

This is the dispensation of the Holy Spirit. He already indwells you and longs to fill you. This is a major phase of His role to you. Would He keep you waiting when you have met God's conditions and when you invite Him to fill you? Oh, believe and receive, and then rejoice.

7. *Rejoice, thank, praise, and testify.* When God has fulfilled His great promise to you and given you the cleansing fullness of His Spirit, when Christ has cleansed you with His blood to make you ready to be His loving bride, when the Holy Spirit has purified you by His cleansing fire, should you not praise, love, adore, and rejoice in God's great goodness to you?

When you have met God's conditions and trusted God's promise with faith, should you not praise the Lord again and again?

Thank God for providing so complete a salvation for both the guilt and the pollution of sin. Thank Jesus for suffering outside the gate for your sanctification. Thank Him for sending the Holy Spirit. Thank the Holy Spirit that He has been so faithful to you in guiding you to this point of full surrender and appropriating faith. Thank God for His promise on which you stand (Luke 11:13).

You have walked in the light God gave you, so thank God that the blood of Jesus has purified you from the sin nature (1 John 1:7). Thank God that He is faithful to His Word. You can one day stand before the throne of God completely resting on His Word.

Sometimes God lets us walk by faith for a few hours or days to strengthen and purify our faith. But God's Word is true; you can place the full weight of your soul on it. When you believe, He does cleanse and fill. At any moment as you rejoice in His Word, He may flood you with the inner assurance, the sense of inner cleanness, the awareness of His power working within you. Don't doubt Him! Rejoice, praise Him, pour out your love to Him. He has come and filled your temple and will prove His presence by His fruit in your life.

There may be many hungry, defeated Christians about you. When God has fulfilled His Word to you, you know He can fulfill it to all. Humbly but joyfully and clearly share your testimony as God guides you.

42

MAINTAINING THE HOLY LIFE

The entire sanctification of your soul by the infilling of the Holy Spirit is not to be compared to a graduation exercise which occurs once and then lives in your memory. It is the entering into a new blessedness of relation with God which is to be maintained the rest of your life. It is not like scaling Mount Everest, after which you must come down from the mountaintop and always rejoice that you once had a "mountaintop" experience. Rather, it is arriving on a new higher plateau on which you now live.

Entire sanctification is not the great final destination of your life of salvation by grace. That is glorification in heaven. It is at last entering into a life of fullness, of holiness and power. You do not enter a Canaan of eternal bliss. You now begin the conquest of Canaan. In other words, the life of holiness is a life to be maintained; the entering into the greatest period of growth, maturing, and spiritual conquest of your spiritual life. Since spiritual conquest is involved, it will include spiritual warfare.

The sanctified life is a life by God's grace and by your willing cooperation. The holy moment must be followed by a lifelong holy walk. You and I are to live and serve by God's grace and the Spirit's power "in holiness and righteousness before him all our days" (Luke 1:75). The holy life is to be maintained by seven aspects of obedient, joyful walking in the light which the Holy Spirit gives you.

1. *Maintain your devotion and intercession.* Prayer is to your soul what breathing is to your body. There is no satisfying spiritual life apart from a life of daily communion with God. All Christian life is dependent on prayer. But after the consecration that leads to the

Spirit's infilling, prayer is even more necessary to maintain your spiritual glow.

Spiritual fire is fueled by prayer. Not only must you set apart regular adequate times for communion with Jesus, but throughout each day prayer should be as natural as breathing. Whenever there are free moments, whenever your heart can be lifted for a moment, love should be expressed to Jesus. Prayers breathed for others as they are called to your attention, and thanksgiving and praise should keep rising from your soul as constantly as your work permits.

Love for Christ is fanned to a flame as your heart communes, loves, and praises Jesus. All the graces of the Spirit and fruit of the Spirit flourish in the climate of devotion. Spiritual maturity depends on placing priority on prayer. Probably the most tragic neglect of the sanctified is in their inadequate prayer life--inadequate devotion and inadequate intercession for others, for Christ's church, and for the unsaved.

Your reading of Scripture devotionally is an essential part of your prayer life. Set Scripture reading goals, and read God's Word consecutively. No literate Christian should read less than a chapter of God's Word a day. That will enable you to complete reading the entire New Testament through every eight months or so. But most Christians can read three chapters a day and five on Sunday. That will take you through the Bible from Genesis to Revelation every year.

When your heart is burning with love for Jesus, the Bible becomes more precious than ever before. Read it; memorize selected verses. Prayer and God's Word are like the two wings of your soul to help it rise above the problems and pressures of life (Ps. 19:10; 119:11, 103; Col. 3:16).

2. *Maintain your faith.* The Spirit-filled life, as all Christian life, is a life of faith (Gal. 3:11; Heb. 10:38). Trusting and obeying go hand in hand. The closer you walk with Jesus the more you look into His face, love Him, and trust Him. Faith, like love and joy, is the natural fruit of the Spirit in the Spirit-filled life (Gal. 5:22). You cannot help but trust Jesus when you love Him with all your heart,

soul, mind, and strength., The more you trust Jesus the more the Spirit keeps filling you. The more you feast on God's Word, the more your faith grows (Rom. 10:17). Faith is your shield in temptation (Eph. 6:16).

You live by faith, not by spiritual feelings of joy or peace. Feelings may come and feelings may go, but your relationship to God is maintained by faith and loving obedience. Spiritual battles in the sanctified life may be stronger than ever before. God is rapidly developing you in character, maturity, and the fruit of the Spirit. Just faithfully trust and obey, and God will fill you again with joyful holy emotion.

3. *Maintain your obedience.* Keep walking in God's light, obeying God's Word as you meditate on it. Spiritual victoriousness is maintained by glad and constant obedience to God. Welcome any new light He sheds upon your pathway. Do not necessarily make the ideas or convictions of other people your guide, but live in God's Word and prayer. The Spirit will guide you in your own convictions and obedience.

Yielding and obeying are the two sides of the same attitude of soul which the Spirit-filled person must maintain. It is a moment and act of surrender, yielding, and consecrating that prepares you for the infilling of the Spirit. Then this experience must be maintained by a continuing attitude of yielding and obeying.

4. *Maintain your spiritual discipline.* It is hoped that you have established firm spiritual habits. But if you have not done so, do so immediately. God provides all that you need for spiritual growth and constant spiritual victory over temptation and sin. But you must appropriate what He provides.

Prayer times must be planned and faithfully maintained. The minimum amount of time for daily prayer, the minimum amount of God's Word you plan to read, your minimum amount of support for the church and God's cause, your minimum attendance in Christian worship--all these standards should be prayerfully set and then observed.

Be constantly alert for a few extra moments to invest in Scripture reading and prayer. Seize every spiritual opportunity to grow in grace, to bless and help others, and to lift your heart to God even for a fleeting moment.

As we have seen, the Bible teaches that sin must be cleansed, removed, destroyed. However, you have a body and nature which are not in themselves sinful but must be disciplined. There is a legitimate place for suppression--not of sin, but of the normal, the natural, the human. Sanctification does not free from temptation. Even Christ was tempted. But Christ disciplined His thoughts.

Paul made his body his slave (1 Cor. 9:27), i.e., subdued it so that good might not become a hindrance to the best. The Holy Spirit gives you power to maintain successful discipline over your body and mind. The desire for food, sleep, society, i.e., association and friendship, conversation, sex, humor--all can have a legitimate and proper place in a sanctified life. But all can become the occasion of sin unless you properly discipline them.

5. *Maintain your fellowship with God and fellow Christians.* Maintain your fellowship with the Lord by expressing your love to Him in prayer moments throughout your day. Learn to take everything to God in prayer and thanksgiving, and keep constantly obeying Him. Feelings may vary from hour to hour, but just maintain your commitment and your prayer fellowship. Then your holy walk with Christ will be unbroken.

Also be sure to maintain your fellowship with your fellow believers. After Pentecost the Christians "devoted themselves to the apostles' teaching (i.e., for us--the Bible), and to the fellowship, to the breaking of bread, and to prayer" (Acts 2:42). This was the key to the rapid spiritual growth of each believer and to the rapid growth of the church.

Christians are to have a communion-fellowship with other believers as real as their communion-fellowship with the Father, Son, and Holy Spirit. Your fellowship implies commitment to your brothers and sisters in Christ. A chief characteristic of your fellowship is "brotherly love."

1 Peter 1:22--"Now that you have purified yourselves by obeying the truth so that you have sincere love for your brothers, love one another deeply, from the heart."

As a believer you need the fellowship (Rom. 12:5), the encouragement (Eph. 5:19), the counsel (Gal. 6:1), the mutual burden sharing (Gal. 6:2), and at times the practical sharing (Rom. 12:13; Heb. 13:16; 1 John 3:16-18) of your fellow believers. At the new birth the Spirit baptizes you into the family of God. You are created for fellowship. It is not normal for any Christian to be without the fellowship of a local church group. The blessings of membership in a Spirit-filled fellowship are the greatest of all, and a Spirit-filled believer should have the most to share spiritually with such a fellowship.

6. *Maintain your active service.* Spiritual service is as important to your spiritual health as exercise is to your physical health. You are "created in Christ Jesus to do good works" (Eph. 2:10). Christ sanctifies you to do good, "To purify for himself a people that are his very own, eager to do what is good" (Titus 2:14). You are to let your light shine by doing good deeds that the unsaved can see (Matt. 5:16), "To be ready to do whatever is good" (Titus 3:1). Your good deeds are to help the unsaved turn to God (1 Peter 2:12), to help stop criticism of the church (1 Peter 2:15).

Christ expects you to be an active representative of His love and a constant demonstration of His grace. He wants your holy life to be seen by the world. You must seek to bless everyone you possibly can by active love in every practical way you can and by blessing in your prayers as many people as possible. The more of God's blessing you pour out on others, the more the Holy Spirit will empower you and keep refilling you if you keep seeking Him. He delights to bless you in what you do (James 1:25).

7. *Be refilled again and again.* The 120 gathered in the Upper Room at Pentecost were all filled with the Spirit as God's Spirit purified them. But power can be renewed again and again. Purity can be preserved as you obey the Spirit. You must keep yourself pure (1 Tim. 5:22; 1 Thess. 5:21-22; 2 Peter 3:14; 1 John 3:3).

Power, however, must be renewed. Power is expended as you serve the Lord. Even Jesus experienced this (Mark 5:30). The sinful environment around you sometimes seems to drain your spiritual resources and the sense of the Spirit's presence and power. Any lack of obedience, any lack of unity with Christian brothers and sisters grieves the Spirit (Eph. 4:30). Self-indulgence, self-sufficiency, or excessive and inappropriate levity can deplete the Spirit's power. You must guard against any sin which would cut off the Spirit's presence and power. If you sense that you have grieved the Spirit, you have instant access to God's forgiveness (1 John 2:1-2).

You need to be refilled again and again as the Holy Spirit keeps filling you and flowing out through you (John 7:38-39). The Greek tense used in Ephesians 3:18 indicates a continually being filled.

The apostles and their associates who were filled with the Spirit at Pentecost (Acts 2:4) were again filled when they confronted special opposition and went to prayer (4:31). Stephen may have had a special refilling as he faced the angry Sanhedrin (7:55). Paul was filled with the Spirit at the house of Judas (9:17), but he seems to have been specially refilled in Cyprus (13:9).

The Holy Spirit wants to keep you full of His presence and power. As you walk in obedience to the Lord, the Spirit will guide you, restrain you, touch you, anoint you, and keep filling you again and again as you have need. If you keep hungering for more of His presence and power, He keeps filling you (Matt. 5:6). When the Spirit has cleansed you, there is nothing to hinder His repeated renewal of His presence and power. Just keep asking for more and more (Luke 11:13) and you will receive God's enablement at every time of need. This is the ultimate secret of maintaining the sanctified life.

43

YOU ARE STILL HUMAN

"We have this treasure in jars of clay to show that this all-surpassing power is from God and not from us" (2 Cor. 4:7). "The Lord . . . knows how we are formed, He remembers that we are dust" (Ps. 103:14). You must not only remember that you are human, but you must be wise in discerning the difference between human reactions which are the result of inbred sin and the human reactions which are the result of your humanness, not your sin.

The fact that you are human, and hence weak, does not detract from God's glory. Rather, it brings ever greater glory to God that in spite of your humanness He can fill you and use you for His purposes (2 Cor. 4:7). God's power is most evident in your weakness. In fact, as you recognize your weaknesses, taking no credit to yourself but giving all the glory for any good you do to God, the Spirit is able to perfect His power working within you (2 Cor. 11:9).

The body itself is not sinful--only the sin nature is sinful. When this is cleansed away, you will be a clean vessel--earthen but clean. Your physical nature includes instincts, drives, emotions, complexes. When the Spirit cleanses and fills you, these do not express the sin nature. However, they can become disordered, undisciplined, and overly dominant. You may then need the help of counseling, medication, or change of occupation or environment.

The cleansing of your soul does not heal faulty patterns of thinking or expressing emotions. It does not change physical or mental habits. It does not correct the chemical imbalance of your physical body. The fullness of the Spirit does not perfect your memory, your thinking process, or your emotional control. It does not change your store of facts, your past experiences which are imprinted on your personality, or your mental ability. It does not give you automatic understanding, automatic emotional control, or automatic self-discipline.

The Holy Spirit does not dehumanize you. He does not make you either an angel or a robot. You still have your basic personality. Some people are inclined to be more optimistic, some to be more pessimistic. Some are inclined to be more fanciful and impractical, and some to be more realistic. Some are more thoughtful and deliberate, and others more hasty and impulsive.

Holiness does not change an introvert into an extrovert, or an extrovert into an introvert. Peter was still Peter after Pentecost, but he was a Spirit-filled, holy Peter. He was still ready to speak or preach at any opportunity, but his sinful fear of people was cleansed away. John was still John, but he was no longer the "son of thunder" (Mark 3:17), jealous and quick to become angry. Now he was cleansed of the sinful anger and jealousy and became the apostle of love.

1. *Sanctification does not remove your humanity.* You have this treasure in a jar of clay (2 Cor. 4:7). While sanctification brings a perfection of love (1 John 4:17-18), yet it does not bring a perfection of body (Phil. 3:11-14). That is given you in glorification and will come at the resurrection when Jesus comes again (1 Cor. 15:42-44, 51-53). Since you are still in your unglorified human body, you are bound by limitations. You forget. You sometimes misunderstand, and you make mistakes. But you can nevertheless by God's grace keep from willfully breaking God's law.

2. *Sanctification does not free from temptation.* Temptation does not involve the necessity of sin. In a moral world you inevitably must make moral choices. Adam and Eve were tempted before they had sin. Christ was tempted, yet He was without sin (Heb. 4:15). The holiest souls are often tempted, but they need not sin. Temptation does not become sin until it is consented to. Sanctification makes victory over temptation easier, because the inner desire for sin is cleansed away and the Holy Spirit fills you, bestowing greater power to overcome temptation.

3. *Sanctification does not free from weaknesses and infirmities.* Sin in others should be rebuked (1 Tim. 5:20). But failings in others should be borne (Rom. 15:1), because they spring from a weakness, rather than from willfulness. Infirmities (failings) are unintentional failures to keep the law of perfect obedience. Sin is the willful transgression of God's law (1 John 3:4). Infirmities are involuntary. Sin is voluntary.

Infirmities are grounded in your physical nature and your intellectual deficiencies. Sin is rooted in your moral nature. Infirmities lead to regret and humiliation. Sin leads to guilt. Infirmities do not interrupt communion with God. Sin breaks communion with God. Infirmities are covered by the blood of Christ as long as you consciously walk in the light you have received (1 John 1:7). Infirmities are consistent with pure love from a pure heart. Sin is not.

4. *Sanctification does not automatically give maturity.* Purity is different from maturity. Maturity is the result of growth. Purity is the result of an act of faith. There are no degrees in spiritual purity. Purity means freedom from all foreign matter. Purity is the freedom from whatever God could not admit into His holy presence, from what would hinder fellowship with Him, i.e., sin. Purity prepares the way for rapid growth. Purity is the foundation upon which character is to be built and goodness added.

Maturity requires time, discipline, prayerfulness, watchfulness, and experience. Purity is available now from God. To be clean and to be mature are different things. Purity is essential to entrance into heaven (Heb. 12:14). Maturity is not, though all sanctified people must seek to grow in grace, maturity, and in the knowledge of God.

Sanctified maturity is your goal as a Spirit-filled, entirely sanctified believer. It is dependent upon the Spirit's filling and controlling your personality and your committed cooperation with the Spirit. It involves at least these seven goals for your prayer and self-discipline:

    a. View yourself, others, the world, and spiritual priorities from God's perspective.

    b. Accept yourself and others as created in God's image,

loved by God, worthy of prayer and loving service, and needed by God and the world.

    c. Discipline your devotional life and seek to manifest observable continuing growth in Christlikeness.

    d. Demonstrate consistent integrity and balanced Christian behavior in all aspects of your life.

    e. Maintain useful wholesome involvement in practical life and daily living as unto the Lord.

    f. Value today and choose God-guided personal goals for the present to move it toward God's tomorrow.

    g. Live today in constant awareness of eternal values and priorities. Constantly choose actions to advance Kingdom goals, and to bless as many people as possible.

    5. *Sanctification does not free from possibility of sinning.* This world is created a moral world, and you are created a moral being. You must make moral choices. As long as you are in the present world you are on probation, and it is possible for you to sin. Victory over temptation is possible to any sanctified person. Victory is easier than for the unsanctified, but sin is always a possibility. Therefore, everyone who thinks he is standing firmly needs to be careful that he does not fall (1 Cor. 10:12).

    The Holy Spirit not only cleanses you, He empowers you. His power is available to help your self-discipline, but you must will to become more self-disciplined. The Spirit is available to help you become more expressive in your loving concern to people, more expressive of forgiveness for those who oppose you, and more expressive of love for those enslaved in sin. But the Spirit will not act for you. You must choose to act, and He then will strengthen and bless you as you act in accordance with His will.

ASPECTS OF SELF-DISCIPLINE

    Suppression. In the new birth you must suppress any sinful inclination. But suppression is not God's full answer to the sin nature. In sanctification you are cleansed from the sin nature, but there is still a very legitimate place for suppression.

Sample tendencies that need to be suppressed include tending (1) to be judgmental of others, (2) to become a frequent conveyor of gossip, (3) to show unwholesome curiosity in the affairs of others, (4) to engage in morbid self-depreciation, (5) to avoid responsibility, (6) to procrastinate, (7) to spend too freely and get into debt, 8) to eat more than is necessary or to eat fattening foods just because you enjoy them, and hence to become overweight, (9) to be restless or hyperactive, (10) to be indolent and waste time.

Suppression can be an acceptable form of self-discipline. The Holy Spirit will gladly assist you control more successfully any tendency to weakness. But you must exercise your will. Ask God to guide you to the areas of your personality or life where you need to use the discipline of suppression.

Substitution. Substitution may be another form of self-discipline in which the Spirit's aid is available. Substitution may guide your emotional response in some more wholesome and helpful action. Are you emotionally bothered over a person's constant interruption? Plan for a way to let that person wholesomely express his opinion. Are you emotionally bothered by an energetic child who is constantly getting into mischief? Plan ways to use that energy more wholesomely. An impulse to criticize can be overcome by deliberately making a list of good qualities of the person you are tempted to criticize and then thank God one by one for these good points. An impulse to remember a temptation may be overcome by quoting to yourself a Scripture you have memorized or by mentally singing over and over a chorus or verse of a Christian song.

Moderation and balance. The Holy Spirit is available to help you with self-discipline in maintaining moderation and balance. It does not honor the Lord when you go to fanatical extremes, but when Satan cannot defeat or stop you he often tries to push you to an extreme.

Have an appropriate balance between time spent in spiritual devotion and ministry and time spent in practical aspects of life, between finance saved and invested in Christ's kingdom and finance used for the legitimate needs of the family, between sacrificial economy in personal dress and expenditures and dressing and living appropriately for your role in life and your ministry, between being separate from the world and yet mixing socially with worldly people so as to influence them and win them to Christ.

The Holy Spirit can help you keep a wholesome balance between avoiding difficult issues and always becoming antagonistic or negative. He can help you avoid both ignoring problems and overreacting to problems. First, ask the Spirit to help you see the other person's situation and viewpoint. Second, avoid rehashing and brooding over situations. Ask the Spirit's help to address situations which you are responsible to change and which can be changed. Commit all other situations to the Lord. Intercede for those for whom you feel a spiritual responsibility.

HOLINESS AND SELF-CONTROL. The new spiritual lifestyle of the born-again Christian is made possible by and is dependent upon the work of the indwelling Holy Spirit. Self-discipline or self-control is one of the beautiful fruits of the Spirit (Gal. 5:23). "God did not give us a spirit of timidity, but a spirit of power, of love and of self-control" (2 Tim. 1:7). Note the role of the Spirit, especially in the life of the sanctified as he develops this fruit of the Spirit.

1. *The Spirit liberates you to exercise self-control.* The unsaved person and even to some extent the unsanctified Christian is under the domination of the sinful self. The law of the Spirit of life sets you free from the law of sin and death (one of the names for the sinful nature) (Rom. 8:2). "Where the Spirit of the Lord is, there is freedom" (2 Cor. 3:17). Where the fullness of the Spirit reigns, there is fullness of freedom. You are liberated to be all God wants you to be and all you hunger to be in Christ.

2. *The Spirit illuminates your mind to understand God's will in self-control.* Among the ways in which the Spirit leads you (Rom. 8:14) are His guiding you into new understandings of God's truth (John 16:13) and how to apply it practically in your life. The Spirit desires to make the witness of your life a great glory to God and a

testimony to the unsaved. He teaches you all you need for your spiritual walk with the Lord (John 14:26).

You often do not realize how much the world about you has influenced you and in how many ways you are almost unconsciously conformed to the culture and ways of the world (Rom. 12:2). If you have been converted to Christ from another religion, you may unconsciously carry over some of the attitudes, beliefs, and lifestyle of your past into your new Christian life. The Holy Spirit gladly illuminates your mind point by point as He progressively educates you in the things of Christ. Then you can discipline your own mind to the life of Christian holiness.

3. *The Spirit gives you the power to discipline your own spiritual life.* The Spirit does not treat you like a robot and make your decisions for you. But He empowers you to do God's will, to walk in the light He is giving you (1 John 1:7).

2 Peter 1:3--"His divine power has given us everything we need for life and godliness through our knowledge of him who called us."

"In order that you may live a life worthy of the Lord and may please him in every way: bearing fruit in every good work" you are "strengthened with all power according to his glorious might" (Col. 1:10-11). Thus the vision of the holy life which the Spirit gives you becomes possible through the Spirit's power within you. He enables you to choose and to do God's good will.

4. *The Spirit gives you power to add more and more self-control to your spiritual life.* You are exhorted to add it; but it is through the Spirit's help that you do so. "Make every effort to add to your faith goodness; and to goodness knowledge; and to knowledge self-control"--for these qualities are to be in your life "in increasing measure" and then you can be effective and productive, says Peter (2 Peter 1:5-8).

WAYS IN WHICH THE SPIRIT CAN HELP AND USE YOUR SELF-DISCIPLINE. Since self-discipline is a fruit of the Spirit, you can be sure it has application and significance in many ways in your life.

1. *Self-discipline in avoiding temptation.* No human being can avoid being tempted. Even Christ was repeatedly tempted, tempted "in every way, just as we are" (Heb. 4:15).

1 Corinthians 10:13--"God is faithful; he will not let you be tempted beyond what you can bear. But when you are tempted, he will also provide a way out (Greek: the way out) so that you can stand up under it."

But you are responsible as far as possible to avoid meeting temptations unless it is in the path of duty. In the Lord's prayer you pray, "Lead us not into temptation" (Matt. 6:13). But you must discipline yourself to avoid temptation as much as you can (Ps. 1:1). Those who were enslaved by sinful habits before they were born again should discipline themselves not to go where they will be specially tempted again.

Every Christian has some weaknesses. If you recognize areas where some sin could be specially attractive, avoid permitting yourself to be in places or situations where temptation could be strong. If you call on the Spirit to strengthen you and do your part in avoiding temptation, you will always be victorious.

2. *Self-discipline in your emotions and moods.* Your emotions are part of your God-given personality. Emotions are God's gift to make life more significant, rewarding, and safe. The Bible gives guidelines to control negative and express positive emotions. Emotions are your perceived feelings, passion is intense emotion, and mood is emotion of long duration.

Emotions, passions, and moods can be holy, normal, and spiritually beneficial. God is moved by holy emotions. It is spiritual to love God and hate sin, to rejoice with those who rejoice, and to mourn with those who mourn (Rom. 12:15). God's children have wholesome emotions.

How wonderful to have a passion for Christ, a passion of love for the unsaved. But how terrible to be possessed with sinful passions. Christians with a joyful mood, a faith-filled mood are a blessing. Christians with a negative or antagonistic mood are a great problem and poor testimony for Christ.

But the world is filled with sorrow, suffering, and chaos because of sinful emotions and lives, as well as personalities that are disordered and destroyed by exaggerated and almost uncontrolled emotions, passions, and moods. These Satan uses in slavery to sin.

The Holy Spirit has a manifold role in guiding, sanctifying, and using your emotions, passions, and moods. He guides you in keeping all in balance and helping you develop a wholesome personality. He restrains you from excessive emotional expression or uncleansed emotional expression. He helps you keep your emotions in balance, spiritually appropriate, and constructively productive. But you must be sensitive to His guidance and restraint.

It is Satan who tries to push people into unreasoned emotion, prejudiced emotion, and fanaticism. The Spirit reminds you of scriptural guidelines, blesses you with Christlike emotions, and helps you discipline your moods.

3. *Self-discipline unto spiritual growth.* Spiritual growth is not automatic. Hebrews 12 tells of Christians who have been Christians long enough to be teachers of others yet "you need someone to teach you the elementary truths of God's Word all over again. You need milk, not solid food" (Heb. 5:12). Three verses later we are urged to "go on to maturity" (Heb. 6:1).

The problem with those Christians was that they had not matured. They had not grown in grace. When such a deplorable condition exists among Christians, there must be one major cause: They have not exercised self-discipline to maintain habits and practices of prayer, fasting, the study of God's Word, witnessing, and seeking to bless and serve others in Christ's name.

Lack of spiritual maturity cannot be blamed on God. You must choose to avail yourself of your Christian privileges. You must choose to walk in God's light and use the means of grace which God has provided. Self-discipline in spiritual matters is up to your choice. Then God will help you develop in holy maturity until your life will be greatly used of God.

44

GROWING IN GRACE

God has created you with amazing capacity for spiritual growth. It is spiritually natural to grow in all aspects of your spiritual life. Growth is a law of life, and salvation is spiritual life. In physical life, you grow to physical maturity. But in spiritual life, you are to grow to Christlikeness, so that spiritual growth is almost endless (Eph. 4:13). This is progressive, positive sanctification.

Jesus, at His return, "will transform our lowly bodies so that they will be like his glorious body" (Phil. 3:21). Then you will be like Him, for you will see Him as He is (1 John 3:2). Since you have this glorious hope, you are to purify yourself even as He is pure (1 John 3:3). Make spiritual preparation for the time when you will be transformed with a glorified body. Then you will share the full likeness of Jesus (1 Cor. 15:49).

This physical transformation into the likeness of Christ's glorified physical body will be instantaneous. "In a flash, in the twinkling of an eye . . . we will be changed" (1 Cor. 15:52). But the spiritual transformation of your personality and character into full Christlikeness now is dependent upon a cleansing crisis experience and progressive growth experience.

Spiritual growth begins at the moment of the new birth. For a time the spiritual picture of the new believer is that of an infant. "Like newborn babes, crave spiritual milk, so that by it you may grow up in your salvation" (1 Peter 2:2). A baby is beautiful to see, a cause of great joy, and there is joy in heaven over the spiritual birth of a new believer (Luke 15:7).

However, a healthy baby begins to grow rapidly and there is continued joy to see the growth and signs of increasing maturity as the infant learns to walk, speak, and develops physically, mentally, and emotionally into an adult with a wholesome personality. If growth stops at any time or is abnormally slow, there is real concern over the health of the child. There should be! Growth is normal. Lack of growth is abnormal.

Similarly, spiritual growth should be rapid after the new birth and should be continuous as long as you live. While physical maturity is reached after a few years, spiritual growth and increasing maturity can and should increase until you reach heaven. You are created in Christ Jesus for lifelong spiritual growth. Observation shows, however, that not all Christians grow equally or continuously.

ENTIRE SANCTIFICATION AND GROWTH. Entire sanctification is not a matter of growth. It is a matter of cleansing and empowering. It is accomplished in you by the Holy Spirit in response to your consecration and faith (Rom. 12:1; Acts 15:9; 26:18). It is not an unending process. It is an experience received at a definite time when you appropriate it by faith. It is of the nature of a spiritual crisis; that is, there is a moment when you receive the Holy Spirit in His fullness.

The cleansing and empowering, however, open the way for much more rapid and unhindered spiritual growth. As weeds hinder the growth of plants or flowers in a garden, so the sinful nature remaining in the heart of the new believer hinders full and constant spiritual growth. As a virus or disease germ or cancerous growth can hinder physical health and normal physical growth, so the sinful nature hinders growth into full Christlikeness.

Holiness is both negative and positive. Negatively, it is cleansing. The cleansing is complete in the moment of consecration and faith. When the Holy Spirit cleanses through the blood of Christ, He cleanses from all sin (1 John 1:7). You do not grow clean. You are washed clean.

Positively, holiness is the power of the Spirit filling you and controlling you. This also occurs in a moment of time, the same moment that you are cleansed. However, positively, holiness is also

Christlikeness. Once you are cleansed from the sin nature and filled with the Spirit's power, you can grow more and more like Christ. Instantly you become pure. Progressively, you grow more Christlike in all the positive fruit of the Spirit (Gal. 5:22-23). The Holy Spirit desires to make each of these kinds of Spirit-fruit more complete, more beautiful, more fragrant, more practical as you live the life of holiness.

The most comprehensive and most manifestly Christlike of these is the first fruit listed--love. Love for God is the first and greatest commandment. Love for others is the second (Matt. 22:37-40). There is no commandment greater than these (Mark 12:31), because love is the very nature of God (1 John 4:8, 16).

In some sense, love includes all the other listed fruit. It has been said that they are all expressions of love: Joy is love rejoicing. Peace is love resting. Patience is love enduring. Kindness is love helping. Goodness is love blessing. Faithfulness is love loyal and dependable. Gentleness is love showing restrained consideration. Self-control is love governing all actions and reactions.

To describe adequately the personal character and personality of Jesus all of the mentioned fruit of the Spirit must be included. You are not fully Christlike unless all of these are manifested and flow from your nature as you relate to others.

HOW WE GROW IN GRACE. Growth in grace is dependent upon the work of the Spirit within you and on your whole-souled cooperation. Thus, the complete surrender of your being in the total consecration that leads to entire sanctification is the prerequisite for the luxuriant growth of the fruit of the Spirit. The Spirit is the infinite source from which the profusion of the graces flow, and your sanctified being as a believer is the clear, unimpeded channel through which the nature of Christ is poured in visible expression into your behavior.

Four primary requirements to growing in grace are:

A. *Drink deeply of the Spirit.* The Holy Spirit is the wonderful Person who is your Guide, your Helper as you grow in Christlikeness, and your Giver of all God's grace and power. He indwells you when you are born again, fills you when He sanctifies you entirely, and rejoices to develop in you the beautiful character of Jesus.

The Holy Spirit takes the things Jesus wants you to know and the beautiful Christly attitudes Jesus wants you to share (Phil. 2:5) and reveals these to you and in you. Jesus promised, "He will bring glory to me by taking what is mine and making it known to you" (John 16:14).

Jesus had just told the disciples that He had much more that He wanted to share with them. That is Jesus' heart's desire today also. He wants you to be like Him in every possible way. So a major role of the Holy Spirit in your life is to transform you more and more into the likeness of Christ. If anyone constantly longs for this, it is surely the pure in heart. How can you cooperate with Christ so as to grow more constantly and beautifully? How can you drink deeply of the Spirit?

1. *Long for the Spirit to make you ever more like Jesus.* Long for the Spirit to possess you and lead you, to reveal Christ in you. Long and hunger to be more Christlike each day.

2. *Appropriate by faith more and more of the Spirit's presence and power.* The promise is yours, "If you . . . know how to give good gifts to your children, how much more will your Father in heaven give the Holy Spirit to those who ask him" (Luke 11:13). Reach out your hand of faith and receive more of the Spirit each day.

3. *Fellowship with the Spirit.* Live in the Spirit. Rejoice in the Spirit. Sing in the Spirit. All this is a part of fellowship. "Spirit of the living God, fall afresh on me." Let that be your daily prayer. Thank the Spirit, just as you thank the Father and Jesus. Live in loving fellowship with all three Persons of the Trinity daily.

B. *Feed constantly upon God's Word.* Spiritual growth depends upon spiritual food. There is no spiritual food so nourishing, so health giving, so conducive to constant growth as the pure Word of God. Other writings can bless and nourish you to the extent they contain and teach God's Word and truth. But the Word itself is the most spiritually nourishing food of all.

1. *Read the Word.* It will be spiritual milk to your soul to help you "grow up" (1 Peter 2:2). The more you read it the more sweet and precious it becomes to you. "How sweet are your words to my taste, sweeter than honey to my mouth" (Ps. 119:103). Spiritual health and growth depend on constant reading and feeding on God's Word.

Read it extensively. Read it consecutively. Repeatedly read your Bible through from beginning to end. Read the New Testament through again and again. It is not enough to read devotional books about the Bible. Read the Bible itself. It is not enough to read a few verses or read a promise or two. You need the whole Word of God to really grow.

Sanctified people should be so hungry for God's Word, so constantly feeding on God's Word that they know the Bible increasingly well and grow rapidly in grace.

2. *Meditate on God's Word.* Meditation is prayerfully considering God's Word. In meditation you concentrate on a verse or verses and prayerfully seek all the wonderful meaning they contain. You can meditate best when you are alone with God. You can also meditate while you do many kinds of work that do not demand close concentration of your thought. You can meditate for some moments several times a day. The Spirit may bring a verse or passage to your mind while you are doing routine work that does not require your close attention.

The godly person meditates on God's Word in free moments day and night (Ps. 1:2; 119:97). He wants his meditation to be pleasing to the Lord (19:14; 104:34). He delights in God's Word (119:16, 24). God's promises bring special blessing as you meditate on them (119:148). Memorizing God's Word also helps plant and hide it in your heart (119:11).

C. *Breathe deeply heaven's spiritual atmosphere as you commune in prayer.* Make communing in prayer your day-long delight. Be ardent in your love to Jesus. On your first waking moment, tell Him you love Him. Again and again throughout your day, talk to Him as you go about your activities. Sometimes you may be able to snatch several minutes to spend with Jesus. At other times you can only lift your heart for a moment or two, expressing again your love, your thanks, your praise.

By all means, reserve one or more times each day for your devotional time, your Bible reading, and more prolonged prayer. But fill your day with dozens of love moments with Jesus. Whenever your mind is free, even for a half minute, commune again briefly with Jesus.

Adore Him, worship Him, praise Him, rejoice in Him, share your love with Him. This is the secret of praying without ceasing, of unbroken communion and fellowship with Jesus. Listen to the words of Jesus, "If anyone loves me, he will obey my teaching. My Father will love him, and we will make our home with him" (John 14:23). "If anyone hears my voice and opens the door, I will come in and eat with him, and he with me" (Rev. 3:20). As you commune and feast with Jesus your soul will grow in grace and Christlikeness. The more you look into His face the more Christlike you will become.

D. *Regularly exercise yourself spiritually.* Jesus wants and deserves your joyous service. Prove your love by your obedience and your serving Him in as many ways as possible. Serving Jesus is as essential to your spiritual growth and health as drinking, eating, and breathing deeply. Every day serve Him by your intercession and blessing others. Seize as many opportunities as you can to serve Him. You serve Jesus by serving His Church, His other children, and the unsaved.

1. *Serve Jesus daily by intercession.* Jesus' priority ministry, His most constant ministry today, is His intercession. Christ's heaviest burden today is His prayer burden for an unsaved and suffering world and for a Church He loves so intensely, yet which responds to His love with such casual indifference and disobedience. If you want to help Jesus most, help Him where He needs help most--in intercession.

God has ordained that your intercession unite with that of Christ. When you fail to do your part, God's intercessory plan is incomplete. Many answers which God would be pleased to grant are never granted because you fail to intercede (James 4:2).

Intercession is the greatest and most strategic way any Christian can serve Christ. No Christian or Christian leader is ever greater than his prayers. But any Christian can be mighty in prayer if he is willing. The more you intercede, the more mighty you become in intercession. Every Christian should use daily prayer lists with names of church leaders, government leaders, the unsaved, mission fields, and a constantly changing list of emergency requests for those ill and for special needs.

You can serve Jesus as fully by prayer as you desire. The more you pray for others, the more you will be blessed and the more your vision, compassion, and Christlikeness will grow. When you put Christ's interests first, He will put your spiritual welfare and your needs on His priority list.

2. *Bless all you can.* God sent Jesus to bless the world (Acts 3:26) because God is a God who blesses. God is love and He loves to bless. He showers blessings on the unsaved as well as on the saved. He wants His Church to bless the world on His behalf. Not only are you to bless the world by being His light and His salt, you are to bless the world with your love and prayer. As Jesus loved our youth, took our children in His arms and blessed them, so you should take people as they are and love them and bless them for Jesus' sake.

When you see a child, a youth, or an adult, love them for Jesus' sake. Breathe a prayer of blessing on as many as you can. Breathe a prayer of blessing on the churches you pass, on the villages or towns you pass through, on the homes you enter. Go through your day blessing people with your brief prayer, your smiles, and your helpfulness.

Jesus went around doing good, healing, and blessing, according to the people's needs (Acts 10:38). Now He sends you in

His name. Encourage, strengthen, help, show kindness, serve, and bless in every way you can. Witness, give, lead to Christ, do all you can to help advance Christ's kingdom. The more you serve others in Jesus' name, the more you will be blessed and the more you will grow spiritually. Be a Barnabas; he was "a good man, full of the Holy Spirit and faith." The result? "A great number of people were brought to the Lord" (Acts 11:24).

GOD'S CALL TO GROWTH. God has a vision of the person you can be through the gracious help of the Holy Spirit. You have never dreamed of the full Christlikeness the Spirit is seeking to develop in you. Entire sanctification starts you in a lifelong pursuit of growth in positive holiness. For this you must daily hunger and pray, and toward this you must strive as a runner in a race.

The constant danger is that you become conformed, molded, shaped in your thinking, lifestyle, and actions by the thought, culture, and manner of living of the unsaved and worldly people about you (Rom. 12:2). To avoid this, Paul says you need to "be transformed by the renewing of your mind. Then you will be able to test and prove what God's will is--His good, pleasing, and perfect will."

In the Greek, the word "transformed" in this verse is "transfigured." It is the same word used of Christ on the Mount of Transfiguration. It is used again in 2 Corinthians 3:18. The holy process of positive transfiguration by the Holy Spirit is progressive sanctification. Thus there is instant initial sanctification in the new birth, instant entire sanctification in the second work of the Holy Spirit, and then a process of transfiguring sanctification--holy growth in Christlikeness.

As God gives you new light on how to please Him more fully, how to be more like Christ, you eagerly walk in this new light. As you do this, the Holy Spirit transforms your inner nature into more and more of the beauty and radiant holiness of Jesus. Your mind is renewed. You catch a vision of new heights in Christ, and by prayer and faith the Spirit leads you to this new higher, more beautiful aspect of the life of holiness.

To put it in other words, Paul says, "We, who with unveiled faces all reflect the Lord's glory, are being transformed into His likeness with ever increasing glory, which comes from the Lord, who is the Spirit" (2 Cor. 3:18). The Berkeley Version translates this, "Into the same likeness from one degree of glory to another."

As the Spirit challenges you with new heights of God's grace, He then leads you into conformity with the new vision, you grow in fuller Christlikeness, and the glory of Christ is reflected in you more beautifully--"from one degree of glory to another." Oh! What a wonderful plan of salvation! Oh! What privileges and possibilities the Spirit holds before you! Praise God for His faithfulness.

Holiness is not a static experience of grace. Entire sanctification begins a thrilling experience of growth in Christlikeness, in fruit of the Spirit, and in God-glorifying living. How long can this continue? "He who began a good work in you will carry it to completion until the day of Christ Jesus" (Phil. 1:6).

45

THE ETHICS OF
THE HOLY LIFE

God not only wills that you be holy in heart, but that you be holy in life. Your outward life must express God's inward grace. You must live like a child of a holy God. Failure to live what you profess would make you a hypocrite. God's grace that cleanses you within is great enough to keep you pure in life. God's power is great enough to make you holy in all your living and in all of your service.

1 Peter 1:15--"Just as he who has called you is holy, so be holy in all you do."

THE IMPORTANCE OF HOLY ETHICS. About one-third of the teachings of Jesus related to Christian life. In the letters of Paul, Peter, James, and John at least half of the content was practical teaching on how to live. Much of New Testament teaching presents clear principles, but it also reports many specific situations which illustrate these principles. The greatest validation of the truth of your gospel should be your holy life.

The ethical instruction in the New Testament is based on the ethical foundations so strongly laid in the Old Testament. The Bible call to holiness began in the Old Testament and is repeated from the Pentateuch to the prophets. God emphasized it to Moses: "I am the Lord your God, consecrate yourselves and be holy, because I am holy. . . . I am the Lord who brought you up out of Egypt to be your God; therefore be holy, because I am holy" (Lev. 11:44-45).

"Consecrate yourselves and be holy, because I am the Lord your God. Keep my decrees and follow them. I am the Lord who makes you holy." "You must not live according to the customs of the nations" (v. 23). "You are to be holy to me because I, the Lord, am holy, and I have set you apart from the nations to be my own" (v. 26). "Be holy because I am the Lord your God" (20:7). Seven times God says, "I am the Lord who makes you holy" or "makes them holy." Therefore, it is not surprising that Peter reiterates this truth in 1 Peter 1:15-16.

Your manifestation of holy ethics is of supreme importance to God and to the testimony of your life. You are called to evidence the character of God in your daily words and acts. Your ethics must be more than the obedience of God's command. It must flow out of God's character which is imparted to you by the Holy Spirit. It is the outflow of the character of God through your new holy nature imparted by the sanctifying, filling work of the Spirit.

You can only be God's salt, God's light, and God's witness to people and society when your ethics is in total conformity with Bible doctrine. You, your God, your doctrine, your church, and Christianity in general are dishonored if your ethics does not validate your testimony to Christ and His salvation.

There is no alternative. You as a holy person must live a holy life. "Everyone who confesses the name of the Lord must turn away from wickedness" (2 Tim. 2:19). How else can you be the light of the world (Matt. 5:14) as Jesus was the Light of the world (John 8:12)? We are to live and serve the Lord "in holiness and righteousness before him all our days" (Luke 1:75).

THE NATURE OF HOLY ETHICS

Your holy ethics must be comprehensive. You are called to be holy in all you do (1 Peter 1:15). If one part of your life is not holy, it contradicts your testimony to having been made holy. If people find one inconsistency, they forget all the good in your character they have seen and point to the obvious failure.

Holy ethics must begin in a holy heart. Its source there is the indwelling Spirit. But it must be demonstrated in your thoughts, your speech, and your actions. It must be demonstrated in your private life, your family life, your church life, and your secular life and work. Holiness must characterize all of your life.

Your holy ethics must be specific. The Bible is highly specific in its requirements. It spells out in hundreds of verses the details in which your holy ethics is to be evident. Holiness is not a mere ideal or beautiful doctrine. It must be lived practically.

If entire sanctification does not make your life holy in specific details, of what value is it? What does 1 Thessalonians 5:23-24 mean if it does not include sanctification in every detail? "May God himself, the God of peace, sanctify you through and through. May your whole spirit, soul and body be kept blameless at the coming of our Lord Jesus Christ. The one who calls you is faithful and he will do it."

The world about you must hear holiness in your words and see holiness in your actions. If holiness is not consistently demonstrated in specific living action, it is valueless.

Your holy ethics must be constant, unchanging, but relevant. Holiness is not defined, measured, or modified by the culture about you, the standards of your day, or by your particular circumstances. It is always God's holiness, Bible holiness, demonstrated holiness.

Yet you must express holiness in your own situation, in your own circumstances. You must mirror God's holiness in your practical life. You must be unchangingly holy in your changing environment, in your context, your day and time. We are to live "godly lives in this present age" (Titus 2:12).

The more positively and evidently holy your life is the greater glory you bring to God, and the greater testimony and conviction of sin you bring to the unsaved. "Live such good lives among the pagans that, though they accuse you of doing wrong, they may see your good deeds and glorify God on the day he visits us" (1 Peter 2:12).

How then can you build a holy testimony into your lifestyle? What are the guidelines you must follow? The instant reply is, "Live according to the Word of God." But how do you apply the Word to specific situations of your day?

Seven simple questions can always help guide you:

1. What does the Bible say? Ps. 119:11, 105, 130; Rom. 15:4; 2 Peter 1:19.

2. What would Jesus do? Rom. 15:5; 1 Cor. 11:1; 1 Peter 2:21.

3. How does the Holy Spirit guide me? John 14:26; 16:13; 1 John 2:27.

4. What does my conscience say? Acts 24:16; Rom. 2:15; 13:5; 2 Cor. 1:12; 1 Tim. 1:5, 19; 1 Peter 3:16.

5. Is this characteristic of the world or of the Father? John 17:14-16; Rom. 12:2; 1 Cor. 10:2; 1 John 2:16.

6. Will this benefit others? Rom. 14:19, 21; 15:2; 1 Cor. 8:9, 12-13; 10:23-24; 14:26; Eph. 4:29.

7. Can I do this for the glory of God? 1 Cor. 10:31; Col. 3:17; 1 Peter 4:11.

Helpful as these seven questions are, you often seek some clear guideline that fits the situation you are facing. The Bible could not go into minute specific details of all the kinds of decisions and choices you will face. Therefore, the Bible gives general principles and occasional illustrations of these principles.

HOLY ETHICS MUST BE GOD-CENTERED. God is the basis of all good. Thus doctrine, for the Christian, cannot be separated from ethics. God is concerned with your life. Salvation changes life. A holy heart is proved by a holy life. The fundamental demand of God is that you be like Him in character. For you as a Christian this means you must be like Jesus (Eph. 5:1-2). Since God's nature is holy love, your ethics must be holy love. There is nothing more basic to all your ethics than for you to love as God loves, as demonstrated by Jesus.

MOTIVES ARE INVOLVED IN HOLY ETHICS. Whatever is contrary to God's holy love is contrary to Bible ethics. But love includes both motive and action. Jesus emphasized that ethics begin in the motive from which the action results. God's judgment, which will be the ultimate recompense or reward, will be primarily based on motive. The deciding factor in righteousness or sin is motive.

Saving faith includes repentance--which aligns the will with God's will and the ethical attitudes with God's attitudes. The total consecration essential in sanctifying faith binds and seals your attitude with God's. Holiness of heart brings holy attitudes which result in holy ethical behavior.

THE HOLY SPIRIT GUIDES IN ETHICS. The Holy Spirit is your ethical light and your ethical guide. He is your ever-present Mentor-Counselor (John 14:16, 26). He seeks to make you Christlike in attitude and action.

The Spirit guides you into all truth (John 16:13) and conforms you to the truth that is in Jesus (Eph. 4:21). The sanctifying Spirit sanctifies the life as well as the heart. Out of the abundance of the heart the mouth speaks (Matt. 12:34), and out of the abundance of the heart the life flows (John 7:38-39). God's righteous (i.e., ethical) requirements are fulfilled in those who have crucified the sinful nature and live "according to the Spirit" (Rom. 8:4). This is possible because their mind is set on what the Spirit desires (v. 5).

The Holy Spirit illumines and guides in how to translate into action and life holy, Christlike love. He shows how to apply the truth of Jesus into holy living and interpersonal relationships with God's family and with the sinners for whom Christ died. Those about you see the fruit of the Spirit in your mind-set, your lifestyle, and your fulfillment of all duty--in the family, in the work place, and in civic and governmental relations.

YOUR ETHICAL GOAL IS CHRISTLIKENESS. You live constantly in the sight of God and as in the light of eternity. You delight to do more than minimum duty. You delight to represent Jesus. You seek to bless as many as you can, for you represent a God who blesses. You seek to scatter light and joy because you represent the God who is light and who is the source of all true joy.

You seek to do good to all people (Gal. 6:10) because God is good to all (Ps. 145:9).

The Spirit delights to transform you into the ethical likeness of Jesus. This is reflected in your face and personality (2 Cor. 3:18) and is demonstrated in Christlike living. Moses prayed, "May the beauty (margin) of the Lord our God rest upon us" (Ps. 90:17). That hunger of his heart was satisfied when on Mount Sinai the Shekinah glory of God temporarily radiated from his face after he left God's presence (Exod. 34:29). We today long that the beauty of Jesus may be seen not merely on our faces but in all we do.

COMMITMENT IS REQUIRED FOR HOLY ETHICS. To live holy ethics requires a fourfold commitment:

1. *You must love God supremely* (Matt. 22:38)--the first and greatest commandment.

2. *You must love people with agape love,* loving others as yourself (Matt. 22:39-40). This is the second great commandment, and Jesus' "new" commandment. "As I have loved you, so you must love one another" (John 13:34).

3. *You must keep separate from sin and the world.* "Do not love the world or anything in the world. If anyone loves the world, the love of the Father is not in him. For everything in the world--the cravings of sinful man, the lust of his eyes and the boasting of what he has and does--comes not from the Father but from the world" (1 John 2:15-17).

4. *You must apply sanctified ethics to the details of your life.* The Spirit enables, guides, and helps you discipline yourself in applying biblical principles, especially New Testament ethical principles, to the details of life.

HOLY ACTION IS REQUIRED FOR HOLY ETHICS. Cleansed from sin, filled with holy, Christlike love, and guided and empowered by the Spirit, you as a Spirit-filled Christian are to demonstrate holiness and love in all you do. You are sent into the world for witness by life as well as word. You are sent for involvement, not avoidance of life (John 17:15-18). You are sent to live as Christ's ambassador (2 Cor. 5:20). You are sent to be busy in good deeds, thus being Christ's light in the world (Matt. 5:16), Christ's salt in the earth (Matt. 5:13). You are purified that you may be eager to do good (Titus 2:14).

As a sanctified person you must take pains to do what is right in the sight of God and people (2 Cor. 8:21; Rom. 12:7). You are "created in Christ Jesus to do good works" (Eph. 2:10). This is the whole purpose of Christian living. You are to be "ready to do whatever is good" (Titus 3:1), to "be careful to devote" yourself to doing what is good (v. 8). Paul says, "Our people must learn to devote themselves to doing what is good" so that they do "not live unproductive lives" (v. 14). God requires you to live a productive life.

God does not want you to be unseen, unheard, and unnoticed. He wants you to be active, so that people see you, see the testimony of your life, see the difference between your life and the lives of non-Christians. You are not to retreat from the world, but to let your light shine in the world. The fire of the Spirit is to fire you to do good in any way you possibly can (2 Tim. 1:6). God has saved you and equipped you to make a difference in your world.

God is constantly blessing the world--the saved and the unsaved. You are to be constantly blessing the world by your life. You are to do what is needed, to go the extra mile, to give your work your best, to be alert, diligent, constantly giving of yourself in good deeds done in a Christlike way, with such overflowing love that the world has to take note that you are a Christian.

Rule-keeping does not make you ethical in the Christian sense unless it is done from the right motive. A person can outwardly seem to be ethical when his heart is unrighteous. A heart filled with holy love is therefore essential to live New Testament ethics. Yet the holy heart love must be expressed in outward observable ways.

Satisfactory ethics require biblical principles to guide, and the Spirit-guided application of these principles in the details of living. Spirit-enabled living out in detail of the basic Bible principles results in Christlikeness of character, life, and service. To be Christlike also involves separation from what is not Christlike--sin, the world, and the principles of the world. Complete holiness of life requires both positive Christlikeness and negative separation.

GENERAL BIBLE PRINCIPLES

1. *Certain clear Bible statements are always true;* e.g., Honor your father and your mother (Exod. 20:12). You shall not give false testimony (Exod. 20:16). Store up treasures in heaven rather than on earth (Matt. 6:19-21). Do not have a judgmental attitude (Matt. 7:1-5).

2. *Some Bible teachings become more clear and specific under New Testament light.* You should live by the fuller light; e.g., Old Testament: "You shall not commit adultery" (Exod. 20:14). New Testament: "Do not lust" (Matt. 5:27-28). OT: "Remember the Sabbath day by keeping it holy" (Exod. 20:8). NT: "It is lawful to do good on the Sabbath" (Matt. 12:12).

3. *You can derive principles from historical incidents in the Bible.* Example 1: In telling the truth it is sometimes wise to conceal part of the facts to protect others. Samuel only told part of the reason he visited Bethlehem. Saul had no right to know all the reasons for Samuel's visit (1 Sam. 16:1-3). Example 2: You should seek to be a blessing to those you meet, especially those who help you with God's work. Elisha sought to bless the home in Shunam, and prayed for the birth of a child (2 Kings 4:1-17).

4. *A general principle can be derived from Bible statements that are for a very specific situation.* Example 1: God is able to heal. The Bible instructs us to pray for healing (James 3:14-18). God used Paul to heal others, so most probably he himself was often healed. Yet Paul told Timothy to use a little wine "because of your stomach and your frequent illnesses" (1 Tim. 5:23). He also took Dr. Luke with him in his travels as a co-worker, and most probably at times used Luke's medical skill. The Christian, like Paul, has full liberty to use medical help, for God has helped medical science to develop.

Example 2: God's call and God's will can take precedence over family interests and desires. The Bible teaches that we have responsibility for our family (Mark 7:9-12; Eph. 6:2; 1 Tim. 5:8). Yet we are not to let this become an excuse for disobeying God. You do not dishonor your parents by putting God first. When a disciple said to Jesus, "Lord, first let me go and bury my father," Jesus replied, "Follow me, and let the dead bury their own dead" (Matt. 8:21-22). Whether the disciple's father was merely in his old age and wanted his son near, or whether he had a lingering illness, Jesus put the claims of God first.

5. *Bible truths cast light on ethical questions.* Example 1: You are created in the image of God. You are Godlike in capacity, are owned by God your creator, and have been purchased by Christ's death on the cross. This casts light on why the sins of murder and abortion are not merely sins against the person and government, but, above all, a sin against God. Since your body and life belong to God, it is your duty to take care of your body for God's sake. You have no right to commit suicide.

Neither do you have a right to shorten your life by alcohol, tobacco, lack of proper exercise, eating foods that are not good for your health, or overeating until you put on excess weight and become more susceptible to diabetes, heart disease, high blood pressure, and other diseases. All these become a matter of holy ethics because you belong to God.

1 Corinthians 6:19-20--"Do you not know that your body is a temple of the Holy Spirit, who is in you, whom you have received from God? You are not your own; you were bought at a price. Therefore, honor God with your body."

Example 2: "Six days you shall labor and do all your work, but the seventh is the Sabbath to the Lord your God" (Exod. 20:9-10). It is normally as much God's command to be usefully busy at work six days a week as it is to rest and worship on the seventh. Every home, church, and community have worthwhile and needed things to be done. When you have spare time, whether you are paid for doing these things or not, you can volunteer and be a help and blessing to others. This can be a great testimony for God. If you have satisfactory health--and since you have a Bible to read, prayers that need to be prayed, good deeds by which you could help extend Christ's kingdom and bless others--it is unethical to waste time or use large amounts of time in ways that have no spiritual or physical benefit and which do not help others.

SELECTED BIBLICAL ETHICAL PRINCIPLES. A brief list of biblical ethical principles to guide you in your moral choices and conduct:

A. In Relation to God

    1. *Be holy in all you do.* 1 Peter 1:15; Isa. 35:8; 1 Thess. 4:7; 1 John 3:3.

    2. *Consecrate yourself and be holy.* Lev. 20:7; Rom. 12:1; 6:13, 16, 19; 1 Peter 2:5.

    3. *Honor God with your body.* Rom. 12:1; 1 Cor. 6:13, 19-20; 9:27. Do nothing which weakens your body or becomes a habit which enslaves your body (1 Cor. 6:12).

    4. *Honor God with your time. Do not be idle.* Matt. 20:6; Prov. 6:9-11; 10:18; 31:27; Eccl. 11:6; 1 Thess. 5:14; 2 Thess. 3:6, 11; 1 Tim. 5:13.

    5. *Honor God with your finance.* Mal. 3:8-12; Acts 20:35; 1 Cor. 16:2; 2 Cor. 9:6-15.

    6. *Imitate God especially by your love.* Eph. 5:1-2; Matt. 5:48; Luke 6:36; John 13:34; 15:12; 1 Thess. 1:6; 1 John 4:10-11.

    7. *Live like Jesus.* 1 John 2:6; 3:3.

B. In Relation to Fellow-Christians

    1. *Serve others in love.* Rom. 12:10; Gal. 5:13; Eph. 4:2; 1 Thess. 4:9; Heb. 13:1; 1 Peter 1:22.

    2. *Honor others above yourself.* Rom. 12:10; 13:7; Phil. 2:3; 1 Peter 5:5.

    3. *Live in harmony with others.* Rom. 12:16; 15:5; 1 Cor. 1:10; 2 Cor. 13:11; Eph. 4:3; Phil. 2:2; Col. 3:14; 1 Peter 3:8.

    4. *Take the initiative in reconciling any interpersonal problems.* Matt. 5:23-24; Ps. 34:14; Rom. 12:17-18; 14:19; 1 Cor. 7:15; 2 Tim. 2:22; Heb. 12:14.

5. *Always be willing to forgive.* Luke 17:1-49; Matt. 6:14-15; Eph. 4:2, 32; Col. 3:13.

6. *Bear with the failings of the weak.* Rom. 15:1; Rom. 14:1; 1 Cor. 8:9-13; 2 Cor. 6:3; Eph. 4:2; 1 Thess. 5:14.

7. *Strive to build up others.* Rom. 14:19; 15:2; 1 Thess. 5:11; Eph. 4:12, 16, 29. Be constructive (1 Cor. 10:23-24).

8. *Confront and then comfort brothers or sisters who sin.* Matt. 18:15-17; Lev. 19:17; Luke 17:3-4; Gal. 6:1; 2 Cor. 2:5-11; James 5:19-20.

9. *Help lift financial loads from fellow-believers in need.* Deut. 15:7-11; Matt. 25:35-36; Luke 16:9; Rom. 12:13; Heb. 13:16; James 2:15-16; 1 John 3:17-18.

10. *Seek practical ways to encourage fellow-believers and help bear their burdens.* Gal. 5:13; 6:2, 10; 2 Cor. 8:11-15; Phil. 4:14; Heb. 10:33-34; 13:3; 1 Peter 3:27.

11. *Maintain a servant-spirit.* John 13:14-17; Matt. 11:29; 20:28; 1 Cor. 9:19; 2 Cor. 4:5; Gal. 5:13; 1 Peter 2:16.

12. *Be completely humble.* Eph. 4:2; Matt. 11:29; Rom. 12:16, 18; 15:5; 1 Cor. 1:10; Phil. 2:3; 5:8; Col. 3:12; Titus 3:2; James 4:6, 8, 10; 1 Peter 3:8; 5:5-6.

13. *Avoid a critical or judgmental spirit.* Rom. 14:1-4, 10, 13; Matt. 7:1-5; Luke 6:41-42; 1 Cor. 4:5; 5:12; James 4:11-12.

14. *Do not go to law against a fellow-Christian.* 1 Cor. 6:1-8.

15. *Make strenuous efforts to maintain peace and harmony.* Eph. 4:3; Rom. 12:16, 18; 14:19-15:7; 15:5; 1 Cor. 1:10; 2 Cor. 13:11; Phil. 2:2; Col. 3:14-15; 1 Peter 3:8; Prov. 20:3.

16. *Avoid sexual sin.* 1 Cor. 6:13, 15-20; Matt. 5:27-30; Eph. 5:3-5; 1 Thess. 4:3-8.

17. *Avoid causing anyone to stumble.* Rom. 14:13; 15:1-2; 1 Cor. 10:32; 2 Cor. 6:3.

18. *Live a life worthy of Jesus.* Phil. 1:27; Col. 1:10; 1 Thess. 1:7; 2 Thess. 1:11; 1 Tim. 4:16; 1 Peter 2:12.

19. *Be content. Avoid complaining.* Phil. 2:14-16; 4:11-13; 1 Tim. 6:6; Heb. 13:5.

20. *Be an encourager.* Heb. 3:13; 10:25.

21. *Love fellow-believers.* John 15:12, 17; 1 Peter 1:22, 2:17; 3:8; 4:8; 1 John 2:10; 3:11, 14, 16-18, 23; 4:7-12, 16, 19-21; 5:1-2; 2 John 5-6.

C. In Relation to Public in General

1. *Whatever your work, be diligent. Do not be idle.* Col. 3:23-24; 2 Thess. 3:6-12; Heb. 6:12.

2. *Be generous to the poor and needy.* Deut. 15:7-11; Ps. 41:1-3; 112:9; Prov. 14:21, 31; 19:17; 31:8-9; Matt. 6:2-3; Luke 6:38; 12:33-34; 14:12-14; 18:22.

3. *Watch your speech.* Ps. 39:1; 141:3; Prov. 10:19; 17:28; 21:23; Matt. 5:33-37; Eph. 4:29; Col. 4:6; Titus 2:8; James 1:19, 26; 3:2-12; 5:12; 1 Peter 3:10, 15.

4. *Be a peacemaker.* Matt. 5:19; James 3:18.

5. *Show no partiality.* James 2:1, 8-9; 3:17.

6. *Be known for doing good.* 2 Tim. 2:21; Titus 2:7, 14; 3:1, 14; Heb. 13:16; 1 Peter 2:12; 3:16.

7. *React as a Christian to unjust suffering.* Matt. 5:11-12; 1 Cor. 1:5; 1 Peter 4:12-19; 3:17.

8. *Be merciful.* Matt. 5:7; Luke 6:36; 10:29-37; James 2:13; Jude 23.

9. *Stand firm under testing.* James 1:2, 12; 5:11; 1 Peter 1:6-7; 3:14; 4:12-16, 19.

10. *Practice your beliefs.* James 1:22-25; 2:14-26; Luke 6:46-49; 8:31; 11:28.

11. *Be gentle.* Isa. 42:2; Phil. 4:5; 1 Peter 3:15.

12. *Be completely separate from all evil.* 2 Cor. 6:17; 7:1; Rom. 12:9; 1 Thess. 5:22.

13. *Keep your lifestyle free of love of the world.* Matt. 5:13-16; 1 John 2:15-17; 5:4-5.

14. *Don't be a stumbling block.* Rom. 14:13; 1 Cor. 8:9; 10:32; 2 Cor. 6:3; 1 John 2:10.

15. *Return good for evil.* Luke 6:27-36; Matt. 5:43-48; Rom. 12:20-21.

16. *Do to others as you would have them do to you.* Luke 6:31; Matt. 7:12.

17. *Be generous.* Luke 6:38.

18. *Love your neighbor as yourself.* Matt. 22:39; 5:43-48.

19. *Be patient.* Rom. 12:12; 1 Cor. 13:4; 2 Cor. 6:6; Gal. 5:22; Eph. 4:2; Col. 1:11; 3:12; 1 Thess. 5:14; 2 Tim. 4:2; James 5:7; Rev. 3:10.

46

YOUR ROLE AS
A HOLY LEADER

God wants sanctified leaders for His Church. The whole world needs sanctified leadership in every area of life. All groups find their closest unity, their most satisfying interpersonal relations, and their most effective growth and activity when led by people characterized by holy love. Every local church and every Christian organization needs a leader or leaders who are (1) holy, (2) loving, and (3) dynamic. That is what the sanctifying fullness of the Holy Spirit helps you become. He helps every leader be a better leader, a biblical leader.

HOLINESS IS ESSENTIAL TO YOU AS A CHRISTIAN LEADER. There is no holiness without a holy heart and holy life. Holiness insures righteousness, honesty, integrity, and that which is acceptable and pleasing to God. Let us define these further.

1. *To be a holy leader you must be righteous.* To be righteous is to be morally right, to be free from all guilt and blame, to do always what you know is just, ethical, and noble.

2. *To be a holy leader is to be honest.* To be honest is always to be truthful, sincere, open, fair, and impartial.

3. *To be a holy leader is to have total integrity.* You must never be false to your responsibility or to one who trusts you. Offers of benefits, position, or reward should never for a moment influence you away from what is right and what is your duty. No one can buy your action.

The more people know you to be a holy leader, the more they trust you. They realize that anyone can make a mistake, but they know their best interests, their reputation, and God's cause are safe in your hands. You must never knowingly go against your conscience or against your best understanding and judgment. You must be true to all those you lead. You must be totally worthy of trust.

AGAPE LOVE IS ESSENTIAL TO YOU AS A CHRISTIAN LEADER. *Agape* is the great New Testament Greek word for love. It is love by choice for God or man. It is self-giving commitment. It is love, not for what you will receive in return but for what you can and long to do for the one loved. God is perfect agape. The Cross is the supreme revelation of agape love (Rom. 5:8-10).

The sanctified leader loves God with all his heart, soul, mind, and strength, and loves everyone he leads as fully and as faithfully as he loves himself (Mark 12:30-31). He loves them because Christ loves them so infinitely. He loves them for Christ's sake and with Christ's love.

Holy agape love is defined and described in 1 Corinthians 13, especially in verses 4-8. Since agape love never fails (verse 8) and always remains (verse 13), this love must always be manifested by a sanctified leader. What does this include?

The sanctified leader has love that is patient with young and old, with all in the group he leads, even those who are not careful to follow his leadership or who reject his leadership. His patience is never exhausted. It always continues (v. 4).

The sanctified leader is always kind (v. 4). He is always gentle with his followers, considerate of them, and always is interested in each of them. He is concerned for their welfare, sympathetic with their interests and problems, and identifies with them in their needs. His unwavering kindness binds their hearts to his.

The sanctified leader never envies others (v. 4). He rejoices in their talents, their blessings, and their successes. He gladly recognizes, appreciates, and commends whatever is true, noble, right, pure, lovely, admirable, excellent, or praiseworthy (Phil. 3:8) in others. Therefore, he gladly makes use of the help of others, seeks to give them opportunities to succeed, and gives them full credit when they do.

The sanctified leader does not boast except in the Lord (v. 4; 1 Cor. 1:31; Gal. 6:14). He does not seek to impress others by his personality, efforts, or accomplishments. He gladly gives credit and thanks to others, and delights to give praise, credit, and thanks to the Lord. He does not seek public recognition for himself, but it is natural to him and real joy to acknowledge God's help, God's guidance, and God's blessing.

The sanctified leader is not proud (v. 4). He does not glory in smug self-satisfaction, self-superiority, or manifest self-assertiveness. He does not parade himself or his possessions or accomplishments. Neither does he grovel in abject self-depreciation. He has appropriate humility and self-esteem. He is modest in his self-evaluation. He is so unconsciously natural that it is easy for others to work with him.

The sanctified leader is not rude, ill-mannered, or impolite (v. 5). Rather, he is considerate of the opinions, desires, and feelings of others. He does not wound others by his thoughtlessness or insensitivity. He is courteous to all, gracious to all--even when they are not courteous or gracious to him. He does not retaliate. Listen to the sanctified leader, Paul: "When we are cursed, we bless; when we are persecuted, we endure it; when we are slandered, we answer kindly" (1 Cor. 4:12-13).

Peter says God has called you to repay evil and insult with blessing (1 Peter 3:9), even when you suffer for doing right (v. 14). When you are questioned or improperly accused, you are to give your reasons with gentleness and respect so that the others may feel ashamed (vv. 15-16). By doing this, you arm yourself with Christ's own attitude (1 Peter 4:1).

The sanctified leader is not self-seeking (v. 5). Paul specifically says, "Nobody should seek his own good, but the good of others" (1 Cor. 10:24). He added, "I try to please everybody in every way. For I am not seeking my own good but the good of many, so that they may be saved. Follow my example, as I follow the example of Christ" (10:33-11:1). A holy leader does not seek honor or position. He does not long to be honored above others or by others. If he desires position or power he is carnal, not holy. If others choose to advance him, he humbly accepts their decision. But he will never make personal efforts or use others to achieve personal position or power. It is better to lose your leadership position than to retain it by carnal means.

The sanctified leader must not be self-centered but Christ-centered and Church-centered (v. 5). He must be careful not to put his own interests above those of others. The shepherd must care for the sheep. "Woe to the shepherds of Israel who only take care of themselves! Should not shepherds take care of the flock?" (Ezek. 34:2). It is fatal to you as a Christian leader if you get the reputation of repeatedly looking to your own advantage, repeatedly seeking your own interests or the interests of your family more than those of the church.

The sanctified leader is not angered (v. 5). The Greek does not include the word "easily" before angered. The only legitimate anger of a Christian leader is with sin and Satan. He does not show anger for his own interests, his own honor, or for himself in any way. Even righteous anger over sin must not be brooded over or rehashed in the mind for an extended time (Eph. 4:26). It will rob you of spiritual joy, anointing, faith, God's nearness, and God's blessing.

Lose your temper and you lose your spiritual power. Lose your temper and you lose the respect of those you seek to lead or help. Should you ever lose your temper, ask God's forgiveness and the forgiveness of those to whom you showed an unChristlike example. Don't delay. Seek to repair the damage as fully and as quickly as possible. The sanctified leader must not show unholy anger.

The sanctified leader keeps no record of wrongs (v. 5). Keeping a record of wrongs is a proof that you have not forgiven. No sin of a Christian is more serious than unforgiveness. Jesus taught that the unforgiving person can lose his own forgiveness (Matt. 18:35). As a Christian leader you may have many things to forgive, for the role of the leader is not easy. But Jesus told Peter he must be willing to forgive the same person 77 times (Matt. 18:22). In other words, the forgiving spirit must never end.

This is not speaking of church discipline. Church discipline must be biblically observed (Matt. 18:15-17). This is the same chapter in Matthew that teaches unlimited forgiveness (v. 22). Christ is speaking of personal unlimited forgiveness. Forgiveness does not eliminate all consequences. You must forgive personally, but a person reaps what he sows. God will see that the unforgiven person reaps eternally, if not before his death (Gal. 6:7).

The sanctified leader does not delight in evil (v. 6). Love can never rejoice in sin. It finds no satisfaction in rumors of the sins of others, in slanderous reports, or sensational stories of others who have fallen into sin. Love sorrows when others are found to have sinned, even if they had been opposing the leader.

The sanctified leader rejoices in truth (v. 6), in good reports of others, and in hearing of their good qualities and commendable acts. He rejoices in the success of others. Love cannot be neutral when truth is in question. The sanctified leader can never be unconcerned about moral issues, but rejoices at all that is just and true and good.

The sanctified leader always protects others (v. 7). He seeks to protect their reputation, to overlook faults, and to bear with others. He keeps things confidential and is slow to expose. He wants to protect the name of Christ and the good name of the church or of any of its members.

He never uses his position or power to get back at others. He leads by love, not fear. He does not use his position to silence opposition. That would be carnal leadership. A holy leader is Christlike with rivals and opponents. The more a holy leader is known by others, the more they respect him. The more a carnal leader is known, the more he is distrusted or feared. A holy leader never uses others to his advantage. He always seeks the good of others.

The sanctified leader always trusts (v. 7). He maintains confidence in others as long as possible. He is eager to believe the best about others. He continues to trust when others give up.

The sanctified leader always hopes regardless of the circumstances (v. 7). He keeps up hope, is optimistic, and is prepared to give others another opportunity as long as it does not seriously risk harm to other people. When the evidence against another is so strong he cannot trust, he still hopes for the best. Love faces reality but refuses to take failure as final.

The sanctified leader always perseveres (v. 7). There is no end to his patience or his endurance. God gives him power to continue on. He stands his ground steadfastly. He does not resign himself to the thought that problems cannot be changed, that people cannot change. He actively does his duty and more, like a soldier of the Cross faithful unto death. He does not give up the battle, but fights on for Christ.

The sanctified leader never stops loving (v. 8). His love never fails, never gives up, never disappears. Holy love faces reality but still loves. The sanctified leader loves Christ so intensely with all his soul and mind and strength that for Jesus' sake he still loves the most unlovable and the most troublesome.

My fellow-leader, I know of no more searching passage in God's Word for you and me than 1 Corinthians 13. The Holy Spirit used this description of holy love many years ago to search my heart and show me my personal need of entire sanctification. None of us will ever get beyond the need to search his heart with this Scripture. Let us teach and preach the "through and through" sanctification of 1 Thessalonians 5:23. But if God shows us we still have personal need, let us run to the Cross. Let us claim God's promise. It is for you and me.

THE FULLNESS OF THE SPIRIT'S POWER IS ESSENTIAL TO YOU AS A CHRISTIAN LEADER. No Christian leader is able to lead acceptably without the fullness of the Spirit's enablement. I cannot and you cannot.

You need the fullness of the Spirit's guidance. No one knows enough to minister without the Spirit's guidance. You need Him daily to guide you in your priorities, contacts, the use of your time, and in all your decisions and ministry.

You need the Spirit's daily empowering of your prayer. You need His guidance in what to pray for and how to pray. You need Him daily to enable and anoint your intercessory prayer. As a leader of your people, perhaps your greatest responsibility to them is your prayer for them and your prayer for your ministry to them. You must schedule adequate daily time for intercession for your people. Labor earnestly in prayer for your people like Epaphras did for his congregation (Col. 4:12-13).

You need the Spirit daily to anoint and empower every aspect of your ministry. Your human best is not enough. You need God's extra enabling and empowering each day. If Paul's priority concern was that divine power constantly rest upon him (2 Cor. 12:9), if Jesus Himself did all in the power of the Spirit's anointing (Luke 4:1, 14, 18), surely a major need, perhaps the greatest need of your leadership each day, is the Spirit's anointing and power upon you.

You need the Spirit's help each day in making leadership holy, loving, and godly. Confess each day your total dependence upon the Spirit. Do not become so self-confident from your training and experience that you unconsciously depend on yourself more than on God. You need the Spirit's guidance and help in applying Bible principles to your ministry. Ask and expect His special help and touch in making your leadership all God wants it to be.

CHRIST'S LEADERSHIP STYLE IS ESSENTIAL TO YOU AS A CHRISTIAN LEADER. Paul exhorted, "Follow my example as I follow the example of Christ" (1 Cor. 11:1). Every Christian leader should be able to say the same.

Christ emphasized leadership by example. To His apostles who were to be the leaders of the church, He presented Himself as an example. "I have set you an example that you should do as I have done to you" (John 13:15). He was a leader who taught prayer by praying, who taught fasting by fasting, who taught sacrifice by sacrificing. He taught humility by being humble (Matt. 11:29) and expected His followers to learn from His example. He taught love by showing them the full extent of His love, by modeling love (John 13:1). Be sure you as a leader live all you preach and teach.

Paul strongly followed Christ's leadership style. Do you? "Join with others in following my example" (Phil. 3:17). "We did this . . . to make ourselves a model for you to follow" (2 Thess. 3:9). "Follow my example as I follow the example of Christ" (1 Cor. 11:1). Don't expect your people to live any higher than the example you set. "Set an example for the believer in speech, in life, in love, in faith, and in purity" (1 Tim. 4:12). "In everything set them an example" (Tit. 2:7).

Christ emphasized servant leadership. "Jesus said to them, 'The kings of the gentiles lord it over them. . . . But you are not to be like that. Instead, the greatest among you should be like the youngest, and the one who rules like the one who serves. . . . I am among you as one who serves'" (Luke 22:25-27).

Peter adds, "Eager to serve; not lording it over those entrusted to you, but being examples to the flock" (1 Peter 5:2-3). The Greek word used here *(kata*--down, plus *kurieo*--lord it over) implies to put down, to exercise rule to your advantage, to display your importance and authority, to domineer.

No Christlike leader will look down upon people, enjoy showing his own authority, or use his authority for his special advantage. No Christlike leader will seek to increase his authority or prestige. That would display a carnal spirit, not a spirit of holiness.

Peter began by saying, "Be shepherds of God's flock" (v. 2), and then reminds in verse four that Christ is the Chief Shepherd. We are only under-shepherds. A Palestine shepherd did not drive the sheep; he led them. Anything that robs us of the Shepherd's loving touch is unChristlike. We must serve those we lead. Paul and Peter delighted to call themselves "a servant" of Christ Jesus. We should never lose the servant spirit or servant attitude. We serve Christ by serving His people. We wound Christ by lording it over His people.

Christ emphasized sacrificial leadership. "Your attitude should be the same as that of Christ Jesus; who, being in very nature God . . . made himself nothing, taking the very nature of a servant . . . he humbled himself and became obedient to death--even death on a cross" (Phil. 2:6-8). Jesus' whole life on earth was one sacrifice. He who was the supreme sacrifice gladly spent His whole life sacrificially. No price was too great to pay if it were for the sake of the world He so loved. No suffering was avoided if it brought blessing to others.

The sanctified leader is to fix his eyes on Jesus, who endured the cross, scorned its shame, and endured opposition from sinful men (Heb. 12:2-3). He is to take up his own cross daily and follow Jesus (Luke 9:23). "Christ suffered for you, leaving you an example, that you should follow in his steps" (1 Peter 2:21). Our leadership style is to offer our bodies and our whole lives as "living sacrifices, holy and pleasing to God" (Rom. 12:2).

SELECTED BIBLE PRINCIPLES OF LEADERSHIP
A. Your Lifestyle as a Holy Leader
    1. *Train yourself to be godly*--1 Tim. 4:7-8; 2:2.
    2. *Practice self-denial.* Daily take up your cross--Luke 9:23-24. Be on your guard against all kinds of greed--Luke 12:15-31. You cannot serve both God and money--Luke 10:13.
    3. *Avoid debt*--Rom. 13:8.
    4. *Avoid idleness.* Work night and day.--1 Thess. 2:9; 2 Thess. 3:7-11.
    5. *Place Christ's kingdom before family*--Luke 9:59-62; 14:25-27.
B. Your Leadership Style
    1. *Give yourself fully to God's work*--1 Cor. 15:58. Sacrifice yourself--John 10:11. Spend yourself in your ministry--2 Cor. 12:15. Work hard at your ministry--1 Thess. 5:12-13. Be diligent in your leadership--Rom. 12:8.
    2. *Guard the purity of your doctrine*--2 Tim. 1:14-2:2; 4:16.
    3. *Be a servant-leader*--Luke 22:24-27; John 13:1-17; Col. 1:25.
    4. *Complete the work God gives to you*--Col. 4:17; 1 Tim. 1:18.
    5. *Evaluate your life and ministry*--Gal. 6:4-5.

6. *Be submissive to authority*--Rom. 13:1-7; 1 Peter 2:13-15.

7. *Do not be dictatorial;* do not rule like a king or lord over God's people--1 Peter 5:3; Lev. 25:43, 46, 53. Let people share in decisions (Acts 14:23 and 2 Cor. 8:19 in the Greek suggest that the people voted and then the leaders approved).

8. *Be gentle in your leadership.* Pursue gentleness--1 Tim. 3:3; 6:11. Be as gentle as a mother caring for her children.--1 Thess. 2:7-9. Be as gentle and comforting as a father--1 Thess. 2:11-12. You can be firm yet gentle.

9. *Avoid arguing*--1 Tim. 2:8; Titus 3:9. Don't quarrel about words--2 Tim. 2:14. The Lord's servant must not quarrel--2 Tim. 2:23-25. Beware of controversies--1 Tim. 1:4.

10. *Do nothing out of selfish ambition*--Phil. 2:3-4. Do not seek honor or position--Luke 14:7-11; 17:7-10.

11. *Do not seek the praise of men*--1 Thess. 2: 5:41-44.

12. *Avoid talking too much about yourself*--2 Cor. 4:5.

13. *Do not love money or prosperity*--Luke 16:13; 1 Tim. 3:3. Be content with what you have--1 Tim. 6:6-10; Heb. 13:5.

14. *Avoid criticism in how you handle money*--2 Cor. 8:20-21.

15. *Do what is right in the eyes of the public*--Rom. 12:17; 2 Cor. 8:21.

16. *Do not become weary or impatient over the results of your ministry*--Gal. 6:9; Heb. 12:3. Do not lose heart--2 Cor. 4:1; Isa. 40:3. You will reap if you don't give up--Ps. 126:5-6; Gal. 6:9.

17. *Remember that one day you will give an account of your leadership at Christ's judgment throne*--Heb. 13:17; 1 Cor. 3:10-15; 2 Cor. 5:10; Acts 2:16.

C. Your Responsibility to Your People

1. *Love your people*--Eph. 5:1-2; 1 Thess. 2:8, 17-20; 3:5-9, 11-12.

2. *Be an example to them*--Phil. 3:17; 2 Thess. 3:9; 1 Tim. 4:12; Titus 2:7; 1 Peter 5:3.

3. *Intercede for your people*--1 Sam. 7:8; 12:23; Rom. 1:9-10; Eph. 1:16; 3:14-21; Phil. 1:4; Col. 1:3, 9-10; 2:1; 4:12-13; 1 Thess. 1:2; 2 Thess. 1:11-12; 2 Tim. 1:3; Philemon 4.

4. *Identify with your people*--Gal. 4:12; John 1:14.

5. *Shepherd your people for God*--Acts 20:28. The Lord is the Chief Shepherd (Ps. 23:1; 1 Peter 5:4; Heb. 13:20), but you are responsible to shepherd God's flock for Him (v. 2). If God's flock is scattered, you may be held accountable by God (Ezek. 34:5-10). As a shepherd, you have awesome responsibility.

6. *Keep clear of the "blood" responsibility of all people.* You must faithfully witness to the unsaved (Acts 18:6), warn any who sin (Ezek. 3:17-19; 33:7-9), teach the full will of God and doctrinal truth to the Church (Acts 20:26-27).

Additional comments: Never avoid responsibilities. If you avoid facing a situation responsibly, you will probably reap an even more difficult situation. Allow full discussion of a situation before you decide (Acts 15:1-32).

7. *Make every effort to keep the unity of the Spirit*--Ps. 133:1-3; Eph 4:3; Luke 9:49-50. Let no root of bitterness grow among your people--Heb. 12:15.

8. *Avoid all partiality*--Deut. 1:17; 2 Chron. 19:7; Mark 12:14; Acts 10:34; Rom. 2:11; Col. 4:25; James 2:1.

9. *Don't be a stumbling block to anyone*--2 Cor. 6:3; Rom. 14:13, 20; 1 Cor. 8:9-13; 9:12; 10:32. Don't just try to please yourself--Rom. 15:1-2.

10. *Encourage and strengthen your people*--Acts 15:32. This was the role of Barnabas--Acts 11:23. Paul wanted the Christians to be encouraged--Eph. 6:22; Col. 2:2; 4:8; 1 Thess. 3:2; 4:18; 5:11. He prayed that they be strengthened and encouraged--2 Thess. 2:17-18. Every Christian should encourage others; how much more a Christian leader--Heb. 3:13; 10:25.

47

THE CONSUMMATION OF GOD'S GREAT SALVATION PLAN

The final consummation of redemption will be the reinstitution of God's original plan for a holy universe, a holy earth, and a holy humanity. God never can be ultimately defeated, nor will He change His eternal goals.

Sin tragically intruded in our universe, as we have seen. It included the fall of Satan and some angelic beings, as well as the fall of Adam and his race. But, thank God, this was countered by God's great plan of incarnation, revelation, atonement, and triumph through Christ.

The God who is always able to work in all things for the good of those who love and obey Him (Rom. 8:28) has been working eternal good. When time is terminated by God and the Judgment Day comes, Satan will have been more than defeated. In spite of Satan and sin, God has been accomplishing great good through this period of earth-time (sin-time, Satan's intrusion-time).

1. *God has been revealing His attributes, perfection, nature, wisdom, love, power, and glory in dimensions of eternal significance* (Rev. 4:11; 5:12-13; 7:10, 12). God's saving acts on behalf of Israel and the world have been giving continual revelation through history as we have seen and learned more about God. These culminated in God's revelation in the cross and resurrection of our Lord Jesus Christ. There has been further demonstration through the history of the Church. All of these have provided evidences in such clarity, beauty, and glory that throughout eternity no one will ever be able to dispute them. This could have been accomplished in no other way.

Throughout the ages of eternity God's created beings will understand God better because of what He has revealed in these ways. Even heaven's angels are learning more about God as they observe His gracious dealings with us (1 Cor. 4:9; Eph. 3:10; 1 Tim. 5:21; 1 Peter 1:12).

2. *God now has a record in the chronicles of heaven and in our inspired Bible which documents for people and for angels these glorious revelations of God and the history of God's holy redemptive acts.* Undoubtedly the libraries of heaven contain innumerable biographies of God's faithful children and how God proved His faithfulness to them. The more this is researched and made known in eternity the more God will be glorified.

But also included in the Bible and in heaven's records are the full account of sin and how impossible it is for any created being to exert his will independent of God and not suffer eternal loss. The history of sin and the resulting suffering and death will be indisputable. The record will be open and available in detailed documentation.

Humanity has tried every form of government, system of society, and variety of philosophy, man-originated religion, and even strenuous efforts at moral reform. All have proved to be failures. God's will is the only way. Everything else is false and every other road leads to destruction. Christ is the only Way (John 14:6).

3. *God has created a new holy family group to dwell with Him in heaven.* We are related to Him in holy covenant, in demonstrated love, and in proved obedience. We are His family. We will throughout eternity provide for Him a love-fellowship group distinct from and more clearly related to Him than any other of heaven's beings. We are related to Him by covenant bonds, by spiritual birth and commitment, and by spiritual experiential maturity. No other group in heaven will have the same affectionate closeness or the same graciously endowed honor and authority as we. We will be God's special glory forever and ever (Eph. 1:11-14). This will all take place "when the times will have reached their fulfillment--to bring all

things in heaven and on earth together under one head, even Christ" (Eph. 1:10).

God's family group has been called, redeemed, and glorified from the Old and New Testament dispensation epochs of time, but especially from New Testament times.

4. *Christ has a special eternal relationship of love, holy commitment, and shared special unity with our chosen group--we who comprise His bride.* We are His New Testament holy ones, the members of His Church. From the moment of our spiritual birth, we have been bonded to Christ by the special love given by the Holy Spirit. We are told very little of Christ's future plans for us, His bride. But it is obviously of great significance to Him and to us. There will be a special bonding celebration of our holy relation known as "the marriage supper of the Lamb" (Matt. 22:2; 2 Cor. 4:14; Eph. 5:15-17, 30, 32; Rev. 19:7, 9).

Christ has plans for us, His bride, to live close to Him (John 14:2). He has Himself made holy preparations for us to live in this close fellowship eternally (v. 3). This is unveiled a little more in the revelation God gave to John on Patmos (Rev. 21:3-5, 9-27; 22:1-6).

We, the bride, will have a special royal function of service to Christ. Unworthy though we are, we will be the elite group in eternity. We will have a kingly role with Christ the King of the universe (Rom. 5:17; 2 Tim. 2:12; Rev. 5:10; 20:4; 22:5). What all this will include has not been revealed to us, but it is important enough to be mentioned repeatedly in God's Word.

Among the things that we know this will involve will be judging the world (Luke 22:30), including judging angels (1 Cor. 6:3). Jesus hinted some of our future role in His parable of Luke 19:12-19. There He said that those who prove faithful will be given a ruling role when He as King takes up His reign.

Undoubtedly part of the rewards which Christ plans for us involve future service for Him. What a joy it will be to serve Him in eternity as His honored special loved ones. Not only will we reign with Jesus, but we will also serve Him (Rev. 5:10; 22:3). Part of our service will be of a worship nature (Rev. 1:6; 7:15). Perhaps we will share in leading some of the worship services in heaven. The service which He assigns to us as His bride will be far different from the service which He assigns to the angels. The rewards He has promised for us are far more diverse and wonderfully special than any mentioned for angels.

God plans to show us "incomparable riches of his grace, expressed in his kindness to us in Christ Jesus." When? "In the coming ages" (Eph. 2:7). So there will be special periods in the unending eternity known as "ages." Throughout them all, God will be fulfilling His eternal plan of love, kindness, and glory.

Then God's great plan of the ages will continue uninterrupted. There will be glory such as only God can plan. Undoubtedly the greatest glory, privilege, and joy will be ours. Of all heaven's beings and of all eternity's participants, we alone will be resplendent in His likeness. We have been created in His likeness as no other beings were created. We alone, of all creation, will share unusual Christ-likeness and glory even in our faces. This must be the meaning of Revelation 22:4. The more fully we have lived for Him here, the more we will be marked by His glory there.

We will shine like stars forever and ever (Dan. 12:3; Matt. 13:43). But the clear implication is that the glory of some will be greater than that of others. Already we are to be so holy and blameless in our earth life now that we shine like stars in the darkness of our environment, and as we hold out to others God's life-saving word (Phil. 2:15-16). We are to be the light of the world (Matt. 5:14). But then we will be God's special glory, His special treasure (Mal. 3:16-18). How grateful you and I will be if we have served God with joyful, lavish, constant, and loving obedience here now.

God's eternal plan would be incomplete without His eternal rewards to those who love and serve Him with exceptional faithfulness here (1 Cor. 3:11-14. Also see Matt. 5:11-12; 6:1; 16:27; Luke 6:35; Col. 3:23-24; Heb. 10:35; 11:26; 2 John 8; Rev. 11:18; 22:12). Costly obedience will be rewarded above all we have ever dreamed.

God's great salvation will be eternally greater than angels or human beings ever realized. It does not end with the return of

Christ, our Bridegroom. That is when its glorious fullness begins. Forever and ever we will rejoice in salvation's unfolding greatness. Oh, let us teach it, preach it, and experience all that God has provided for us now, so that we can experience greatest fullness then.

1 Corinthians 2:9--"No eye has seen, no ear has heard, no mind has conceived what God has prepared for those who love him."

And what about God's original plan? It will be perfectly fulfilled. There will be new heavens and a new earth (Isa. 65:17-25; 66:22). Only righteousness will remain there.

2 Peter 3:13-14--"In keeping with his promise we are looking forward to a new heaven and a new earth, the home of righteousness. So then, dear friends, since you are looking forward to this, make every effort to be found spotless, blameless and at peace with him."

There will be new nations of saved ones bringing their glory into the New Jerusalem, our home and the capital of God's holy, united universe (Rev. 21:24). Christ our crucified Savior will then be the glorious Sovereign King of the universe. Satan will have been cast out of God's universe forever (Rev. 20:16). Every sinner who failed to repent and receive Christ will be cast with Satan into the lake of fire (Rev. 20:15). There will never again be any sin, curse, or death (Rev. 20:14; 21:27; 22:3).

Perhaps earth's new inhabitants will, like Enoch and Elijah, be translated after faithful holy mortality into holy immortality without having to face death. But whatever the glory of the inhabitants of the new earth, our glory will be separate and greater. We will be the battle-tested immortal heroes and heroines of eternity. We will be Christ's own bride--the wonder of the ages to angels and to earth's new inhabitants. And probably we will share with Jesus His rule over them. The Father and Son will reign supreme forever, and we will be like Jesus and reign with Jesus as His eternal bride (Rev. 22:3-4).

Revelation 22:20--"He who testifies to these things says, 'Yes, I am coming soon.' Amen. Come, Lord Jesus."

Appendix A

BIBLE TERMS AND
DEFINITIONS FOR SIN

To understand the Bible doctrine of sin we need to note the words used for sin by the Hebrew in the Old Testament and the Greek in the New Testament. Sin is so fundamental in our understanding of God, sin, and salvation that numerous words are used. Only three words are used to express grace (two in the Old Testament and one in the New Testament), but at least eight basic words are used for sin in the Old Testament and some 12 in the New Testament.

OLD TESTAMENT TERMS

1. *Hata.* This root occurs about 580 times in the Old Testament and is its principal word for sin. It means to miss a mark or way. It is failure to observe God's laws, failure to reach God's goal or standard. It is to miss or fall short of God's standard. The equivalent Greek word is *hamartano.* The concept is not merely to miss the right mark but to hit the wrong mark. Note: Exod. 20:20; Lev. 5:16; Judges 20:16.

2. *Ra.* This root occurs some 444 times. It can be translated "bad, evil, wicked." It suggests violence or breaking out of evil. It is mainly unethical or immoral activity against other people. It can be used for inner attitudes. It is often translated "wicked." It is the equivalent to the Greek words *kakos* or *poneros.* Note: Ps. 34:15; Isa. 31:2; Amos 5:14-15.

3. *Pasha.* The basic idea of this word is to rebel. It is a breach of relationships between two parties. Israel rebels against God (Isa. 48:8). Note: Isa. 1:28; Dan. 8:23; Hosea 7:13.

4. *Awon.* This word occurs 231 times as a noun and 17 times as a verb. It suggests crookedness or perverseness. It means iniquity, sin, guilt, or punishment for guilt. It is a collective noun (Isa. 53:6). Because of *awon* punishment is due (Job 31:11; Ezek. 44:12).

5. *Shaga.* This verb occurs 21 times. It means to go astray, to stray, to err. A sheep or a drunkard goes astray. The emphasis is on a non-deliberate sin, a "sin of ignorance." Note: Lev. 4:2; Num. 15:22; Deut. 27:18; Ps. 119:10.

6. *Taa.* This means to err, stagger, stray, wander. It can be physical, mental, moral, or spiritual. Note: Isa. 53:6; Ps. 58:3.

Thus sin in the Old Testament can take many forms. The Old Testament is rich in ethical terms. Sin is primarily a rupture of relations between the person and God, disobedience resulting in estrangement. It is a breach of Israel's covenant with God. The prophets saw sin as open rebellion against God. Every Jew familiar with the Old Testament knew sin was against God and that the sinner needed to repent for his sin.

NEW TESTAMENT TERMS. The New Testament uses eight different Greek roots from which 28 different synonyms are derived. These occur 386 times.

1. *Hamartia* (Compare *hata* in Hebrew). This is the most frequently used word for sin and occurs in its various forms at least 214 times. It is the most comprehensive word for moral sin. In the Bible the word suggests not merely failure to hit the mark, but a decision to miss the mark. The wicked misses the mark because he has chosen to do so. The wicked misses the correct path because he deliberately chooses to take the wrong one. The verb is used about 40 times in this moral sense. This word is not only used for the act of sin, but also for the governing principle or power of sin, for the sinful state or condition.

Romans 6:6--"That the body of sin might be done away with."
Romans 6:18--"You have been set free from sin."
1 John 1:7--"The blood of Jesus, his Son, purifies us from all sin."

Note also: John 8:34; 15:22; Rom. 6:12; 7:17; Heb. 4:15; 1 John 3:4; 5:17.

2. *Parabasis.* This word means a transgression (always a breach of law, a violation of God's law). The law of God is written in conscience (Rom. 2:15) or in Scripture. Where there is a law there must be a Lawgiver. A transgression is thus an act not merely against the law but also against the Lawgiver. Thus every sin against the law of God is a sin against God Himself. This term is used for an act which is only possible to a rational moral being. An animal may do wrong but cannot be said to sin in the sense of this word.

Romans 5:14--"Sin by breaking a command."

1 Timothy 2:14--"The woman who was deceived and became a sinner."

Note also: Matt. 15:3; Rom. 4:15; Heb. 2:2.

3. *Adikia.* This word means injustice, unrighteousness, wickedness, iniquity. It is wrongness of character, life, or act. It can point to moral, social, and physical wrong. The word in its various forms occurs 66 times in the New Testament.

Whatever is a transgression of God's law is against God. It is inherently wrong. It is not right. It is unjustly displeasing God in the soul and life, and giving love and obedience to someone else--self or Satan. The basis of obedience to all God's commands is love; "Love is the fulfillment of the law" (Rom. 13:10). Love is the great command that fulfills all others (Matt. 22:37-40). Love is the goal or purpose of all God's commands (1 Tim. 1:5).

To act on the basis of self-love instead of love to God is wrong, unrighteous, and sinful. Such sinful, unrighteous love supplants God and obedience to God. *Adikia* can refer to an act or to a state of the soul.

Romans 1:29--"They have become filled with every kind of wickedness."

1 John 1:9--"Faithful and just to . . . purify us from all unrighteousness (*adikias*)."

1 John 5:17--"All wrongdoing (*adikia*) is sin (*hamartia*)."

Note also: Rom. 1:18; 2:8; 6:13; 2 Tim. 2:19.

4. *Anomia.* This Greek word means without law, not subject to law, hence, lawlessness. It is a much stronger word than *adikia*. It

not only refers to a wrong, unrighteous, wicked act or state, but an actual state of rebellion, of being lawless. The sinner, in this sense, not only transgresses God's law but is hostile to it and hostile to God. He refuses to be subject to God. 1 John 3:4 tells us that all sin is serious. "Everyone who sins (*hamartia*) breaks the law (*anomia*), for sin (*hamartia*) is lawlessness (*anomia*).

Furthermore, all that is unrighteous or wrong is rebellion, the extreme lawlessness. "All wrongdoing (*adikia*) is sin (*hamartia*)," and 1 John 3:4 says all *hamartia* is *anomia*. No sin is small in the sight of God. All sin expresses soul rebellion against God. Sin cannot be excused as a mere mistake or weakness, something so much a part of our humanity that God overlooks it. God says every sin is open rebellion against Him.

This is why the Bible says, "The sinful mind is hostile against God. It does not submit to God's law, nor can it do so" (Rom. 8:7). Therefore God provides salvation not merely for the committed acts of sin but also for the sinful nature. No salvation could be complete which only dealt with the acts of sin and left untouched by redeeming grace this inward nature, this rebellious hostility.

This strong term *anomia* is used at least 11 times in the New Testament.

1 John 3:4--"Sin (*hamartia*) is lawlessness (*anomia*)."

Note also: Mark 15:28; 1 Tim. 1:9.

5. *Asebeia*. This word means godlessness, impiety. It is the opposite of *eusebeia*--godliness. *Asebeia* is extreme disrespect for God. God is not only completely absent, He is defied. It is the attitude toward God that *anomia* is to God's laws. This word is used 18 times in the New Testament and expresses utter wickedness. It is a life that sin has made totally unlike God--God is completely absent from it. It is used in 2 Peter and in Jude for godless apostates.

Romans 5:6--"Christ died for the ungodly."

Jude 4--"They are godless men who . . . deny Jesus Christ."

Jude 15--"To convict all the ungodly (*asebeis*) of all the ungodly acts (*asebeias*) they have done in the ungodly way (*asebasan*), and of all the harsh words ungodly (*asebeis*) sinners (*hamartoloi*) have spoken against him."

Note also: Rom. 1:18; Titus 2:12; 1 Peter 4:18; 2 Peter 3:7.

Appendix B

OUR SECURITY IN CHRIST

The believer has a blessed security in Christ. "This world in its present form is passing away" (1 Cor. 7:31). The things of earth provide only temporary and relative security. People are mortal and our human relationships are often not as permanent or secure as we had expected. Praise God for full and eternal unchangeableness in Christ.

Scripture teaches the spiritual security of the believer as he remains in Christ. We are not insecure in Christ. No one, not even Satan, can snatch us out of God's hand (John 10:28). After we have known Christ as Savior, the only thing that can separate us from Christ is our deliberate sin if not repented and forgiven.

Paul asks, "Who shall separate us from the love of Christ? Shall trouble, or hardship or persecution or famine or nakedness or danger or sword? . . . No, in all these things we are more than conquerors through him who loved us. For I am convinced that neither death nor life, neither angels nor demons, neither the present nor the future, nor any powers, neither height nor depth, nor anything else in all creation, will be able to separate us from the love of God that is in Christ Jesus our Lord" (Rom. 8:35-39).

God's desire and plan for every believer is constant walking in the light, unbroken communion with God, continued growth in grace. God's provision is for constant spiritual obedience and victory over temptation. All the provisions of grace and instant forgiveness are available should we ever fall into sin but return instantly to God (1 John 2:1-2). The possibility of apostasy is present, but the probability is that the Christian truly born again and filled with the Spirit will persevere in God's grace faithfully until the end. But can anyone

who was once truly born again turn his back on God and separate
himself from God's saving grace? Let us see what the Scripture
teaches.

**THE NATURE OF SIN AND ITS RESULTS ARE THE
SAME FOR ALL.** Sin is sin. It always has the same nature and
effect, whether in a man or woman. Whether in a person who has
never come to Christ or a person who has made a commitment to
Christ, sin is sin. It blinds anyone who sins. It deceives anyone who
sins (Heb. 3:13). The wages of sin is death--this is God's universal
law (Rom. 6:23). Sin not repented of will lead to the spiritual death
of a Christian as surely as to the death of a sinner who never knew
Christ. Sin "leads to death" (Rom. 6:16). Paul was writing to
Christians when he wrote that. Sinful things result in death (v. 21).

Ezekiel is very clear. "The soul who sins is the one who will die"
(Ezek. 18:4, 20). "If a righteous man turns from his righteousness
and commits sin and does the same detestable things the wicked man
does, will he live? None of the righteous things he has done will be
remembered. Because of the unfaithfulness he is guilty of and
because of the sins he has committed, he will die" (Ezek. 18:24).
Again Ezekiel says, "If a righteous man turns from his righteousness
and commits sin, he will die for it; because of the sin he has
committed he will die" (v. 26). Yes, the wages of sin is death for the
sinner and for the Christian alike.

If a Christian lives according to the sinful nature, he will die
(Rom. 8:13). Any person who sins will reap what he sows, and if he
sows to please his sinful nature, from that nature he will reap
destruction (Gal. 6:7-8). Sin, when full grown, in any person gives
birth to death (James 1:15).

LIFE IS A PERIOD OF MORAL PROBATION FOR ALL.
We must not confound the blessed security of the believer in Christ
with what some call "eternal security." The purpose of the Atonement was not to make us happy, cancel our punishment, and let us

continue in sin. Neither was it to make us happy and free from our sins for a short period of time.

The plan of God was to create man in His image so that man could become holy like God and could qualify as an eternal companion of God. Earth life is the period of preparation for the life of eternity which will never end. Adam was created with Godlike personality so that he might be indwelt by the Holy Spirit and so that Christ could become the incarnate Son of Man. Forevermore throughout all eternity He will continue to be united to us in our redeemed, glorified humanity as our Bridegroom.

God has made every provision for us to be victorious over sin. But God also has provided for our forgiveness in case we do sin but then truly repent. However, it would be impossible for God to be infinitely holy and yet have eternal companionship with those who are unholy in nature, rebellious in attitude, and filled with unholy thoughts, desires, and deeds. This would bring constant infinite sorrow and pain into the infinitely loving and holy heart of God. Sin in us, if we were in heaven, would cause heaven to cease to be heaven, for sin is what brought the curse and reign of death on earth.

God in His grace has ordained earth life as a period of probation when anyone can receive salvation and develop personal character through choice, through deliberately devoting love, worship, faith, and obedience to Him. Probation continues for every person until death. Until then he can yield to or resist the Spirit. He can believe or reject. He can obey or cease to obey. Moral choice, that is, probation, does not cease at conversion. Therefore until death, salvation for the individual is conditional upon his continuing to believe and obey. The Holy Spirit strives with each person until death (Gen. 6:3), seeking to bring him to Christ, and seeking to conform the Christian more and more into the image of Christ (Eph. 4:13).

There is no further opportunity to accept God's plan of salvation or to grow in holiness or character through victory over sin after this life. Every Scripture exhortation is therefore addressed to us in the now. "Now is the time of God's favor (grace), now is the day of salvation" (2 Cor. 6:2; Heb. 3:13-15).

In accordance with God's eternal plan, God saves us with the purpose of our remaining secure in His grace, love, and holiness from the moment of our initial salvation until death, and then on throughout all eternity. Israel was unconditionally God's chosen people. But each Israelite was conditionally a part of redeemed Israel and assured of heaven if he obeyed God and walked in the Old Testament light. Similarly, the Church is unconditionally chosen for God's plan and each individual is chosen conditionally, subject to his fulfilling God's conditions for spiritual sonship, for membership in the Church, the Bride.

The Christian can rejoice and rest securely in God's love. But he cannot deliberately and persistently sin against that love and remain secure. God will remain the holy God, even if sorrowfully He must separate unrepentant backsliders from His Church, His Bride. Professing Christians who live in sin are in one of two categories:

1. Perhaps they never truly were saved (1 John 2:19).

2. Perhaps they truly were saved but turned back from God's will and now persist in their backsliding and apostasy. They are salt which has lost its saltiness, "No longer good for anything, except to be thrown out and trampled by men" (Matt. 5:13). They are a branch which was a part of the vine, but became fruitless and God, the Gardener, cut them off the vine (John 15:1-2). They are then, said Jesus, "Like a branch that is thrown away and withers; such branches are picked up, thrown into the fire and burned" (v. 6). Why? Jesus explains it is because they do not remain in Him (v. 6).

The forgiveness of sins covers the past. You cannot forgive sins not yet committed. At the time of Luther the Roman Catholic Church sold "indulgences," which promised forgiveness of future sins. This doctrine is contrary to Scripture. Similarly, it is contrary to Scripture to say that a person who was forgiven of his past sins will remain forgiven regardless of what he does in the future. Salvation is not an indulgence to permit the Christian to start living again in constant willful sin.

Justification by faith covers the sins of the past that God forgave. The forgiven sinner is declared righteous on the basis of his faith. If he stops believing, he is no longer a believer. If he willfully and persistently sins after justification, he is no longer just (i.e., right-eous) and he is again a sinner. "No one who lives in him keeps on sinning. . . . He who does what is right is righteous, just as he is right-eous. He who does what is sinful is of the devil" (1 John 3:6-8). No matter how wonderfully a person was once saved, if that person persists in sin he no longer is righteous (i.e., justified by faith). He is no longer believing or obeying; but he is now "of the devil."

> 1 John 3:9-10--"No one who is born of God will continue to sin. . . . This is how we know who the children of God are and who the children of the devil are: Anyone who does not do what is right is not a child of God."

THE ILLUSTRATIONS GOD USES. No human illustration is a perfect and complete description of God or of God's salvation. Each illustration, like each parable, teaches one or more aspects of truth. But each illustration must be understood in harmony with all other parts of God's Word. It must be interpreted in the light of the total Word of God. We dare not interpret the whole of Scripture in the light of one verse or one illustration or one parable. Each illustration is true for the purpose God intended, but no interpre-tation of Scripture is true if it contradicts other plain scriptural statements.

Birth. Birth is a Bible illustration of receiving spiritual life. But every aspect of birth does not teach spiritual truth. That is taking a simple illustration too far. Salvation is called being born again. It brings spiritual life. But salvation is birth from one parent only--God. Human birth requires two parents. You dare not say spiritual birth is the result of two parents--God and the Church, or God and bap-tism. That is to take the illustration too far. Salvation is all of God. We must meet God's conditions of repentance and faith, but only God can save.

In the same way, to say that once you have been born again and are a child of God you can never lose spiritual life or be unborn is to stretch the illustration too far. Scripture never makes that statement. An analogy assumes similarity, it does not prove it.

Washed. Salvation is also called being washed (Titus 3:5). Can a person once washed ever become dirty again? Can you insist that once a person is clean he will always be clean? Of course not. Sin always brings the need of cleansing (2 Peter 2:22).

Life. Salvation is also called life. Can you say a person who was once alive can never die? Of course not. Physical life is subject to the law of death, and spiritual life is subject to the law of spiritual death (Rom. 6:23; 8:13). Sin, if persisted in, destroys spiritual life.

Branch of the Vine. Salvation is like being a branch of the vine (Christ) (John 15:5). If a branch is once a part of the vine, is it always a part of the vine? No. Jesus says that if a saved person does not remain in Him (v. 6) he is like a branch that is no longer bearing righteous fruit. Jesus does not say he was never in the vine. He says the Father cuts him off the vine of which he was once a part (v. 2).

Life by Faith. Spiritual life is a life of faith. A person is a believer only as long as he believes. Continuing faith is essential to final salvation (1 Peter 1:5). A believer is a believer only as long as he obeys, for obedience is an element of saving faith. The two are shown to be equivalent to each other in John 3:36. Obedience proves the presence of saving faith. Disobedience proves the absence of saving faith. Any person with so-called faith who does not obey has the same kind of faith that demons have (James 2:19). It is not saving faith.

ETERNAL LIFE IS CHRISTLIKE. What does the Bible mean by "eternal life"? We do not need to come to Christ to receive endless existence. God created man with endless existence--spirit, once created, can never die. The endless existence of every being, whether saved or lost, is clearly taught in Scripture (John 5:28-29). Eternal life is not synonymous with endless existence. It is much greater than that. Eternal life is a life with an essential godly quality from God the Eternal One. It is a gracious participation in the life of Christ, the eternal Son of God. It is spiritual life, holy life.

Eternal life is obtained by coming to Christ (John 5:40). Christ came that we might have this life (10:10). He gives eternal life (10:28). Believing in Christ, the Son of God, bestows eternal life (6:40). By believing we have life in His name (20:31). He is the Bread of Life (6:35, 48, 51). As we partake of Christ we partake of eternal life (6:53-58). Christ's words, as obeyed, give spiritual life (v. 63). "This is eternal life: that they may know you, the only true God, and Jesus Christ, whom you have sent," prayed Jesus (17:3). "I am the way and the truth and the life" said Jesus (14:6).

Spiritual life continues as we continue to eat Christ's flesh and blood (i.e., obey His words). Such feeding on Christ is not automatic. The thought of John 6:56-57 is that whoever continues to eat will continue in union with Christ, just as Christ continued in union with the Father. There must be constant appropriation of Christ, even as Christ the Son constantly lived because of the Father. It is tragically possible and all too common for some to backslide into apostasy and no longer feed on and remain in Christ.

WE CAN CEASE TO REMAIN IN CHRIST. Jesus tells us the condition of His remaining in us is our remaining in Him (John 15:4). But if He does not remain in us, we have no eternal spiritual life (1 John 5:11-12).

The alternative is clear. We must choose to remain (abide) in Christ, remain in His will, continue to feed on His Word, eat His flesh and blood, and partake of His holy nature, remain in union with Him, and thus continue to share spiritual unity with Him and spiritual life in Him. Otherwise, we choose to stop feeding on Christ, stop remaining in His will, thus become separated from Christ-life, become cut off from the vine, and forfeit eternal Christ-life (not endless life, but the life the Holy Spirit gives).

WE CAN FAIL TO CONTINUE TO BELIEVE. Jesus said the same in Luke 8:13. Some people, He says, "receive the word with joy when they hear it," "believe for a while, but in the time of testing they fall away." Is Jesus talking about saving faith? Yes. "Believe and be saved" (v. 12). Although they believed for a time and were saved, they fell away. These true believers who fell away are contrasted with the true believers who persevered (v. 15) because they hear the same word, but "retain" it. Jesus explained in John 8:51, "If a man keeps my word, he will never see death" (referring to spiritual death).

Paul explains the same in 1 Corinthians 15:2, "By this gospel you are saved, <u>if you hold firmly</u> to the word I preached to you. <u>Otherwise, you have believed in vain</u>." He does not say, otherwise you never really believed, but otherwise you believed in vain. How is it possible to truly believe but believe in vain? By not continuing to obey the Word.

John adds, "See that what you have heard from the beginning remains in you. <u>If it does, you also will remain in the Son</u> and in the Father. And this is what he promised us--even eternal life" (1 John 2:24-25). Yes, eternal life is sure upon one condition: remaining in Christ by staying obedient to His Word. That is how we make our calling and election sure (2 Peter 1:10).

WE CAN BACKSLIDE. The writer to Hebrews says, "My righteous one will live by faith. And <u>if he shrinks back</u>, I will not be pleased with him" (Heb. 10:38). God's own righteous one (quoting from Habakkuk 2:4) can shrink back from his righteous walk and, if so, will forfeit God's favor. To shrink back is to cease to be an active believer, to cease to live by faith.

Paul said this was possible for himself: "So that after I have preached to others, I myself will not be disqualified for the prize" (1 Cor. 9:27). What prize? The crown that will last forever (v. 25). The full significance is even further clarified by Paul in the verses that follow immediately in chapter 10:1-14. He points to Israelites who were saved out of Egypt, baptized into Moses (v. 2), shared the same spiritual food and drink as Moses, for they were really partaking of Christ (vv. 3-4). Yet they displeased God (v. 5), fell into grievous sins (vv. 6-8), and were punished by God's judgments and destroyed by God's angels (v. 10). Paul emphasizes that these events were "written down as warnings for us" (v. 11). "So, if you think you are standing firm, <u>be careful that you don't fall</u>!" (v. 12). Paul clearly believed that if either he or the Corinthian true believers failed to persevere in walking in obedience to Christ he or they would be lost.

Jesus teaches the same truth in the parable of the lord and his appointed administrator in Luke 12:42-46: If the lord's faithful and wise manager sins against his lord and his fellow servants, he will be destroyed and share the place (hell) of the unbelievers (v. 46).

WE CAN LOSE FORGIVENESS. We can lose our status as a forgiven person. It is possible to forfeit God's forgiveness, said Jesus in Matthew 18:21-35, if the forgiven one who owed all to his lord's mercy then fails to forgive his fellowmen. The clear meaning of the parable is that God's mercy, grace, and forgiveness are conditional. Even though a person may once have been forgiven, if that person then becomes unforgiving, God's mercy, grace, and forgiveness cease to be applied to him. This is in harmony with the petition we make in the Lord's prayer: "Forgive us our sins, for we also forgive everyone who sins against us" (Luke 11:4; Matt. 6:14-15). "This is how my heavenly Father will treat each of you," concluded Jesus, "unless you forgive your brother from your heart" (Matt. 18:35).

Man has no inherent right to eternal life. He does not own it. He has life only as he partakes of the life of the Son of God. In Him alone is life. "With you is the fountain of life" (Ps. 36:9). Union with Christ is a faith union--not just an imputed union, but a real union. Christ is our life (Col. 3:4). "The gift of God is eternal life in Christ Jesus our Lord" (Rom. 6:23). If we turn from Christ we break that faith union.

GOD AND THE CHRISTIAN WHO SINS. The primary relationship which God has to a person who has been born of the Spirit is that of being his Father. True, God is also his Creator, sovereign King, and Judge. Jesus Christ came to reveal God to us as our Father.

God is not a sovereign tyrant with a worldwide network of angelic spies reporting to Him. We are not to picture God as a frowning God ready to cut off our relationship the first moment that we think a thought, speak a word, or commit a deed that grieves Him. He is a Father-Savior. He is watching with a Father's heart. His angels are all ministering spirits to help us, to seek to restrain us from sin, and to help us to do God's will.

The moment we stumble or fall into temptation or sin God is there as our saving Father to grasp our hand and lift us up again. The moment we fall into sin our Advocate at the right hand of the Father, Jesus Christ, his holy Son and our crucified Savior, pleads on our behalf (1 John 2:1). His blood is available to cover our sin, His advocacy on our behalf before the Father secures instant forgiveness of our sin, if we but turn to Him in confession. 1 John 1:9 is instantly available to the erring child of God. Instant restoration to God's full favor is available to us because of the Cross.

The Holy Spirit is also instantly available and is always present as our Helper. He will convict us of sins of commission and sins of omission. If we sin and turn to Christ our Advocate, confessing our sin and need, the Spirit will instantly reassure us of God's forgiveness and our continuing acceptance. He is there to help us be watchful so we do not fall a second time into the same temptation. His power is always available to make us victorious over every temptation and sin.

GOD DEALS WITH US ACCORDING TO OUR PRESENT RELATIONSHIP TO HIM. The whole teaching of Scripture is in agreement with 2 Corinthians 13:5, where Paul exhorts the Christian believers: "Examine yourselves to see whether you are in the faith; test yourselves. Do you not realize that Christ Jesus is in you--unless, of course, you fail the test." What should we examine if we are believers in Christ? We should examine whether the faith we profess continues to be matched by the walk of obedience, for faith without a holy life that proves the genuineness of our faith is useless

(James 2:20). Faith in Christ and a Christlike life go hand in hand (vv. 23-24).

God deals with us according to our present relationship to Him, not according to our past. The sinful past can be forgiven and the righteous past can be canceled by now plunging into a life of sin. "If a righteous man turns from his righteousness and commits sin, he will die for it; because of the sin he has committed he will die. But if a wicked man turns away from the wickedness he has committed and does what is just and right, he will save his life. Because he considers all the offenses he has committed, and turns away from them, he will surely live; he will not die. . . . Therefore . . . I will judge you, each one according to his ways, declares the Sovereign Lord" (Ezek. 18:26-30).

FURTHER WARNINGS AGAINST BACKSLIDING. Here is
a sample selection from the many Scriptures that warn the believer not to backslide. The warnings are Bible truth. God does not threaten us with what is not really possible or a danger.

Matthew 24:4, 12-13--"Watch out that no one deceives you . . . because of the increase of wickedness, the love of most will grow cold, but he who stands firm to the end will be saved."

Colossians 1:21-23--"Once you were alienated from God and were enemies in your minds because of your evil behavior. But now he has reconciled you by Christ's physical body through death to present you holy in his sight, without blemish and free from accusation--if you continue in your faith, established and firm, not moved from the hope held out in the gospel."

1 Timothy 4:1, 16--"The Spirit clearly says that in later times some will abandon the faith and follow deceiving spirits and things taught by demons. . . . Watch your life and doctrine closely. Persevere in them, because if you do, you will save both yourself and your hearers."

1 Timothy 6:10-12--"Some people, eager for money, have wandered from the faith. . . . But you, man of God, flee from all this, and pursue righteousness. . . . Take hold of the eternal life to which you were called."

James 5:19--"My brothers, if one of you (not the unsaved) should wander from the truth and someone should bring him back, remember this: Whoever turns a sinner away from his error will save him from death and cover over a multitude of sins."

2 Peter 1:9-11--"If anyone does not have them, he is nearsighted and blind, and has forgotten that he has been cleansed from his past sins. Therefore, my brothers, be all the more eager to make your calling and election sure. For if you do these things, you will never fall, and you will receive a rich welcome into the eternal kingdom of our Lord and Savior Jesus Christ."

2 Peter 3:17-18--"Since you already know this, be on your guard so that you may not be carried away by the error of lawless men and fall from your secure position. But grow in the grace and knowledge of our Lord and Savior Jesus Christ."

Jude 21, 24--"Keep yourselves in God's love as you wait for the mercy of our Lord Jesus Christ to bring you to eternal life. . . . (He) is able to keep you from falling."

1 John 2:24--"See that what you have heard from the beginning remains in you. If it does, you also will remain in the Son and in the Father."

Hebrews 2:1--"We must pay more careful attention, therefore, to what we have heard, so that we do not drift away."

Hebrews 3:6-14--"Christ is faithful as a son over God's house. And we are his house, if we hold on to our courage and the hope of which we boast. So, as the Holy Spirit says: 'Today, if you hear his voice, do not harden your hearts'. . . . See to it, brothers, that none of you has a sinful, unbelieving heart that turns away from the living God . . . so that none of you may be hardened by sin's deceitfulness. We have come to share in Christ if we hold firmly till the end the confidence we had at first."

Hebrews 6:4-6 warns that it is possible to have been "enlightened," "have tasted the heavenly gift," "have shared in the Holy Spirit," "have tasted the goodness of the word of God and the powers of the coming age" and yet for that person to "fall away" and crucify the Son of God "all over again" by his sins.

Hebrews 10:26-27--"If we deliberately keep on sinning <u>after we have</u> <u>received</u> the knowledge of the truth, no sacrifice for sins is left, but only a fearful expectation of judgment and of raging fire.

Such a person "<u>has trampled the Son of God under foot</u> . . . has treated as an unholy thing the blood of the covenant <u>that sanctified</u> <u>him</u>, and . . . <u>has insulted the Spirit of grace</u>" (v. 29).

Who are the ones to whom this is spoken? They are the ones addressed in verse 19 as "brothers" who "have confidence to enter the Most Holy Place by the blood of Jesus, by a new and living way opened for us" and who "have a great priest over the house of God." They are urged to "draw near to God with a sincere heart in full assurance of faith," having hearts cleansed by the blood of Jesus, to "hold unswervingly" to the faith they profess, and to "encourage one another" as they see Christ's coming drawing near (vv. 19-25). If such people turn back to the practice of sin (v. 26), there is "only a fearful expectation of judgment and of raging fire" (v. 27) awaiting them. Solemn warning indeed!

These are the people to whom the writer urges, "<u>Do not throw</u> <u>away your confidence</u>; it will be richly rewarded. <u>You need to</u> <u>persevere</u> so that when you have done the will of God, you will receive what he has promised" (vv. 35-36). They are urged not to shrink back from living a life of righteous faith (v. 38), thus incurring God's displeasure; for <u>those who shrink back will be "destroyed"</u> (v. 39).

SUMMARY. The Christian is not insecure in Christ; he is secure, eternally secure as he remains in Christ, walks in the light, and continues to trust and obey. He has no other security. His security does not lie in an experience in his past, but in his present relationship to Christ. Earth time is given to man as probation time to walk in the light, grow in grace, and become more and more Christlike. God is committed to conform every believer more and more unto the full measure of the fullness of Christ (Eph. 4:13).

The Holy Spirit has been given to secure our constant growth in grace and Christlikeness and to prepare us to be a part of Christ's eternal bride, the Church, in heaven. As we yield to the Spirit's guidance, we are increasingly transformed into His image.

But until death ushers us into heaven, we are responsible to love and obey Christ, and to follow as the Spirit leads. "If by the Spirit you put to death the misdeeds of the body, you will live, because those who are led by the Spirit of God are sons of God" (Rom. 8:13-14). Over the door of Spurgeon's College in London was written, "Holding, I am held."

Appendix C

THE GIFTS OF THE SPIRIT

Some Christians teach that the proof of the fullness of the Spirit is that the person speaks in tongues. They consider tongues-speaking the witness to "the baptism of the Spirit." This is obviously incorrect. The Holy Spirit is Himself the great Witness to Christ and to the Christian. He the great Witness needs no gift to witness to Him. He is His own witness.

Furthermore, the Bible says the gift of tongues is not a sign to believers but to unbelievers (1 Cor. 14:22); that is, it is to be used in evangelism, enabling you to witness to the person in his own language.

Although we do not agree with the Pentecostal interpretation of the gift of tongues, we thank God that Pentecostal people are generally evangelical in doctrine and often very zealous in evangelism. However, we need to understand the Bible reasons why we do not agree with their emphasis, which has brought division to so many churches.

Unfortunately, although there are many godly people who claim to speak in tongues, many other tongues-speakers still show clear evidences of the sinful nature, and spiritual defeats. Some even show moral weakness. They have not yet had their hearts cleansed by the Spirit, for when the Spirit fills He cleanses. Yet they insist they are speaking or praying in tongues. We have shown in chapter 36 that the terms "baptized with the Holy Spirit" and "filled with the Spirit" refer to the same experience and that Peter says it results in the heart being purified by faith (Acts 15:9). A pure heart is not defeated by sin. So whatever those "tongues" are, in their case they certainly do not witness to being filled or baptized with the Spirit.

Other people urge all Christians to seek a tongues manifestation which they call a "prayer language." This term does not even occur in the Bible and was not thought of the first 1900 years of the Christian Church.

This chapter is written to give a brief answer to the people who place emphasis upon the gift of tongues, speaking in tongues, or tongues as a "prayer language." While Paul emphasizes that biblical tongues is a lesser gift, it has become unbiblically the main emphasis of many people.

GIFTS AND THE GIFT OF TONGUES. All of the ministry of the Spirit related to salvation and living in the Spirit is equally available to every Christian. The Holy Spirit's conviction, regeneration through the Spirit, the witness of the Spirit, the fullness of the Spirit, the empowering of the Spirit, the guidance of the Spirit, the anointing of the Spirit, the Spirit's assistance in prayer, and the fruit of the Spirit are all equally available to you.

Each Spirit-filled person will have some of each of the fruit of the Spirit listed in Galatians 5:22-23. But no person will have all of the gifts of the Spirit (1 Cor. 12:8-11). The fruit of the Spirit results in spiritual growth and maturity. The gifts of the Spirit are not primarily for yourself but for the service of others (1 Cor. 12:7). Every Christian needs every fruit of the Spirit to become more Christlike. No person needs any gift of the Spirit except as he or she uses it in ministry. Every Christian should be a ministering Christian as the Spirit guides. A gift of the Spirit is to be used to be more effectively a salt, light, witness, and ambassador for Christ, and to be a strength and blessing to the Church.

The Holy Spirit will impart some gift to you (1 Cor. 7:7), but there is no gift of the Spirit which is promised to all. The choice of which gift you receive or how God uses you is not based upon your asking, but upon the decision and choice of the Holy Spirit (1 Cor. 12:11).

Lists of the gifts of the Spirit are found in Romans 12:6-8, 1 Corinthians 12:7-10, 28; Ephesians 4:7-8, 11-13; 1 Peter 4:10-11. Some gifts are listed several times, and some only once.

Those listed in the Bible are sometimes listed by the kind of ministry (prophecy, teaching, serving, encouraging), and sometimes by the role of the person (apostles, pastors, evangelists). Thus, those to whom the Holy Spirit gives a gift then become themselves God's gift to the Church and the world. The gifts listed in the above passages include: prophecy, four times; teaching, three times; apostles, two times; healings (plural), two times; interpretations of languages (plural), two times; kinds of languages (plural), two times; miraculous powers (plural), two times; serving, two times. The following are listed one time: gifts of administration (plural), discerning of spirits, encouraging, evangelists, faith, giving, helps (plural), knowledge, leadership, showing mercy, pastors, speaking, wisdom. Undoubtedly there are other gifts, such as hymnwriting, singing, and writing.

Whatever gift you receive, use it to serve others (1 Peter 4:10; Eph. 4:12). The whole body of Christ grows as each believer faithfully uses his or her gift for the others (Eph. 4:16).

Some of the gifts listed in the Bible seem related to natural abilities (serving, gifts of administration, helps, leadership, knowledge). When the Holy Spirit specially anoints, guides, and blesses the use of these abilities, they become His gift.

No gift permanently resides in any one person. A God-appointed prophet could not prophesy whenever he wanted to. He had to be "carried along" (the literal meaning of the Greek) by the Holy Spirit (1 Peter 1:21). Balaam testified he could not prophesy whenever he wanted to (Num. 22:38). Jeremiah could not immediately give God's prophetic answer when he wanted to do so (Jer. 42:4). On one occasion he had to wait ten days before the prophecy came (v. 7).

The same is true with gifts of healing or miracles. Paul had the gift of healing (Acts 14:8-11), but he could not heal Epaphroditus (Phil. 2:25-30) or Trophimus (2 Tim. 4:20) or Timothy (1 Tim. 5:23).

We do not use the Holy Spirit whenever we desire. He uses us when He so desires.

A person can teach from his purely human abilities, but he cannot choose when the Spirit anoints him in teaching and makes this his gift. The same is true of preaching. This keeps us humble. We are totally dependent upon God. If we depend on ourselves, God will withdraw His power from us and there will be little permanent spiritual benefit.

This is also true with healing or any other gift. No one can heal whenever he chooses. No one can pray and see every person for whom he prays healed. It is not his gift; it is the gift of the Holy Spirit. The Spirit is always in charge and chooses when to heal, according to God's will.

The gift of languages (sometimes called the gift of tongues) is the same as any other gift. It is not given to every Christian any more than any other gift (1 Cor. 12:29-30). The main purpose of the gift of tongues is to evangelize when the person does not already know the language of the one God wants to reach. This was true at Pentecost, and there are strong reasons to believe it was true at the house of Cornelius and at Ephesus.

The main purpose of tongues is not to testify to God's grace at work in your soul. It is not a sign for believers but for unbelievers (1 Cor. 14:22); that is, it is for evangelism. Persons can manifest a gift and yet be spiritually immature and carnal. This was true at Corinth. God sometimes uses carnal people to help others. But a gift is never a measure of grace.

Some well-meaning Pentecostal friends try to teach a person how to speak in tongues. Anything taught is psychological and not divine, not a gift of the Spirit. If they can teach a genuine gift, let them teach their own people when they go out as missionaries. Then they will not have to spend months learning the language! But it is not being done.

You can no more teach a person to have a genuine gift of language than you can teach a person how to heal or how to perform a miracle. God is sovereign over the use of all His own gifts. No one can choose when to use a genuine gift of the Spirit. A person who claims to speak in tongues whenever he wants to in prayer or in public may love the Lord and have good intentions, but he does not have a genuine gift of the Spirit. He has developed a psychological habit.

God wants all His children to be His witnesses, but no one has the right to speak in God's name claiming to be God's voice apart from God's authorization. No one dare claim to have a prophecy, "word of knowledge," or "revelation" on his own. If anyone who claims to speak under such circumstances makes any incorrect statement which fails to come true, it proves that the person was mistaken or was used by an evil spirit (Deut. 18:22). In the Old Testament such a person was termed a false prophet, and the penalty for the false prophet was death.

IS THERE SUCH A THING AS A "PRAYER LANGUAGE"?
In recent years, beginning in the United States, some people have changed their emphasis from speaking in tongues to using what they call a "prayer language," i.e., praying in tongues. They have called it a superior or more effective way to pray, a more direct way to the heart of God, a way to get answers to prayer that you cannot get in other ways. Is this biblical? reasonable? true?

Reasons why this emphasis cannot be correct:

1. *Prayer is too basic to the spiritual life.* Prayer is the most important, most basic aspect of the Christian's life. We are to pray always (Luke 18:1), continually (1 Thess. 5:17). If prayer is that important to us, why did God hide this superior way to pray from His people for 1900 years until the Pentecostal Movement began? Why does He give it only to certain people? The Spirit chooses to whom He gives the gift of tongues (1 Cor. 1:11). The vast majority of God's great prayer warriors over the ages have never used a prayer language or even thought of such a thing. This emphasis cannot be right.

2. *Jesus never taught or encouraged the use of a "prayer language."* Jesus was deeply concerned for His disciples. In the last days and

hours before the cross He taught them the deep things of the Spirit. He told them to pray in His name, but He never told them to pray in a "prayer language." When His disciples asked Him to teach them how to pray (Luke 11:1), He did not even mention a "prayer language."

3. *The Holy Spirit never inspired any emphasis upon a "prayer language."* There are only two verses in the Bible which mention praying in tongues (1 Cor. 14:14-15), and neither suggests that people should pray in a "prayer language." The Bible is our rule for faith and practice. All necessary spiritual truth is included in the Bible, but the Holy Spirit did not mention a "prayer language" once in the Bible.

4. *The Bible gives no example of the use of a "prayer language."* The great Bible prayer warriors--Moses, Elijah, David, Hezekiah, and Daniel--never used a "prayer language." There is no proof that Jesus ever did. When the Scripture is silent on this subject, the people teaching a "prayer language" should also be silent.

5. *The Bible does not hint of a "prayer language" to be used in private devotion.* Jesus told us how to pray in private (Matt. 6:6) but did not mention this. He told us not to babble (v. 7). The Greek word here suggests sounds imitating speech but having no meaning. It is like the sounds made by an infant who has not yet learned to speak intelligently. What better word could be used to describe the sounds you hear in a "prayer language." These sounds mean nothing to the one praying. Paul says the mind is fruitless (1 Cor. 14:14), unless that person can interpret his own sounds. Jesus says not to pray like this, not to make sounds which have no understandable content. In the very next verse He tells us how to pray, and He gives us the Lord's prayer as our model and in a language we understand.

6. *You require no heavenly language to pray more acceptably to God.* Only one language was used till Babel (Gen. 11:1-8). Probably only one language will be used in heaven. Whenever God or an angel speaks to a person in Bible records, it is always in the person's own language. God does not miraculously give a new language so this person can talk to the angel or talk to Him. God understands

our hearts and our words. He does not require a separate prayer language.

7. *You cannot truly pray or love God without your mind.* We are to love God with all our heart, soul, mind, and strength (Mark 12:30). Your deepest love to God cannot be expressed without your mind. You cannot pray with all your desire if you do not know what you are saying. The Holy Spirit does not manipulate your mouth to make sounds that do not express your heart. Evil spirits manipulate. God uses our mind. No form of prayer is deeper or more acceptable to God than that which expresses your mind and heart.

8. *You cannot express faith without your mind.* The real "you" cannot ask for anything without your mind. The real "you" cannot believe for anything without your mind. But you are commanded to believe. That means you are commanded to use your mind when you pray. Real Bible faith includes three aspects: First, mental acceptance of the fact. You cannot do this without your mind. Second, consent of your will. Your will cannot consent without your mind. Third, personal appropriation. You cannot personally appropriate without your mind. An unfruitful mind (1 Cor. 14:14) cannot believe God.

9. *You cannot intercede for others without your mind.* Intercession is a vital part of the prayer life of a Christian. Christ lives to intercede (Heb. 7:25), and we are to be His fellow-intercessors as priests to God (Rev. 1:6). How can you express love for a person, intelligently bring that person's needs to God, or exercise faith for him when you do not know the meaning of the sounds you are making?

10. *You cannot test your own "prayer language."* The Holy Spirit knows the dangerous possibility of an evil spirit acting like an angel of light to deceive a person through a demonic tongue (2 Cor. 11:14). Some have been thus deceived (1 Cor. 12:3). That is why one gift of the Spirit is "the distinguishing between spirits" (1 Cor. 12:10). But that distinguishing has to be done by someone else, and when you pray in private there is no one to check. But we are commanded to test the spirits (1 John 4:1; 1 Thess. 5:21). A "prayer language"

permits undetected deception by an evil spirit masquerading as the Holy Spirit.

11. *"Prayer language" is not intended to be a primary means of edification.* Paul wrote 1 Corinthians 14 to correct a serious problem of wrong emphasis in the Corinthian church. It was not written to teach how to pray or how to edify one's self. In verse four, Paul points out that unless there is interpretation the tongues-speaker does not edify anyone but himself.

The goal of Paul in this chapter is the edification of others, not personal edification. Thus, a tongues manifestation does not benefit anyone unless it is interpreted. The only one who can benefit is the person himself, but that benefit is almost nil since his mind is unfruitful (v. 14).

Whenever you try to please the Lord you have the inner satis- faction that God sees and knows your heart, even if you should make a mistake. This is the only kind of benefit you have when you pray in a tongue. Praying in a tongue is not a primary way to become edified. Edification is growth in character. It is not a mysterious infusion of power. All growth in grace is growth in character, in Christlikeness. All growth in character involves choice, obedience, expressions of love, and all this requires the mind. Since the mind is not involved in tongues-speaking, it cannot be a major way to edification. However, how a person worships God privately is between him and the Lord.

Spiritual growth, edification, and maturity come as your whole being, including your mind, makes use of the means of grace, obeys God, and reaffirms commitment to God. This is impossible apart from the involvement of the mind.

12. *Prayer is natural to every believer; "prayer language" is not.* Even little children can pray and tell Jesus what is on their hearts. A new Christian can begin to pray as soon as he is born again. It is natural to a new believer to pray. When has a new believer begun to pray in a "prayer language" without hearing about it or hearing someone else demonstrate what they claim to be a "prayer language"? Anything that requires others to teach us is not a divine gift. A

"prayer language" is not spiritually natural. Prayer in one's own language is.

13. *If "prayer language" is the Bible manifestation of tongues, it is not for all believers."* Yet prayer is essential for all. See 1 Corinthians 12:10, 30. If it is not the Bible gift of tongues, then it should not be taught, recommended, or practiced. If it is a scriptural gift, then it cannot be used whenever the person desires to do so. The manifestation of the Spirit in 1 Corinthians 12:7 (Greek: *phanerosis*) is the action of the Spirit. We do not control that. It is under the sovereign control and sovereign initiative of the Holy Spirit. But normal prayer is our action at our own initiative.

Incidentally, "praying in the Spirit" does not mean praying in tongues. Paul says, "Pray in the Spirit on all occasions with all kinds of prayers and requests" (Eph. 6:18). If this means tongues or a "prayer language," then all other prayer is wrong. But God has answered billions of prayers by people in their own language. Obviously, you can pray in the Spirit without praying in a tongue, as has been constantly demonstrated in the nearly 2,000 years since Christ died. When you are born of the Spirit and indwelt by the Spirit, you can pray in the Spirit regardless of any gift of the Spirit.

15. *All manifestation of tongues is to be less desired than some other activity or gift of the Spirit.* Holy Spirit-given love is superior to all other gifts (1 Cor. 12:31-13:13). But love is never contrasted with prayer. Prayer is as important as love. We are to pray continually (1 Thess. 5:17), but we are nowhere told to use a gift of the Spirit continually. Thus, "prayer language" cannot be a necessary gift of the Spirit. We are to desire greater gifts rather than tongues (1 Cor. 12:31; 14:1-12), but we are never to desire gifts more than prayer.

PAUL'S USE OF TONGUES. Some point to Paul's statement that he spoke in tongues more than others (1 Cor. 14:18). When and how did he do that? There are four possible ways to express tongues: in messages or testimony, in prayer, in song, or in personal witnessing.

Paul presents his example to the Corinthians for them to follow:

1. His great use of tongues is not in public messages or testimony. (V. 19--"In the church I would rather speak five intelligible words to instruct others than ten thousand in a tongue.")

2. It is not in prayer. (Vv. 14-15--"If I pray in a tongue my spirit prays, but my mind is unfruitful. So what shall I do? I will pray with my spirit but I will also pray with my mind.") This can mean either of two things:

   a. It can mean that the only way he will pray with his spirit is when he uses his mind at the same time; that is, not in tongues. (F. F. Bruce: "Let my prayer and praise be Spirit-inspired, indeed, but let it be intelligent too.") Paul discourages uninterpreted prayer in a tongue.

   b. Some think Paul means he will pray in two ways--either in tongues or with his mind, i.e., in the understood language. They believed he prayed in tongues in private devotion but with his mind in a known language in public. This cannot be correct. Paul would not contradict himself. He teaches that all prayer should be in the Spirit. "Pray in the Spirit on all occasions" (Eph. 6:18). Hence, it is clear that Paul did not practice tongues as his method of prayer or private devotion.

3. Paul says he does not use tongues in singing (v. 15). The same reasoning used above for prayer applies here.

4. Then it is evident that Paul's great use of tongues was in personal witnessing. That is the way it was used on the Day of Pentecost. God had given him the gift to use in his personal evangelism. Paul was probably the greatest personal soul-winner in the Bible. He preached in the synagogues on the Sabbath and wherever he found crowds of people. But most of his soul-winning was probably in private: in homes of notable people (Acts 13:7-12); in the marketplace (14:8-11); by the riverside (16:13); in the street (16:17); in the marketplace (17:17); house to house (20:20), and in his own house (28:30).

Paul's strategy was to go from city to city, emphasizing those centers where garrisons of Roman soldiers were stationed. The Roman army was made up of soldiers from all nationalities. It is always most effective to evangelize a person in his mother tongue. God gave Paul the gift of tongues so he could most effectively evangelize the people heart to heart in their own tongue.

SUMMARY. The gift of tongues has three possible forms:

a. A genuine gift of the Spirit, the purpose of which is to benefit an unbeliever, not a believer (as at Pentecost). See 1 Corinthians 14:22. This can be evangelizing a person or praying with and for a person when neither of you knows the other's language. A genuine gift of tongues would enable you to speak or pray so the other could understand. God has done this from time to time.

b. A demonic counterfeit (1 Cor. 12:3; 1 John 4:1). Demonic tongues are manifested in other religions as well as those appearing from time to time in deceived Christians.

c. A psychological manifestation. No doubt there is much of the psychological involved. It is an unessential emotional response which has been unconsciously developed or consciously learned. It is not sinful. Neither does it accomplish what the person thinks it does. The fact that the tongues speaker is sincere does not prove that he is right in his understanding. God still loves him and no doubt longs for him to get over his childish approach and become more spiritually mature. Note that in 1 Corinthians 13 the most excellent way is given in the center of the discussion of tongues (1 Cor. 12-14). It is an essential part of this discussion. The childishness that Paul wanted the Corinthian church to put away was their childish attitude regarding tongues (1 Cor. 13:11; 14:20).

When Christians do not understand this truth correctly and biblically, pray for them, love them, but do not let them divide the church by their doctrine and practice. Again and again this manifestation of tongues has divided churches instead of promoting the unity of the Spirit.

INDEX

importance of doctrine, 2-4
origin of, 6
original (see Original sin)
possibility of, 249
terms for, 40-41, 293-97
transmission of, 66-68
twofold nature, 163-67, 172,
    188-89
victory over, 73, 112-13, 130,
    138-40
Sinful nature, 51, 54-59, 64, 130,
    164-66, 173, 181, 183,
    185-86, 188-89, 198, 217,
    219, 230, 235, 256
    terms for, 54-55, 168-70
    transmission of, 66-68
Singleness of heart, 64, 223-24
Sonship, 144-45
Sorrow for sin, 89, 98-99
Soul-winning, 186-87
Sovereignty of God, 79, 117
Spirit, 21
    angels as spirit beings, 5
    man as, 5, 191
    nature of, 21
Steps in temptation, 32-34
Steps to entire sanctification,
    232-39
Substitution, 70-73, 250
Suppression, 243, 249-50
Surrender, 41, 109, 110, 112, 218,
    219
Symbolism, 28-29, 70-74
Synergism, 85

Temptation, 26, 247
    and Fall, 22-37
    avenues of, 33-34
    avoiding, 253
    role of, 35-37, 247
    steps in yielding, 30-34
Terminology
    of atonement, 70, 72-75
    of carnality, 168-70
    of depravity, 54-55
    of grace, 82, 84
    of entire sanctification,
        151-53, 192, 193-96,
        221-22, 313
    of new birth, 87, 88-89, 104,
        114-116, 125, 143, 191
    of Satan, 8
    of sin, 40-41, 166, 293-97
Testimony, 239
Time, 5, 6, 272-73
Tongues, gift of, 214, 312-22
Total depravity, 55-59, 166
Transfiguration, 262-63
Trinity, 5-6, 11, 77, 81, 146
Trust, 109-11, 120, 159
Truth, 222, 251

Unbelief, 32, 38

Victory over sin, 73, 112, 130,
    138-40, 175-76

Will, 25, 26, 33, 85-86
    and Holy Spirit, 87, 249

OTHER BOOKS BY
DR. DUEWEL

Touch the World through Prayer--A challenging, very readable manual on prayer that has been used by God to "revitalize" the prayer life of thousands. A Christian "best-seller."

Let God Guide You Daily--A manual on guidance to help you enter into the joy of God's guidance as the daily experience of your life.

Ablaze for God--A book to challenge all Christians, especially Christian workers and lay leaders to a life and service Spirit-filled, Spirit-empowered, and mightily used by God.

Mighty Prevailing Prayer--Let the Spirit use this powerful volume to make your intercession mighty before God. A guide to intensified intercession and prayer warfare.

Measure Your Life--Seventeen ways God is measuring your life as He prepares for your eternal reward.

Some 300,000 of Dr. Duewel's books are already in circulation. Available from the author and Christian bookstores.